Instructor's Manual
to Accompany

International Financial Management

FOURTH EDITION

Jeff Madura
Florida Atlantic University

West Publishing Company
Minneapolis/St. Paul New York Los Angeles San Francisco

WEST'S COMMITMENT TO THE ENVIRONMENT

In 1906, West Publishing Company began recycling materials left over from the production of books. This began a tradition of efficient and responsible use of resources. Today, up to 95% of our legal books and 70% of our college texts and school texts are printed on recycled, acid-free stock. West also recycles nearly 22 million pounds of scrap paper annually—the equivalent of 181,717 trees. Since the 1960s, West has devised ways to capture and recycle waste inks, solvents, oils, and vapors created in the printing process. We also recycle plastics of all kinds, wood, glass, corrugated cardboard, and batteries, and have eliminated the use of Styrofoam book packaging. We at West are proud of the longevity and the scope of our commitment to the environment.

Production, Prepress, Printing and Binding by West Publishing Company.

Printed in the United States of America
02 01 00 99 98 97 96 95 8 7 6 5 4 3 2 1 0

ISBN 0–314–05376–X

Contents

Chapter 1 Multinational Financial Management: An Overview 1
Chapter 2 International Flow of Funds 9
Chapter 3 International Financial Markets 17
Chapter 4 Exchange Rate Determination 25
Chapter 5 Currency Futures and Options 33
Chapter 6 Government Influence on Exchange Rates 43
Chapter 7 International Arbitrage and Interest Rate Parity 51
Chapter 8 Relationships Between Inflation, Interest Rates, and Exchange Rates 63
Chapter 9 Forecasting Exchange Rates 69
Chapter 10 Measuring Exposure to Exchange Rate Fluctuations 75
Chapter 11 Managing Transaction Exposure 83
Chapter 12 Managing Economic Exposure and Translation Exposure 95
Chapter 13 Financing International Trade 101
Chapter 14 Short-Term Financing 109
Chapter 15 International Cash Management 117
Chapter 16 Direct Foreign Investment 125
Chapter 17 Multinational Capital Budgeting 131
Chapter 18 Multinational Cost of Capital and Capital Structure 141
Chapter 19 Country Risk Analysis 147
Chapter 20 Long-Term Financing 153
Chapter 21 Global Strategic Planning 157
Chapter 22 International Banking 161
Chapter 23 The International Debt Crisis and Bank Assessment of Country Risk 167

Chapter 1

Multinational Financial Management: An Overview

Lecture Outline

Objective of MNC
- Conflicts Against the MNC Goal
- Constraints Interfering with the MNC Objective

Theories of International Business
- Theory of Comparative Advantage
- Imperfect Markets Theory
- Product Cycle

Methods of Conducting International Business

Increasing Globalization
- Growth in International Trade
- Growth in Direct Foreign Investment

International Opportunities and Risk

Organization of the Course

Chapters 2-8:	Macro-Oriented
	Provide Background
Chapters 9-23:	Micro-Oriented
	Managerial Implications

Chapter Theme

This chapter introduces the multinational corporation as having similar goals to the purely domestic corporation, but a wider variety of opportunities. With additional opportunities come potential increased returns and other forms of risk to consider. The potential benefits and risks are introduced.

Topics to Stimulate Class Discussion

1. What is the appropriate definition of an MNC?
2. Why does an MNC expand internationally?
3. What are the risks of an MNC which expands internationally?
4. Why do you think European countries rely on international trade more than the U. S.?
5. Why must purely domestic firms be concerned about the international environment?

Answers to End Of Chapter Questions

1. Explain the agency problem of MNCs. Why might agency costs be larger for the MNC as opposed to a purely domestic firm?

   ANSWER: The agency problem reflects a conflict of interests between decision-making managers and the owners of the MNC. Agency costs occur in an effort to assure that managers act in the best interest of the owners.

   The agency costs are normally larger for MNCs than purely domestic firms for the following reasons. First, MNCs incur larger agency costs in monitoring managers of distant foreign subsidiaries. Second, foreign subsidiary managers raised in different cultures may not follow uniform goals. Third, the sheer size of the larger MNCs would also create large agency problems.

2. Explain how the theory of comparative advantage relates to the need for international business.

   ANSWER: The theory of comparative advantage implies that countries should specialize in production, thereby relying on other countries for some products. Consequently, there is a need for international business.

3. Explain how the existence of imperfect markets had led to the establishment of subsidiaries in foreign markets.

   ANSWER: Because of imperfect markets, resources cannot be easily and freely retrieved by the MNC. Consequently, the MNC must sometimes go to the resources rather than retrieve resources (such as land, labor, etc.).

4. If perfect markets existed, would wages, prices, and interest rates among countries be more similar or less similar than under conditions of imperfect markets? Why?

   ANSWER: More similar. Resources would be more mobile and could therefore be transferred to those countries more willing to pay a high price for them. As this occurred, shortages of resources in any particular country would be alleviated and the costs of such resources would be similar across countries.

5. Explain how the product cycle theory relates to the growth of the MNC.

   ANSWER: The product cycle theory suggests that at some point in time, the firm will attempt to capitalize on its perceived advantages in markets other than where it was initially established.

6. How does access to international opportunities affect the size of corporations? Describe a scenario wherein the size of the corporation is not affected by access to international opportunities.

   ANSWER: Additional opportunities will often cause a firm to grow more than if it did not have access to such opportunities. Thus, a firm which considers international opportunities has greater potential for growth. Yet, some firms may avoid opportunities because they lack knowledge about foreign markets or expect that the risks are excessive. Thus, the size of these firms is not affected by the opportunities.

7. What factors cause some firms to become more internationalized than others?

   ANSWER: The operating characteristics of the firm (what it produces or sells) and the risk perception of international business will influence the degree to which a firm becomes internationalized. Several other factors such as access to capital could also be relevant here. Firms that are labor-intensive could more easily capitalize on low-wage countries while firms that rely on technological advances could not.

8. What are some potential disadvantages of international business that are often not relevant to domestic business? Briefly state how an MNC can be adversely affected by these disadvantages.

   ANSWER: First, exchange rate fluctuations can adversely affect cash flows of an MNC. Second, foreign economies could weaken, thereby reducing foreign business. Third, host countries could enforce barriers which hamper foreign business. These barriers include foreign exchange restrictions, tax regulations, etc. The MNC's cash flow could be reduced if such barriers exist.

9. Briefly describe the change in the importance of world trade over time. If the trend continues, what does this suggest about the importance of international financial management?

   ANSWER: When comparing the 1980s, trade as a percentage of GNP has increased. Consequently, international financial management has become more important than ever. It should be mentioned that U. S. trade has been somewhat stable over time. Yet, even firms that do not engage in international trade must understand international financial management so that they can compete against foreign competitors in their home country.

10. As an overall review of this chapter, identify possible reasons for growth in international business. Then, list the various disadvantages that may discourage international business.

    ANSWER: Growth in international business can be stimulated by (1) access to foreign resources which can reduce costs, or (2) access to foreign markets which boost revenues. Yet, international business is subject to risks of exchange rate fluctuations, foreign exchange restrictions, a host government takeover, tax regulations, etc.

11. Describe constraints that interfere with the MNC objective.

    ANSWER: The constraints faced by financial managers attempting to maximize shareholder wealth are:

    a. Environmental constraints—countries impose environmental regulations such as building codes and pollution controls, which increase costs of production.

    b. Regulatory constraints—host governments can impose taxes, restrictions on earnings remittances, and restrictions on currency convertibility, which may reduce cash flows to be received by the parent.

c. Ethical constraints—U. S.-based MNCs may be at a competitive disadvantage if they follow a worldwide code of ethics, because other firms may use tactics that are allowed in some foreign countries but considered illegal by U. S. standards.

12. Describe the trends in the volume of U. S. direct investment abroad over time.

ANSWER: The value of U. S. direct investment abroad has increased throughout the 1980s.

13. The managers of Loyola Corporation recently had a meeting to discuss new opportunities in Europe as a result of the recent integration between European countries. They decided not to penetrate new markets because of their present focus on expanding market share in the U.S. Financial managers of Loyola Corporation developed forecasts for earnings based on Loyola's 12 percent market share (defined here as its percentage of total European sales) that it presently has in Europe. Is 12 percent an appropriate estimate for next year's European market share? If not, would it likely overestimate or underestimate the actual European market share next year?

ANSWER: It would likely overestimate its market share because the competition should increase as barriers between European countries are reduced.

14. Would the agency problem be more pronounced for Berkely Corporation, which has its parent company make most major decisions for its foreign subsidiaries, or Oakland Corporation, which has a decentralized approach?

ANSWER: The agency problem would be more pronounced for Oakland because of a higher probability that subsidiary decisions would conflict with the parent. Assuming that the parent attempts to maximize shareholder wealth, decisions by the parent should be compatible with shareholder objectives. If the subsidiaries made their own decisions, the agency costs would be higher since the parent would need to monitor the subsidiaries to assure that their decisions were intended to maximize shareholder wealth.

15. Explain why more standardized product specifications across countries can increase global competition.

ANSWER: Standardized product specifications allow firms to more easily expand their business across other countries, which increases global competition.

16. How can German subsidiaries of U.S.-based MNCs capitalize on the removal of the Berlin Wall that separated East and West Germany?

    ANSWER: West German firms could capitalize by exporting to East Germany, or by targeting their products for people from East Germany that cross the border.

17. Describe privatization and explain why it may allow for a greater degree of international business.

    ANSWER: Privatization involves the sale of government operations to corporations and other investors, which promotes more free enterprise. To the extent that these operations can be purchased by foreign firms, privatization can induce international business.

18. Describe the Single European Act and explain how it may affect international business by U.S. firms.

    ANSWER: The Single European Act (1987) was intended to make regulations more uniform across European countries. Some U. S. firms attempted to capitalize on this act by increasing their business in Europe. Because of the act, they can more efficiently spread their business throughout Europe.

19. Review the table of contents and identify whether each of the chapters from Chapter 2 through Chapter 21 have a macro or micro perspective.

    ANSWER: Chapters 2 through 8 are macro, while Chapter 9 through 21 are micro.

20. Explain why MNCs such as Coca Cola and PepsiCo. Inc. still have numerous opportunities for international expansion.

    ANSWER: Countries are at various stages of development. Some countries have just recently opened their borders to MNCs. Many of these countries do not offer sufficient food or drink products to their consumers.

21. An MNC desires to penetrate a foreign market with either a licensing agreement with a foreign firm or the acquisition of a foreign firm. Explain the differences in potential return and risk between a licensing agreement with a foreign firm, versus the acquisition of a foreign firm.

ANSWER: A licensing agreement has limited potential for return, because the foreign firm will receive much of the benefits as a result of the licensing agreement. Yet, the MNC has limited risk, because it did not need to invest substantial funds in the foreign country.

An acquisition by the MNC requires a substantial investment. If this investment is not a success, the MNC may have trouble selling the firm it acquired for a reasonable price. Thus, there is more risk. However, if this investment is successful, all of the benefits accrue to the MNC.

Solution to WSJ Case: Anheuser Busch's Joint Venture in Japan

1. Explain how the joint venture can enable Anheuser Busch to achieve its objective of maximizing shareholder wealth.

   ANSWER: The joint venture creates a way for Anheuser Busch to distribute Budweiser throughout Japan. It enables Anheuser Busch to penetrate the Japanese market without requiring a substantial investment in Japan.

2. Explain how the joint venture can limit the risk of the international business.

   ANSWER: The joint venture has limited risk because Anheuser Busch does not need to establish its own distribution network in Japan. Thus, Anheuser Busch may be able to use a smaller investment for the international business, and there is a higher probability that the international business will be successful.

3. Many international joint ventures are intended to circumvent barriers that normally prevent foreign competition. What barrier in Japan is Anheuser Busch circumventing as a result of the joint venture? What barrier in the U. S. is Kirin circumventing as a result of the joint venture?

   ANSWER: Anheuser Busch is able to benefit from Kirin's distribution system in Japan, which would not normally be so accessible. Kirin is able to learn more about how Anheuser Busch expanded its product across numerous countries, and therefore breaks through an "information" barrier.

4. Explain how Anheuser Busch could lose some of its market share in countries outside of Japan as a result of this particular joint venture.

ANSWER: Anheuser Busch could lose some of its market share to Kirin as a result of explaining its worldwide expansion strategies to Kirin. However, it appears that Anheuser Busch expects the potential benefits of the joint venture outweigh any potential adverse effects.

Solution to Case Problem: Ranger Supply Company

This case is simply intended to force students to think about reasons for or against international business. As with most cases, there are no perfect solutions, but there are some general conclusions that can be drawn.

a) Some of the more obvious factors to consider are:

1. Competition. There are similar distributors in Canada, whereas Eastern Europe may not have an organized system for the distribution of office supplies. Yet, some European firms (like the British competitor) may attempt to pursue the Eastern European market.

2. Transportation Costs. The costs of transporting office supplies to Eastern Europe would be high, placing Ranger at a relative disadvantage compared to other European firms.

3. Export Barriers. Either country could impose tariffs or quotas on the exports. Canada is less likely than Eastern European countries to impose such restrictions.

4. Marketing Characteristics. Ranger would have an easier time adapting to the Canadian market. The information about Eastern Europe firms would be more limited. Thus, Ranger would be unable to identify many of the firms that may need office supplies, unless it expended funds to search for newly opened retail stores. Furthermore, these stores may prefer to deal with a supplier that is not so distant. For example, they may have connections with Western Europe suppliers. Since Ranger has no experience in Eastern Europe, it may be at a disadvantage in attempting to penetrate that market.

5. Exchange Rates. The future exchange rates of the Canadian dollar and currencies of Eastern European countries could be relevant. Even if Ranger plans to invoice the exports in dollars, the future exchange rates will influence the amount of foreign currency needed by the firms in Canada or Eastern Europe to purchase the supplies. Therefore, foreign demand for the supplies will be influenced by the exchange rates. The future East European currency values are more uncertain. In fact, the governments may even prevent conversion of these currencies into U. S. dollars.

Overall, most of the factors would favor Canada as the more reasonable market to pursue.

b) Recall that the reason for Ranger to expand overseas was to offset the anticipated U. S. demand for its supplies. In this way, it could maintain its present production level and avoid problems with excess employment. Establishing a subsidiary in another country defeats the idea of maintaining the production level in the U. S. Many employees would probably not be willing to relocate without substantial compensation. The firm would now have two plants instead of one, which could prevent it from fully capitalizing on economies of scale.

Project

1. Look in a recent annual report of an MNC which interests you. Summarize any comments made in the annual report about:

   - the MNC's level of international sales
   - the MNC's plans to expand overseas in the future
   - the impact of the MNC's foreign business on its recent performance

   Does it appear that the MNC has benefited from its international operations? Explain.

   Results of the project will vary with the MNC chosen. This project allows students to realize how significant the international business can be for some MNCs.

Chapter 2

International Flow of Funds

Lecture Outline

Balance of Payments
- Current Account
- Capital Account

Factors Affecting the Current Account
- Impact of Inflation
- Impact of National Income
- Impact of Government Restrictions
- Impact of Exchange Rates
- Interaction of Factors
- Correcting a Balance of Trade Deficit
- Why a Weak Home Currency is not a Perfect Solution

Factors Affecting the Capital Account Balance
- Impact of Taxes
- Impact of Capital Controls
- Impact of Exchange Rates
- Agencies that Promote International Flows

Chapter Theme

This chapter provides an overview of the international environment surrounding MNCs. Foreign exchange as well as foreign lending and borrowing are available in the international financial markets. The chapter is macro-oriented in that it discusses international payments on a country by country basis. This macro discussion is useful information for an MNC since the MNC can be affected by changes in a country's current account and capital account positions.

Topics to Stimulate Class Discussion

1. Is a current account deficit something to worry about?

2. If a government wants to correct a current account deficit, why can't it simply enforce restrictions on imports?

3. Why don't exchange rates always adjust to correct current account deficits?

Answers to End of Chapter Questions

1. What is the current account generally composed of?

   ANSWER: The current account balance is composed of 1. the balance of trade, 2. the net amount of payments of interest to foreign investors and from foreign investment, 3. payments from international tourism, and 4. private gifts and grants.

2. What is the capital account generally composed of?

   ANSWER: The capital account is composed of all capital investments made between countries, including both direct foreign investment and purchases of securities with maturities exceeding one year.

3. Discuss the trend in the U.S. current account position since 1980. How can you explain the trend?

   ANSWER: The U.S. current account deficit increased over the period 1980-84. This is largely due to the strong dollar which increased U.S. imports and decreased U.S. exports. In the 1985-87 period the current account deficit continued to increase, even though the dollar weakened. Some foreign exporters reduced their prices to compensate U.S. importers for the weak dollar. In addition, some U.S. importers shifted their purchases to those countries (such as South Korea) in which the dollar did not weaken. Thus, the weak dollar caused a shift in the U.S. demand for imports among countries, but the total demand for imports was still very high. In the late 1980's and early 1990's current account deficit was smaller than it was in 1987, but was still very large.

4. How would a relatively high home inflation rate affect the home country's current account, other things being equal?

   ANSWER: A high inflation rate tends to increase imports and decrease exports, thereby increasing the current account deficit, other things equal.

5. How would a weakening home currency affect the home country's current account, other things being equal?

   ANSWER: A weakening home currency increases the prices of imports purchased by the home country and reduces the prices paid by foreign businesses for the home country's exports. This should cause a decrease in the home country's demand for imports and increase in the foreign demand for the home country's exports, and therefore increase the current account. However, this relationship can be distorted by other factors. For example, when the dollar weakened during the 1985-87 period, the current account deficit became larger. Foreign exporters to the U.S. offset the weak dollar effect by reducing their prices, so that they could retain the U.S. demand for their goods, In addition, while the dollar weakened against major currencies, it strengthened against some other currencies. This encouraged U.S. importers to purchase more goods denominated in currencies that weakened against the dollar.

6. How can government restrictions affect international payments among countries?

   ANSWER: Governments can place tariffs or quotas on imports to restrict imports. They can also place taxes on income from foreign securities, thereby discouraging investors from purchasing foreign securities. If they loosen restrictions, they can encourage international payments among countries.

7. Is a negative current account harmful to a country? Discuss.

   ANSWER: This question is intended to encourage opinions and does not have a perfect solution. A negative current account is thought to reflect lost jobs in a country, which is unfavorable. Yet, the foreign importing reflects strong competition from foreign producers which may keep prices (inflation) low.

8. More than 500 U.S. firms have developed offices or factories in China. Many other U.S. firms have become exporters to China in recent years. However, the U.S. government has periodically threatened to restrict business between the U.S. and China until China improves its human rights record. The U.S. Chamber of Commerce has estimated that heavy restrictions of U.S. - China business could cause layoffs of 150,000 U.S. workers. Should the U.S. use trade restrictions as a means of encouraging improvements in human rights in some countries? If so, how will this affect U.S. firms that are considering business in less developed countries?

ANSWER: There is no perfect solution, but the tradeoff should be recognized. When trade is used as the means to correct human rights problems, those firms that initiated their business in China (or other countries) will suffer major losses. These firms may argue that they are mistreated by such restrictions, and that the country of concern will not necessarily improve its human rights record even with the restrictions.

9. It is sometimes suggested that a floating exchange rate will adjust to reduce or eliminate any current account deficit. Explain why this adjustment would occur. Why does the exchange rate not always adjust to a current account deficit?

   ANSWER: A current account deficit reflects a net sale of the home currency in exchange for other currencies. This places downward pressure on that home currency's value. If the currency weakens, it will reduce the home demand for foreign goods (since goods will now be more expensive), and will increase the home export volume (since exports will appear cheaper to foreign countries). In some cases, the home currency will remain strong even though a current account deficit exists, since other factors (such as international capital flows) can offset the forces placed on the currency by the current account.

10. What are some of the major objectives of the IMF?

    ANSWER: Major IMF objectives are to 1. promote cooperation among countries on international monetary issues, 2. promote stability in exchange rates, 3. provide temporary funds to member countries attempting to correct imbalances of international payments, 4. promote free mobility of capital funds across countries, and 5. promote free trade.

11. From 1985 to 1987 the dollar substantially depreciated but the U.S. demand for particular foreign imports was not significantly affected. Explain why.

    ANSWER: Some foreign exporters reduced the prices of their goods to U.S. importers in order to compensate for the weak dollar. This offsetting effect allowed U.S. importers to purchase some foreign goods for about the same price as before, even though the dollar was worth less.

12. If a U.S. importer is charged higher prices for its imported supplies, what will influence its decision to switch to a U.S. supplier?

    ANSWER: A U.S. importer will more seriously consider switching to a U.S. supplier if 1. the higher import prices are expected to continue, and 2. if a U.S. supplier can offer similar quality.

13. From 1986 to 1988 the dollar depreciated against most major currencies but not against the currencies of South Korea and Singapore. Explain why the balance of trade between the United States and these countries would shift in reaction to the dollar's depreciation against major currencies. Would the U.S. balance-of-trade deficit have been larger or smaller if the dollar depreciated against all currencies during this period? Explain.

    ANSWER: The dollar's weakness against major currencies encouraged U.S. importers to shift away from imports denominated in those major currencies (unless the exporters reduced prices to offset the effect of the weak dollar). Some U.S. importers shifted to imports from South Korea and Singapore, since the dollar did not weaken against the currencies of those countries.

    If the dollar weakened against all currencies, the U.S. balance of trade deficit would likely have been smaller. Some U.S. importers would have more seriously considered purchasing their goods in the U.S. rather than shifting from major foreign countries to South Korea and Singapore if the dollar had weakened against these currencies as well.

14. Explain how a country can assess the historical impact of exchange rate movements on its imports. How can we use this information to forecast the expected impact of exchange rate movements on future imports?

    ANSWER: To assess the historical impact of exchange rates on imports, regression analysis can be used (as discussed in the "Applied Research" box). Regression analysis estimates regression coefficients, which measure the sensitivity of one variable to changes in other variables.

    If the exchange rate movements have a lagged impact on imports, the recent percentage change in the exchange rate could be used along with the estimated regression coefficient to forecast the future percentage change in imports.

15. In 1989 South Korea's export growth stalled. Some South Korean firms suggested that South Korea's primary export problem is the weakness in the Japanese yen. How would you interpret this statement?

    ANSWER: One of South Korea's primary competitors in exporting is Japan, which produces and exports many of the same types of products to the same countries. When the Japanese yen is weak, some importers switch to Japanese products in place of South Korean products. For this reason, it is often suggested that South Korea's primary export problem is weakness in the Japanese yen. In 1988, when the Japanese yen was strong, South Korea's exports grew by 29 percent. However, in 1989 the yen weakened, and the growth in South Korea's exports stalled.

16. In 1990, the U.S. balance of trade deficit was about $100 billion, which was the smallest deficit in several years. The smaller trade deficit was attributed to a strong demand for U.S. exports. What do you think is the underlying reason for the strong demand for U.S. exports?

    ANSWER: The strong demand for U.S. exports in 1990 was at least partially attributed to the U.S. dollar's weakness against most currencies. Thus, U.S. goods were relatively cheap from the perspective of non-U.S. countries because the dollar was cheap. [Answer is based on opinion]

17. In recent years there has been considerable momentum to reduce or remove trade barriers in an effort to achieve "free trade." Yet, one disgruntled executive of an exporting firm stated "Free trade is not conceivable; we are always at the mercy of the exchange rate. Any country can use this mechanism to impose trade barriers." What does this statement mean?

    ANSWER: This statement implies that even if there were no explicit barriers, a government could attempt to manipulate exchange rates to a level that would effectively reduce foreign competition. For example, a U.S. firm may be discouraged from attempting to export to Japan if the value of the dollar is very high against the yen. The prices of the U.S. goods from the Japanese perspective are too high because of the strong dollar. The reverse situation could also be possible in which a Japanese exporting firm is priced out of the U.S. market because of a strong yen (weak dollar). [Answer is based on opinion]

18. The Single European Act was expected to promote more cross- border trade within Europe. Yet, there was some concern that firms exporting to Europe would lose business. Why?

    ANSWER: There was some concern about a so-called "Fortress Europe" in which only firms within Europe could trade without excessive restrictions. European businesses could be protected from competition by non-European firms if trade barriers were imposed on any exports to Europe.

19. Explain why events in Japan can influence financial markets in the United States.

    ANSWER: Japan is a major investor in the U.S. financial markets. Consequently, the U.S. financial markets now rely on Japanese investment. For example, Japanese investors account for between 15 and 30 percent of the purchases of U.S. Treasury bonds. If the Japanese investors discontinued their investment, U.S. interest rates would be higher.

20 Explain how the German reunification could affect U.S. interest rates.

ANSWER: The German reunification caused an increase in the German demand for loanable funds (in response to preparing for more opportunities in East Germany, and financial support for improving economic conditions there). Capital flows from the U.S. to Germany (to capitalize on high interest rates) caused a reduction in funds available in the U.S., which placed upward pressure on U.S. interest rates.

Solution to WSJ Case: International Financial Flows

1. It was mentioned that expectations of a strong dollar can affect the tendency of U.S. investors to invest abroad. Explain this effect.

   ANSWER: A weak dollar would discourage U.S. investors from investing abroad. It can cause the investors to purchase foreign currency (when investing) at a higher exchange rate than the exchange rate they would sell the currency (when the investment is liquidated).

2. It was mentioned that low U.S. interest rates can affect the tendency of U.S. investors to invest abroad. Explain this effect.

   ANSWER: Low U.S. interest rates can encourage U.S. investors to invest abroad, as investors seek higher returns on their investment than they can earn in the U.S.

3. In general terms, what is the attraction of the foreign investments to U.S. investors?

   ANSWER: The main attraction is potentially higher returns. The sales of government-owned industries in Third-World countries create opportunities for U.S. investors that are not available in the U.S. In addition, the international stocks can outperform U.S. stocks, and international bonds can outperform U.S. bonds. However, there is no guarantee that the returns on international investments will be so favorable. Some investors may also pursue international investments to diversify their investment portfolio, which can possibly reduce risk.

Solution to Case Problem: Mapleleaf Paper Company

This case reflects the actual experience of a Canadian exporting firm (although the name and industry have been changed) to the free-trade agreement on January 2, 1989. The appreciation in Canadian dollars (resulting from the agreement) offset the tariff, so that the firm was no better off with the free-trade agreement. The case shows that the effects of free trade are not always so obvious and may differ across firms.

a) While the tariff allowed for a 12 percent decline in price, the U.S. clients will have to pay more dollars to obtain Canadian dollars in the future, based on the forecast of the exchange rate. The exchange rate is expected to rise by 13.15 percent. Given that the 12 percent tariff is removed along with the exchange rate movement, the net effect will be an increase in price to U.S. clients of about one percent. Based on the relationship between the price and U.S. demand, the U.S. demand for Mapleleaf paper should decline 3 percent in response to the one percent increase in price. This implies a U.S. demand of 174,600 rolls of paper per year.

   In Canada, the 20 percent increase in demand (provided in the case) implies an annual demand of 24,000 rolls. Therefore, the total demand for Mapleleaf paper should be around 198,600 rolls, which is slightly less than the total demand in the past.

b) The precise forecast is not as important as the general concept here. What seemed to be a favorable event does not benefit Mapleleaf. While the free-trade agreement allows for the removal of tariffs, it causes a shift in international trade flows, which places upward pressure on the Canadian dollar's value. The appreciation of the Canadian dollar is expected to overwhelm the effect of removing the tariff, forcing the price in U.S. dollars to rise.

c) The U.S. exporting firm is not directly affected by the removal of the tariff on Canadian exports, but would benefit from the appreciation of the Canadian dollar.

Project

1. Once a month, the U.S. balance of trade figures are announced. Look in the *Wall Street Journal* or other business periodicals to determine how the U.S. trade deficit has changed in the last month. What explanation is given for the change in the trade deficit? Is the change in the trade deficit attributed to a change in the U.S. dollar's value? Explain.

   The intent of this project is to realize how trade flows can be affected by the value of the dollar. A weaker dollar can sometimes reduce the balance-of-trade deficit in the U.S., unless other factors offset this effect.

Chapter 3

International Financial Markets

Lecture Outline

Foreign Exchange Market
- Bank Participation
- Bid/Ask Spread
- Exchange Rate Risk at Banks
- Forward Contracts
- Interpreting Foreign Exchange Quotations
- Cross Exchange Rates
- Currency Futures and Options Markets

Eurocurrency Market
- Development of the Eurocurrency Market
- Asian Dollar Market

Eurocredit Market

Eurobond Market

International Stock Markets

Use of International Financial Markets

Chapter Theme

This chapter identifies and discusses the various international financial markets used by MNCs. These markets facilitate day-to-day operations of MNCs, including foreign exchange transactions, investing in foreign markets, and borrowing in foreign markets.

Topics to Stimulate Class Discussion

1. Where is the foreign exchange market?

2. Why does a foreign exchange market exist?

3. Which international financial markets are most important to a firm that consistently needs short-term funds? What about a firm that needs long-term funds?

Answers to End of Chapter Questions

1. List some of the important characteristics of bank foreign exchange services that MNCs should consider.

   ANSWER: The important characteristics are (1) competitiveness of the quote, (2) the firm's relationship with the bank, (3) speed of execution, (4) advice about current market conditions, and (5) forecasting advice.

2. Assume that a bank's bid price for Canadian dollars is $.7938 while its ask price is $.81. What is the bid/ask percentage spread?

   ANSWER: ($.81 - &.7938)/$.81 = .02 or 2%

3. Compute the forward discount or premium for the French franc whose 90-day forward rate is $.102 and spot rate is $.10. State whether your answer is a discount or premium.

   ANSWER: [($.102 - $.10)/$.10] x 360 = .08 or 8% (premium)

4. Of what use is a forward contract to an MNC?

   ANSWER: The forward contract can hedge future receivables or payables in foreign currencies to insulate the firm against exchange rate risk.

5. How can a forward contract backfire?

   ANSWER: A forward contract can backfire when the forward rate at the time a forward contract is negotiated is (1) less than the spot rate that exists when receivables arrive, or (2) more than the spot rate that exists when payables are due.

6. If a dollar is worth 1.7 German marks, what is the dollar value of a mark?

   ANSWER: (1/1.7) = about $.5882

7. Assume that a French franc is worth $.17 and a Japanese yen is worth $.008. What is the cross rate of the French franc with respect to yen? That is, how many yen equal a franc?

   ANSWER: ($.17/$.008) = 21.25

   1 French franc = 21.25 yen

8. Explain how the Eurocurrency, Eurocredit, and Eurobond markets differ from one another.

   ANSWER: The Eurocurrency market focuses on short-term deposits and loans, while the Eurocredit market is used to tap medium- term loans, and the Eurobond market is used to obtain long- term funds (by issuing long-term bonds).

9. Briefly describe the historical developments that led to floating exchange rates as of 1973.

   ANSWER: Country governments had difficulty in maintaining fixed exchange rates. In 1971, the bands were widened. Yet, the difficulty of controlling exchange rates even within these wider bands continued. As of 1973, the bands were eliminated so that rates could respond to market forces without limits (although governments still did intervene periodically).

10. What is the function of the Eurocurrency market?

    ANSWER: The function of the Eurocurrency market is to efficiently facilitate the flow of international funds from firms or governments with excess funds to those in need of funds.

11. Briefly describe the reasons for growth in the Eurocurrency market during the last twenty years.

    ANSWER: Growth was largely due to (1) regulations in the U.S. which limited foreign lending by U.S. banks; (2) regulated ceilings placed on interest rates of dollar deposits in the U.S., which encouraged deposits to be placed in the Eurocurrency market where ceilings were nonexistent, and (3) zero reserve requirements of dollars deposited in Eurobanks which allowed Eurobanks to offer attractive rates on deposits and on loans.

12. Why do interest rates vary among countries?

    ANSWER: Interest rates in each country are based on the supply of funds and demand for funds within that country. Supply and demand conditions vary among countries.

13. With regard to Eurocredit loans, who are the common borrowers?

    ANSWER: Large corporations and some government agencies commonly request Eurocredit loans.

14. What is LIBOR and how is it used in the Eurocredit market?

    ANSWER: LIBOR (London interbank offer rate) is the rate of interest at which Eurobanks lend to each other. It is used as a base from which loan rates on other loans are determined in the Eurocredit market.

15. Why would a bank desire to participate in syndicated Eurocredit loans?

    ANSWER: No single bank would be totally exposed to the risk that the borrower may fail to repay the loan. The risk is spread among all lending banks within the syndicate.

16. Discuss some reasons for the popularity of the Eurobond market.

    ANSWER: This market can sometimes avoid regulations required for domestic bonds and may allow borrowers to obtain funds at lower interest rates.

17. Compute the forward discount or premium for the British pound whose 180-day forward rate is \$1.75 and spot rate is \$1.78. State whether your answer is a discount or premium.

    ANSWER: $\text{Forward Discount} = \frac{1.75 - 1.78}{1.78} \times \frac{360}{180} = -3.37\%$ (minus sign implies discount)

18. The Wolfpack Corporation is a U.S. exporter that invoices its exports to the United Kingdom in British pounds. If it expects that the pound will appreciate against the dollar in the future, should it hedge its exports with a forward contract? Explain.

    ANSWER: Wolfpack Corporation should not hedge because it would benefit from appreciation of the pound when it converts the pounds to dollars.

19. Explain why firms may consider issuing stock in foreign markets.

    ANSWER: Firms may issue stock in foreign markets when they are concerned their home market may be unable to absorb the entire issue. In addition, these firms may have foreign currency inflows in the foreign country that can be used to pay dividends on foreign-issued stock. They may also desire to enhance their global image. Other reasons are also provided in text.

20. Bullet Inc., a U.S. firm, is planning to issue new stock in the United States during this month. The only decision it has left is the specific day in which the stock should be issued. Why do you think this firm monitors results of the Tokyo stock market every morning?

    ANSWER: The U.S. stock market prices sometimes follow Japanese market prices. Thus, the firm would possibly be able to issue its stock at a lower price in the U.S. if it can use the Japanese market as an indicator of what will happen in the U.S. market. However, this indicator will not always be accurate.

Solution to WSJ Case: Impact of the ERM on Foreign Exchange Services

1. Explain why the widening of the ERM bands causes a greater need for foreign exchange traders.

   ANSWER: As the ERM bands widen, there is more potential for a European currency to deviate from its present position. Thus, the banks that speculate on currency values may have more opportunities. Also, corporations may be more likely to hedge their positions (because of the higher risk), which provides more business to foreign exchange traders.

2. If Europe ever adopts a single currency, how would the demand for foreign exchange traders be affected?

   ANSWER: With a single European currency, there would be less need for foreign exchange traders, because all European transactions could be handled without exchanging currencies. Also, foreign exchange traders would not be switching positions among European currencies (as a speculative strategy) if there was only one European currency.

3. Explain the comment from Lehman Brothers that some countries were previously viewed as a single entity when ERM bands were tight, but now each country must be accessed individually.

   ANSWER: When the ERM bands were tight, European currencies would move in tandem against other currencies. However, as ERM bands widened, each European currency began to move independently and could no longer be assessed along with other European currencies.

4. Describe the recent increase in international financial flows throughout Europe, and how these flows affect the need for foreign exchange traders.

   ANSWER: There are more financial flows into Europe to purchase European securities. There are also more international alliances and partnerships between European firms and other firms. These transactions require the exchange of foreign currencies, causing an increased need for foreign exchange traders.

Solution to Case Problem: Gretz Tool Company

a) Citicorp could facilitate the following financial transactions:

   1. Foreign Exchange. Citicorp could provide whatever currency was needed by Gretz in the foreign exchange market.

   2. Short-Term Financing. Citicorp could provide short-term loans to Gretz in whatever currency is desired through the Eurocurrency market. (Citicorp would be the creditor

here.) Citicorp could also accept short-term deposits in various currencies through the Eurocurrency market.

3. Medium-Term Financing. Citicorp could provide mediumterm loans to Gretz in whatever currency is desired through the Euro-Credit Market (Citicorp would be the creditor here).

4. Long-Term Financing. Citicorp could place bonds issued by Gretz in the Eurobond market (Citicorp would normally serve as an intermediary rather than the creditor here). Citicorp could also help Gretz place newly issued stock in foreign stock markets.

b) Citicorp and other U.S. banks have historically been restricted from providing securities-related services in the U.S. (although these restrictions have been reduced over time). Therefore, Gretz may need to hire an investment banking firm to issue large amounts of stock in the U.S.

c) Normally, a subsidiary would prefer to borrow the currency that it uses to invoice its products. Thus, the future cash inflows would be in the same currency that is needed to pay back the loan, and exchange rate risk is avoided. Since the French subsidiary probably invoices its products in French francs, this is the logical currency to borrow.

However, the high interest rate on the French franc may cause the subsidiary to consider borrowing a different currency. Yet, it must recognize the risk involved. The currency borrowed would initially be converted to francs. At a future point in time, francs will be converted to that currency to repay the loan. Thus, the risk is that the currency borrowed appreciates against the franc over the period of concern. This concept is covered in detail in later chapters. At this point, the objective is to simply make the student aware of the possible alternatives and the risk-return tradeoff involved.

Project

1. Look at a recent copy of *The Wall Street Journal*, and fill in the quotes for spot and forward rates in the following table. Also compute the forward rate premiums in this table.

	Currency					
	British pound	Canadian dollar	French franc	Japanese yen	Swiss franc	German mark
Spot rate						
30-day forward rate						
30-day forward premium or discount						
90-day forward rate						
90-day forward premium or discount						
180-day forward rate						
180-day forward premium or discount						

This project gives students experience at finding exchange rate quotes and computing forward rate premiums.

Chapter 4

Exchange Rate Determination

Lecture Outline

Measuring Exchange Rate Movements

Exchange Rate Equilibrium

Demand for a Currency
Supply of a Currency for Sale

Factors That Influence Exchange Rate Movements

Relative Inflation Rates
Relative Interest Rates
Relative Income Levels
Governmental Controls
Expectations
Interaction of Factors
How Factors Have Influenced Exchange Rates

Speculating on Anticipated Rates

Chapter Theme

This chapter provides an overview of the foreign exchange market. It is designed to illustrate (1) why a market exists, (2) the use of spot and forward transactions, and (3) why exchange rates change over time.

Topics to Stimulate Class Discussion

1. Why does a foreign exchange market exist?

2. What is the use of a forward contract?

3. Show the class a current exchange rate table from a periodical-identify spot and forward quotations; then show class an exchange rate table from a date a month ago, or three months ago. The comparison of tables will illustrate how exchange rates change, and how forward rates of the earlier date will differ from the spot rate of the future date for a given currency.

4. Make up several scenarios, and ask the class how each scenario would, other things equal, affect the demand for a currency, the supply of a currency for sale, and the equilibrium exchange rate. Then integrate several scenarios together to illustrate that in reality other things are not held constant, which makes the assessment of exchange rate movements more difficult.

Answers to End of Chapter Questions

1. Assume the spot rate of the British pound is $1.73. The expected spot rate one year from now is assumed to be $1.66. What percentage depreciation does this reflect?

   ANSWER: ($1.66 - $1.73)/$1.73 = -4.05%

   Expected depreciation of 4.05% percent

2. Assume that the U.S. inflation rate becomes high relative to German inflation. Other things being equal, how should this affect the (a) U.S. demand for German marks, (b) supply of marks for sale, and (c) equilibrium value of the mark?

   ANSWER: Demand for marks should increase, supply of marks for sale should decrease, and the mark's value should increase.

3. Assume that the U.S. interest rates fall relative to British interest rates. Other things being equal, how should this affect the (a) U.S. demand for British pounds, (b) supply of pounds for sale, and (c) equilibrium value of the pound?

ANSWER: Demand for pounds should increase, supply of pounds for sale should decrease, and the pound's value should increase.

4. Assume that the U.S. income level rises at a much higher degree than does the German income level. Other things equal, how should this affect the (a) U.S. demand for German marks, (b) supply of marks for sale, and (c) equilibrium value of the mark.

   ANSWER: Assuming no effect on U.S. interest rates, demand for marks should increase, supply of marks for sale may not be affected, and mark's value should increase.

5. Assume that the Japanese government relaxes its controls on imports by Japanese companies. Other things equal, how should this affect the (a) U.S. demand for Japanese yen, (b) supply of yen for sale, and (c) equilibrium value of the yen.

   ANSWER: Demand for yen should not be affected, supply of yen for sale should increase, and the value of yen should decrease.

6. What is the expected relationship between the relative real interest rates of two countries and the exchange rate of their currencies?

   ANSWER: The higher the real interest rate of a country relative to another country, the stronger will be its home currency, other things equal.

7. Discuss the historical trend of the dollar's value from the middle 1970s to the early 1990s.

   ANSWER: The dollar has generally been strong in the early years of the floating exchange rate system (1973-1976), weak in 1977-1980, strong during the 1981-1984 period, weak during the 1985-1988 period, somewhat mixed in 1989, and weak in 1990. The dollar was erratic in the early 1990s

8. Explain why a public forecast by a respected economist about future interest rates could affect the value of the dollar today. Why do some forecasts by well-respected economists have no impact on today's value of the dollar?

   ANSWER: Interest rate movements affect exchange rates. Speculators can use anticipated interest rate movements to forecast exchange rate movements. They may decide to purchase securities in particular countries because of their expectations about currency movements, since their yield will be affected by changes in a currency's value. These purchases of securities require an exchange of currencies, which can immediately affect the equilibrium value of exchange rates

   If a forecast of interest rates by a respected economist was already anticipated by market participants or is not different from investors original expectations, an announced forecast does not provide new information. Thus, there would be no reaction by investors to such an announcement, and exchange rates would not be affected.

9. Assume that substantial capital flows occur between the United States, County A, and Country B, in all directions. If interest rates in Country A declined, how could this affect the value of Currency A against the dollar? How might this decline in Country A's interest rates possibly affect the value of Currency B against the dollar?

ANSWER: If interest rates in Country A declined, then Country A investors may attempt to capitalize on higher U.S. interest rates, while U.S. investors do not invest in Country A's securities. This places downward pressure on Currency A's value.

If Country A's interest rates declined, U.S. investors that previously invested in Country A may shift to Country B. Yet, Country B's investors that had previously invested in Country A may shift to the U.S. These shifts are somewhat offsetting. There is an increase in investment in both directions between the U.S. and Country B. Thus, we can not determine the direction of Currency B's value against the dollar.

10. Tarheel Company plans to determine how changes in U.S. and German real interest rates will affect the value of the U.S. dollar. (See Appendix B)

a. Describe a regression model that could be used to achieve this purpose. Also explain the expected sign of the regression coefficient.

ANSWER: Various models are possible. One model would be:

$$\text{\% Change in DM} = a_0 + a_1(r_{U.S.} - r_G) + u$$

Where $r_{U.S.}$ = real interest rate in the U.S.

r_G = real interest rate in Germany

a_0 = intercept

a_1 = regression coefficient measuring the relationship between the real interest rate differential and the percentage change in the mark's value

u = error term

Based on the model above, the regression coefficient is expected to have a negative sign. A relatively high real interest rate differential would likely cause a weaker mark value, other things being equal.

An appropriate model would also include other independent variables that may influence the percentage change in the mark's value.

b. If Tarheel Company thought that the existence of a quota in particular historical periods may have affected exchange rates, how might this be accounted for in the regression model.

ANSWER: A dummy variable could be included in the model, assigned a value of one for periods when a quota existed and a value of zero when it did not exist.

11. From 1985 through 1987 the dollar weakened against most major currencies. Why do you think the dollar weakened over this period?

ANSWER: The dollar could have weakened because of the large U.S. balance of trade deficit, which reflects more U.S. demand for foreign goods than the foreign demand for U.S. goods. In some periods, this could be offset by large demand for U.S. dollar-denominated securities. However, during 1985-1987, it appears that the trade flows overwhelmed any other factors.

12. Blue Demon Bank expects that the French franc (FF) will depreciate against the dollar from its spot rate of $.15 to $.14 in 10 days. The following interbank lending and borrowing rates exist:

	Lending Rate	Borrowing Rate
U.S. dollar	8.0%	8.3%
French franc	8.5%	8.7%

Assume that Blue Demon Bank has a borrowing capacity of either $10 million or FF70 million in the interbank market, depending on which currency it wants to borrow.

a. How could Blue Demon Bank attempt to capitalize on its expectations without using deposited funds? Estimate the profits that could be generated from this strategy.

ANSWER: Blue Demon Bank can capitalize on its expectations as follows:

1. Borrow FF70 million

2. Convert the FF70 million to dollars:

FF70,000,000 x $.15 = $10,500,000

3. Lend the dollars through the interbank market at 8.0% annualized over a 10-day period. The amount accumulated in 10 days is:

   $10,500,000 x [1 + (8% x 10/360)] = $10,500,000 x [1.00222] = $10,523,333

4. Repay the franc loan. The repayment amount on the franc loan is:

   FF70,000,000 x [1 + (8.7% x 10/360)]=FF70,000,000x [1.002417]=FF70,169,167

5. Based on the expected spot rate of $.14, the amount of dollars needed to repay the franc loan is:

   FF70,169,167 x $.14 = $9,823,683

6. After repaying the loan, Blue Demon Bank will have a speculative profit (if its forecasted exchange rate is accurate) of:

   $10,523,333 - $9,823,683 = $699,650

b. Assume all the preceding information with the exception: assume that Blue Demon Bank expects the French franc to appreciate from its present spot rate of $.15 to $.17 in 30 days. How could it attempt to capitalize on its expectations without using deposited funds? Estimate the profits that could be generated from this strategy.

ANSWER: Blue Demon Bank can capitalize on its expectations as follows:

1. Borrow $10 million

2. Convert the $10 million to francs:

   $10,000,000/$.15 = FF66,666,667

3. Lend the francs through the interbank market at 8.5% annualized over a 30-day period. The amount accumulated in 30 days is:

   FF66,666,667 x [1 + (8.5% x 30/360)] = FF66,666,667 x [1.0071]= FF67,138,889

4. Repay the dollar loan. The repayment amount on the dollar loan is:

   $10,000,000 x [1 + (8.3% x 30/360)] = $10,000,000 [1.0069] = $10,069,000

5. Convert the francs to dollars to repay the loan. The amount of dollars to be received in 30 days (based on the expected spot rate of $.17) is:

   FF67,138,889 x $.17 = $11,413,611

6. The profits are determined by estimating the dollars available after repaying the loan:

   $11,413,611 - $10,069,000 = $1,344,611

13. Assume that the United States heavily invests in government and corporate securities of Country K. In addition, residents of Country K heavily invest in the United States. Approximately $10 billion worth of investment transactions occur between these two countries each year. The total dollar value of trade transactions per year is about $8 million. This information is expected to also hold in the future.

    Because your firm exports goods to Country K, your job as international cash manager requires you to forecast the value of Country K's currency (the "kranc") with respect to the dollar. Explain how each of the following conditions will affect the value of the kranc, holding other things equal. Then aggregate all of these impacts to develop an overall forecast of the kranc's movement against the dollar.

    a. The U.S. inflation has suddenly increased substantially, while Country K's inflation remains low.

       ANSWER: Increased U.S. demand for the kranc. Decreased supply of krancs for sale. Upward pressure in the kranc's value.

    b. The U.S. interest rates have increased substantially, while Country K's interest rates remain low. Investors of both countries are attracted to high interest rates.

       ANSWER: Decreased U.S. demand for the kranc. Increased supply of krancs for sale. Downward pressure on the kranc's value.

    c. The U.S. income level increased substantially, while Country K's income level has remained unchanged.

       ANSWER: Increased U.S. demand for the kranc. Upward pressure on the kranc's value.

    d. The U.S. is expected to place a small tariff on goods imported from Country K (assume that there will be no retaliation).

       ANSWER: The tariff will cause a decrease in Country K's desire for U.S. goods, and will therefore reduce the supply of krancs for sale. Upward pressure on the kranc's value.

    e. Combine all expected impacts to develop an overall forecast.

       ANSWER: Three of the scenarios described above place upward pressure on the value of the kranc. However, these scenarios are related to trade and trade flows are relatively minor between the U.S. and Country K. The interest rate scenario places downward pressure on the kranc's value. Since the interest rates affect capital flows, and capital flows dominate trade flows between the U.S. and Country K, the interest rate scenario should overwhelm all other scenarios. Thus, when considering the importance of implications of all scenarios, the kranc is expected to depreciate.

14. Every month, the U.S. trade deficit figures are announced. The foreign exchange traders often react to this announcement and even attempt to forecast the figures before they are announced.

    a. Why do you think the trade deficit announcement sometimes has such an impact on foreign exchange trading?

    ANSWER: The trade deficit announcement may provide a reasonable forecast of future trade deficits and therefore has implications about supply and demand conditions in the foreign exchange market. For example, if the trade deficit was larger than anticipated, and is expected to continue, this implies that the U.S. demand for foreign currencies may be larger than initially anticipated. Thus, the dollar would be expected to weaken. Some speculators may take position in foreign currencies immediately and could cause an immediate decline in the dollar.

    b. In some periods, foreign exchange traders do not respond to a trade deficit announcement, even when the announced deficit is very large. Offer an explanation for such a lack of response.

    ANSWER: If the market correctly anticipated the trade deficit figure, then any news contained in the announcement has already been accounted for in the market. The market should only respond to an announcement about the trade deficit if the announcement contains new information.

15. As the barriers are removed to allow free trade and capital flows across European countries, there is much interest in creating a single European currency that would be used by all countries by 1997. The German government stated that a single European currency would only be appropriate if those European countries with relatively high inflation are able to reduce their inflation rates. Why do you think this would be a necessary condition for the implementation of a single European currency?

    ANSWER: If some European countries can not maintain low inflation, and there was a single European currency, these countries would probably experience major balance of trade deficits. There would be no self-correcting mechanism since these countries would not have their own currencies. [Answer is based on intuition, is not directly from the text.]

16. The currencies of some Latin American countries depreciate against the U.S. dollar on a daily basis. What do you think is the major factor that places such severe downward pressure on the value of these currencies? What obvious change in Latin American economic policy is needed to prevent further depreciation of Latin American currencies?

ANSWER: These countries have very high inflation, which places downward pressure on their currencies. Effective anti-inflationary policies are needed to prevent further depreciation.

17. As the "Iron Curtain" separating East and West Germany was removed in the fall of 1989, would you have anticipated appreciation or depreciation of the German mark against the dollar? Why?

    ANSWER: As the "Iron Curtain" was removed, the most appropriate expectation is that the German mark would appreciate against the dollar. The removal of the "Iron Curtain" opened up new opportunities in West Germany, causing an immediate increase in capital flows from the U.S. to West Germany. In addition, there was an increase in U.S. direct foreign investment in West Germany. These actions require the exchange of dollars for marks.

    Some students may suggest that higher national income and higher inflation will result from the German reunification, which ultimately will cause the mark to depreciate. However, these factors affect the mark through trade flows, which occur with a lag. The capital flows occurred immediately, and therefore had an immediate impact on the mark's value.

18. Analysts commonly attribute the appreciation of a currency to expectations that economic conditions will strengthen. Yet, this chapter suggests that when the factors are held constant, increased national income could increase imports, and cause the local currency to weaken. In reality, other factors are not constant. What other factor is likely to be affected by increased economic growth, which could place upward pressure on the value of the local currency?

    ANSWER: Interest rates tend to rise in response to a stronger economy, and higher interest rates can place upward pressure on the local currency (as long as there is not offsetting pressure by higher expected inflation).

19. In the early 1990s, Russia was attempting to import more goods, but had little to offer other countries in terms of potential exports. In addition, Russia's inflation rate was high. Explain the type of pressure that these factors placed on the Russian currency.

    ANSWER: The large amount of Russian imports and lack of Russian exports placed downward pressure on the Russian currency. The high inflation rate in Russia also placed downward pressure on the Russian currency.

Solution to WSJ Case: Foreign Exchange Trading During the ERM Crisis

1. Explain why the spread between the bid and the offering (ask) prices may widen during a period when exchange rate movements are volatile.

ANSWER: Commercial banks stand ready to buy or sell currencies, but may be less comfortable accommodating orders when exchange rate movements are volatile. Therefore, they lower their bid (relative to the offering price) to compensate for the risk of receiving a currency that may abruptly decline in value.

2. What is meant by the comment that traders at Chase Manhattan are swapping prices and orders?

   ANSWER: As one trader at Chase Manhattan receives an order over the phone to buy a specific currency, he or she may shout the order to other traders in the trading room, to see if any other traders at Chase are receiving an opposite order. In this case, the trader can buy the currency at one exchange rate (the bid price) and be assured that the currency will be sold by another trader at Chase (at the offering price). Thus, Chase does not expose itself to exchange rate risk in this case.

3. Why did Chase Manhattan attempt to execute a large order (a customer wanting to sell £100 million) in pieces rather than all at once. Do you think Chase was the ultimate purchaser of the British pounds?

   ANSWER: Chase likely executed the order in pieces because it searched for other offsetting order to match up with the large order. That is, as a buy order for £5 million came in, it executed a £5 million sell order simultaneously as a piece of a large order) to match the two orders. In this way, it is not exposing itself to exchange rate risk. It is only serving as an intermediary, and benefits from the difference between its bid price quoted when buying the pounds to accommodate the sell order, versus the offering price quoted when selling pounds to accommodate the buy order. As more orders came in to buy pounds over the next few minutes, Chase matched these orders up with the large sell order. In other words, it may have taken Chase 10 orders on the buy side to completely offset the one large order on the sell side.

Solution to Case Problem: Bruin Aircraft, Inc.

a. Some of the more commonly cited factors are listed below. This exercise forces students to recognize how factors influence the value of each currency.

Factors That Can Affect the Value of the Pound	Check (X) Here if the Factor Influences the U.S. Demand for Pounds	Check (X) Here if the Factor Influences the Supply of Pounds for Sale
$i_{U.S.} - i_{U.K.}$	X	X
$INF_{U.S.} - INF_{U.S.}$	X	X
Income Growth Differential	X	X
New U.S. Quotas on Imports from U.K.	X	
U.S. Tariffs on Imports from U.K.	X	
New U.K. Quotas on Imports from U.S.		X
New U.K. Tariffs on Imports from U.S.		X
Government Intervention to Purchase $ with Pounds		X
Government Intervention to Purchase Pounds with $	X	
Government Tax to be Imposed on Interest Income Earned by U.K. Investors from Future U.S. Investments		X
Government Tax to be Imposed on Interest Income Earned by U.S. Investors from Future U.K. Investments	X	

Project

1. Use the *Wall Street Journal* or some other business periodical to obtain the recent spot rate and the spot rate one year ago for major currencies. Compute the percentage change in the currency and offer reasons why the change may have occurred. Use the following table:

	Currency			
	British pound	Canadian dollar	Japanese yen	German mark
Recent spot rate				
Spot rate last year				
Percentage change				
Reason for change				

This project is intended to demonstrate how volatile currency values can be and to force students to apply theory to actual examples.

Chapter 5

Currency Futures and Options

Lecture Outline

Currency Futures Market
- Currency Futures Contracts Versus Forward Contracts
- Pricing Currency Futures
- Interpreting Currency Futures Contracts Information
- Closing Out a Futures Position
- Credit Risk of Currency Futures Contracts
- Corporate Use of Currency Futures
- Speculation With Currency Futures

Currency Call Options
- Factors Affecting Call Option Premiums
- Hedging With Currency Call Options
- Speculating With Currency Call Options

Currency Put Options
- Factors Affecting Currency Put Option Premiums
- Hedging With Currency Put Options
- Speculating with Currency Put Options

Contingency Graphs for Options

European Currency Options

Chapter Theme

This chapter provides an overview of markets related to foreign exchange which are sometimes referred to as "speculative." Yet, firms are increasing their use of these markets for hedging. The chapter does give speculation some attention, since this is a good way to illustrate the use of a particular instrument based on certain expectations. However, the key is that students have an understanding why firms would consider using these instruments and under what conditions they would use them. This objective is realized to a greater degree in Chapter 10 on hedging. At this point, students need to at least get a feel for what currency futures and options are, and how they can be used.

Topics to Stimulate Class Discussion

1. Why would a firm ever consider futures contracts instead of forward contracts?

2. What advantage do currency options offer that are not available with futures or forward contracts?

3. What are some disadvantages of currency option contracts?

4. Why do currency futures prices change over time?

5. Why do currency options prices change over time?

6. Set up several scenarios, and for each scenario, ask students to determine whether it would be better for the firm to purchase (or sell) forward contracts, futures contracts, call option contracts, or put options contracts.

Answers to End of Chapter Questions

1. Compare and contrast the forward and futures contracts.

   ANSWER: Because currency futures contracts are standardized into small amounts, they can be valuable for the speculator or small firm (a commercial bank's forward contracts are more common for larger amounts). However, the standardized format of futures forces limited maturities and amounts.

2. How can currency futures be used by corporations?

   ANSWER: U.S. corporations which desire to lock in a price at which they can sell a foreign currency would sell currency futures. U.S. corporations which desire to lock in a price at which they can purchase a foreign currency would purchase currency futures.

3. How can currency futures be used by speculators?

   ANSWER: Speculators who expect a currency to appreciate could purchase currency futures contracts for that currency. Speculators who expect a currency to depreciate could sell currency futures contracts for that currency.

4. What is a currency call option?

   ANSWER: A currency call option provides the right to purchase a specified currency at a specified price within a specified period of time.

5. What is a currency put option?

   ANSWER: A currency put option provides the right to sell a specified currency for a specified price within a specified period of time.

6. When should a firm consider purchasing a call option for hedging?

   ANSWER: A call option can hedge a firm's future payables denominated in a foreign currency. It effectively locks in the maximum price to be paid for a currency.

7. When should a firm consider purchasing a put option for hedging?

   ANSWER: A put option can hedge a firm's future receivables denominated in a foreign currency. It effectively locks in the minimum price at which a currency can be sold.

8. When should a speculator purchase a call option on German marks?

   ANSWER: Speculators should purchase a call option on marks if they expect the mark value to appreciate substantially over the period specified by the option contract.

9. When should a speculator purchase a put option on German marks?

   ANSWER: Speculators should purchase a put option on marks if they expect the mark value to depreciate substantially over the period specified by the option contract.

10. List the factors that affect currency call options and briefly explain the relationship that exists for each.

ANSWER: These factors are listed below:

- The higher the existing spot rate relative to the strike price, the greater is the call option value, other things equal.
- The longer the period prior to the expiration date, the greater is the call option value, other things equal.
- The greater the variability of the currency, the greater is the call option value, other things equal.

11. List the factors that affect currency put options and briefly explain the relationship that exists for each.

ANSWER: These factors are listed below:

- The lower the existing spot rate relative to the strike price, the greater is the put option value, other things equal.
- The longer the period prior to the expiration date, the greater is the put option value, other things equal.
- The greater the variability of the currency, the greater is the put option value, other things equal.

12. Assume a speculator purchased a call option on Swiss francs for $.02 per unit. The strike price was $.45 and the spot rate at the time the franc was exercised was $.46. Assume there are 62,500 units in a Swiss franc option. What was the net profit on this option to the speculator?

ANSWER:

Profit per unit on exercising the option	= $.01
Premium paid per unit	= $.02
Net profit per unit	= -$.01
Net profit per option = 62,500 units x (-$.01)	= -$625

13. Assume a U.S. speculator purchased a put option on British pounds for $.04 per unit. The strike price was $1.80 and the spot rate at the time the pound was exercised was $1.59. Assume there are 31,250 units in a British pound option. What was the net profit on the option?

ANSWER:

Profit per unit on exercising the option	= $.21
Premium paid per unit	= $.04
Net profit per unit	= $.17
Net profit for one option = 31,250 units x $.17	= $5,312

14. Assume that a U.S. speculator sold a call option on German marks for $.01 per unit. The strike price was $.36 and the spot rate at the time the option was exercised was $.42. Assume the speculator did not obtain marks until the option was exercised. Also assume that there are 62,500 units in a German mark option. What was the net profit to the seller of the call option?

ANSWER:

Premium received per unit	= $.01
Amount per unit received from selling marks	= $.36
Amount per unit paid when purchasing marks	= $.42
Net profit per unit	= -$.05
Net Profit = 62,500 units x (-$.05)	= -$3,125

15. Assume that a U.S. speculator sold a put option on Canadian dollars for $.03 per unit. The strike price was $.75 and the spot rate at the time the Canadian dollar was exercised was $.72. Assume the speculator immediately sold off the Canadian dollars received when the option was exercised. Also assume that there are 50,000 units in a Canadian dollar option. What was the net profit to the seller of the put option?

ANSWER:

Premium received per unit	= $.03
Amount per unit received from selling C$	= $.72
Amount per unit paid for C$	= $.75
Net profit per unit	= $0

16. What are the advantages and disadvantages to a corporation that uses currency options rather than a forward contract to hedge against exchange rate fluctuations?

ANSWER: A currency option allows more flexibility since it does not commit one to purchase or sell a currency (as is the case with a futures or forward contract). Yet, it does allow the option holder to purchase or sell a currency at a locked-in price.

The disadvantage of a currency option is that the option itself is not free. One must pay a premium for the call option, which is above and beyond the price specified in the contract at which a currency could be purchased.

17. Assume that the transactions listed in Column 1 of the following table are anticipated by U.S. firms that have no other foreign transactions. Place an "X" in the table wherever you see a possible way to hedge each of the transactions.
    a. Georgetown Company plans to purchase German goods denominated in marks.
    b. Harvard Inc. sold goods to Japan, denominated in yen.
    c. Yale Corporation has a subsidiary in France that will be remitting funds to the U.S. parent.
    d. Brown Inc. needs to pay off existing loans soon that were denominated in French francs.
    e. Princeton Company may purchase a company in Japan in the near future (but the deal may not go through).

ANSWER:

	Forward contract		Futures contract		Options contract	
	Forward Purchase	Forward Sale	Buy Futures	Sell Futures	Purchase calls	Purchase puts
a.	X		X		X	
b.		X		X		X
c.		X		X		X
d.	X		X		X	
e.					X	

18. Assume that the British pound's spot rate has moved in cycles over time. How might you try to use futures contracts on pounds to capitalize on this tendency? How could you determine whether such a strategy would have been profitable in previous periods?

    ANSWER: Use recent movements in the pound to forecast future movements. If the pound has been strengthening, purchase futures on pounds. If the pound has been weakening, sell futures on pounds.

    A strategy's profitability can be determined by comparing the amount paid for each contract to the amount for which each contract was sold.

19. Assume that on November 1, the spot rate of the British pound was $1.58 and the price on a December futures contract was $1.59. Assume that the pound depreciated over November, so that by November 30 it was worth $1.51.

    a. What do you think happened to the futures price over the month of November? Why?

ANSWER: The December futures price would have decreased, because it reflects expectations of the future spot rate as of the settlement date. If the existing spot rate is $1.51, the spot rate expected on the December futures settlement date is likely to be near $1.51 as well.

b. If you had known that this would occur, would you have purchased or sold a December futures contract in pounds on November 1? Explain.

ANSWER: You would have sold futures at the existing futures price of $1.59. Then as the spot rate of the pound declined, the futures price would decline and you could close out your futures position by purchasing a futures contract at a lower price. Alternatively, you could wait until the settlement date, purchase the pounds in the spot market, and fulfill the futures obligation by delivering pounds at the price of $1.59 per pound.

20. Assume that a March futures contract on marks was available in January for $.54 per unit. Also assume that forward contracts were available for the same settlement date at a price of $.55 per mark. How could speculators capitalize on this situation, assuming zero transaction costs? How would such speculative activity affect the difference between the forward contract price and the futures price?

    ANSWER: Speculators could purchase mark futures for $.54 per unit, and simultaneously sell marks forward at $.55 per unit. When the marks are received (as a result of the futures position) on the settlement date, the speculators would sell the marks to fulfill their forward contract obligation. This strategy results in a $.01 per unit profit.

    As many speculators capitalize on the strategy described above, they would place upward pressure on futures prices and downward pressure on forward prices. Thus, the difference between the forward contract price and futures price would be reduced or eliminated.

21. LSU Corporation purchased German mark call options for speculative purposes. If these options are exercised, LSU will immediately sell the marks in the spot market. Each option was purchased for a premium of $.03 per unit, with an exercise price of $.55. LSU plans to wait until the expiration date before considering whether to exercise the options. Of course, it will exercise the options at that time only if it is feasible to do so. In the following table, fill in the net profit (or loss) per unit to LSU Corporation based on the listed possible spot rates of the mark that may exist on the expiration date.

ANSWER:

Possible spot rate of the mark on the expiration date	Net profit (or loss) per unit to LSU Corporation if that spot rate occurs
$.56	$.02
.58	.00
.60	.02
.62	.04
.65	.07
.67	.09

22. Auburn Company has purchased Swiss franc put options for speculative purposes. Each option was purchased for a premium of $.02 per unit, with an exercise price of $.66 per unit. Auburn Company will purchase the francs just before it exercises the options (if it is feasible to exercise the options). It plans to wait until the expiration date before considering whether to exercise the options. In the following table, fill in the net profit (or loss) per unit to Auburn Company based on the listed possible spot rates of the franc that may exist on the expiration date.

ANSWER:

Possible spot rate of the mark on the expiration date	Net profit (or loss) per unit to LSU Corporation if that spot rate occurs
$.56	$.08
.59	.05
.64	.00
.67	- .02
.69	- .02
.71	- .02

23. Bama Corporation has sold British pound call options for speculative purposes. The option premium was $.06 per unit and the exercise price was $1.58. Bama will purchase the pounds on the day the options are exercised (if the options are exercised) in order to fulfill its obligation. In the following table, fill in the net profit (or loss) to Bama Corporation if the listed spot rate exists at the time the purchaser of the call options considers exercising them.

ANSWER:

Possible spot rate of the pound on the expiration date	Net profit (or loss) per unit to Bama Corporation if that spot rate occurs
$1.53	$.06
1.55	.06
1.57	.06
1.60	.04
1.62	.02
1.64	.00
1.68	-.04

24. Bulldog, Inc. has sold French franc put options at a premium of $.01 per unit, and with an exercise price of $.16 per unit. It has forecasted the French franc's lowest level over the period of concern as shown in the following table. If that level occurs and the put options are exercised at that time, determine the net profit (or loss) per unit to Bulldog Inc.

ANSWER:

Possible spot rate of the franc on the expiration date	Net profit (or loss) per unit to Bulldog Corporation if that spot rate occurs
$.12	- $.03
.13	- .02
.14	- .01
.15	.00
.16	.01

25. A U.S. professional football team plans to play an exhibition game in the United Kingdom next year. Assume all expenses will be paid by the British government, and a check of 1 million pounds will be provided to the team. The team anticipates that the pound will depreciate substantially by the scheduled date of the game. In addition, the National Football League must approve the deal, and approval (or disapproval) will not occur for three months. How could the team hedge its position? What is there to lose by waiting three months to see if the exhibition game is approved before hedging?

ANSWER: The team could purchase put options on pounds in order to lock in the amount at which it could convert the 1 million pounds to dollars. The expiration date of the put option should correspond to the date in which the team would receive the 1 million pounds. If the deal is not approved, the team could let the put options expire.

If the team waits three months, option prices will have changed by then. If the pound has depreciated over this three-month period), put options with the same exercise price would command higher premiums. Therefore, the team may wish to purchase put options immediately. The team could also consider selling futures contracts on pounds, but it would be obligated to exchange pounds for dollars in the future, even if the deal is not approved.

Solution to WSJ Case: Panic in Currency Futures Trading

1. Explain the logic of how central bank intervention caused sheer panic for currency futures traders with long positions.

   ANSWER: Futures prices on marks and other European currencies rose in tandem with the values of these currencies. However, when central banks intervened to support the dollar, the values of these currencies declined, and so did values of futures contracts on these currencies. So traders with long (buy) positions in these contracts experienced losses because the contract values declined.

2. Explain the concern caused when a floor broker was willing to sell 700 mark futures contracts (representing a value of about $50 million of marks) at the going market rate. What might this action signal to the brokers?

   ANSWER: Normally, this order would have been sold in pieces. This action could signal a desperate situation in which many investors sell futures contracts at any price, which places more downward pressure on currency future prices, and could cause a crisis.

3. Explain why speculators with short (sell) positions could benefit as a result of the central bank intervention.

   ANSWER: The central bank intervention placed downward pressure on the mark and other European currencies. Thus, the values of futures contracts on these currencies declined. Traders that had short positions in futures would benefit because they could now close out their short positions by purchasing the same contracts that they had sold earlier. Since the prices of futures contracts declined, they would purchase the contracts for a lower price than the price at which they initially sold the contracts.

4. Some traders with long (buy) positions may have responded immediately to the central bank intervention by selling futures contracts. Why would some speculators with long positions leave their positions unchanged or even increase their positions by purchasing more futures contracts in response to the central bank intervention?

ANSWER: Central bank intervention sometimes has only a temporary effect on exchange rates. Thus, the European currencies could strengthen after a temporary effect caused by central bank intervention. Traders have to predict whether natural market forces will ultimately overwhelm any pressure induced as a result of central bank intervention.

Solution to Case Problem: Capital Crystal, Inc.

This case is designed to give students more insight on the advantages and disadvantages of currency futures and options. More comprehensive questions on this subject are offered in Chapter 11.

a) To hedge with futures, the cost of the imports will be $295 million ($.59 x DM500 million). To hedge with call options, the cost per unit (including the premium paid) is $.61, so that the cost of the imports if the option is exercised is $305 million. Since the mark's spot rate is expected to be above the call option's exercise price, the call option would likely be exercised. In this case, hedging with futures will cost $10 million less than hedging with call options.

   Since the future spot rate is likely to exceed the futures price, hedging with futures would likely be less costly than not hedging. Even if it was more costly, it might be wise to hedge in keeping with the conservative management style of Capital Crystal Corp.

   This part of the case illustrates that currency call options may not always be the best choice, even though they offer more flexibility than currency futures.

b) Based on the new information, the cost of importing when using futures is still $295 million. When using the call option, if the forecast of the mark's future spot rate is correct, the option would not be exercised. Thus, the amount paid per unit would be the future spot rate of $.57 plus the $.01 premium paid per unit for the option. Therefore, the cost of imports would be $290 million, or $5 million less than when using the futures hedge.

   Assuming the forecast is correct, the cost of importing when not hedging is $285 million ($.57 x DM500 million), which is less than the cost of either hedge. However, given the conservative management style of Capital Crystal Corp., a hedge may still be appropriate. If the mark's value is just $.02 higher than forecasted in three months, Capital will have to pay $5 million more than if it had hedged with a call option. This issue normally generates much discussion. The key question is whether a manager should take the risk of not hedging? While this strategy is expected to save the firm $5 million, it could backfire if the mark appreciates over the period (in which case the manager may be reprimanded). This part of the case attempts to show that hedging is sometimes used even if it is expected to be more costly than not hedging, because of the desire to avoid risk.

If students put themselves in the position of the managers (bonus is received if a minimum level of performance is achieved), they would probably hedge. However, it is questionable whether this strategy would satisfy shareholder wealth. One could argue that there are agency problems, because managers are forced by the bonus system to avoid risk. Therefore, managers may use more conservative strategies than what is desired by shareholders in some situations.

This case is realistic, although the name of the firm has been changed. The manager decided to use the call options in order to avoid risk; based on the firm's policy, he would not have benefited directly by not hedging even if it reduced the firm's costs. There was no real incentive to take any chances.

Projects

1. Using recent quotes from the *Wall Street Journal*, select a currency call option with an expiration date that occurs before the end of your school term. On that date, assume you will either (1) exercise your call option and sell the currency in the spot market or (2) let the option expire. Just before the end of your school term, determine your net profit or loss from this strategy as a percentage of your initial investment (the premium you originally paid).

   This project allows students to determine actual profits and losses on currency option positions. Furthermore, they will realize how changes in the spot rate over the school term affect option profits by periodically assessing their position.

2. Repeat the preceding project using a currency put instead of a currency call option.

   This project has the same objectives as Project Number 1.

3. Look in a recent *Wall Street Journal* at Japanese yen call options. For any single expiration date, assess the relationship between exercise prices and premiums. Explain that relationship.

   This project demonstrates that call option premiums for a given expiration date are inversely related to the exercise price. That is, the higher the exercise price on a currency call option, the lower is the premium paid. The reason for this relationship should be obvious.

4. Repeat the preceding project using puts rather than calls.

   This project demonstrates that put option premiums for a given expiration date are positively related to the exercise prices. That is, the higher the exercise price, the higher is the premium paid for put options.

5. Look in a recent *Wall Street Journal* and compare the Japanese yen call options that are available with a specific exercise price. Assess the relationship between the remaining time to the expiration date and the premium. Explain the relationship.

   This project demonstrates that currency call options with more time remaining until the expiration date have high premiums, other things being equal. The relationship exists because sellers of call options incur higher risk on options with a longer time to the expiration date.

6. Repeat the preceding project using puts instead of calls.

   This project demonstrates that currency put options with more time remaining until the expiration date have higher premiums, other things being equal. The relationship exists because sellers of put options incur higher risk on options with a longer time to the expiration date.

Integrative Problem for Part I

The International Financial Environment

Mesa Company specializes in the production of small fancy picture frames, which are exported from the U.S. to the United Kingdom. Mesa invoices the exports in pounds and converts the pounds to dollars when they are received. The British demand for these frames is positively related to economic conditions in the United Kingdom. Assume that British inflation and interest rates are similar to the rates in the U.S. Mesa believes the U.S. balance of trade deficit from trade between the U.S. and the United Kingdom is expected to adjust to changing prices between the two countries, while capital flows will adjust to interest rate differentials. Mesa believes that the value of the pound is very sensitive to changing international trade flows. The following information was considered by Mesa:

- The U.K. inflation is expected to decline, while the U.S. inflation is expected to rise.
- British interest rates are expected to decline, while U.S. interest rates are expected to increase.

1. Explain how the international trade flows should initially adjust in response to the changes in inflation (holding exchange rates constant). Explain how the international capital flows should adjust in response to the changes in interest rates (holding exchange rates constant).

   ANSWER: The U.S. balance of trade deficit should increase in response to the changes in inflation, since prices of U.S. exports will increase if U.S. inflation rises, causing a decline in the British demand for U.S. exports. In addition, the U.S. demand for British exports should increase if U.S. prices increase.

The capital flows from the U.S. to the U.K. should decrease in response to lower British interest rates, while the capital flows from the U.K. to the U.S. should increase (assuming exchange rates are held constant).

2. Using the information provided, will Mesa expect the pound to appreciate or depreciate in the future? Explain.

   ANSWER: The pound's equilibrium value will change in response to changes in the capital flows and changes in the trade flows. The information on interest rates suggests that capital flows from the U.S. to the U.K. will decrease, (because British interest rates are expected to decline), while flows from the U.K. to the U.S. will increase (because U.S. interest rates are expected to rise). These forces will place downward pressure on the pound's value.

   The information on inflation rates suggests that the U.S. will purchase more British goods (increased U.S. demand for pounds) and will sell less goods to the U.K. (reduced supply of pounds to be exchanged for dollars), based on the relative changes in prices in the two countries. These forces will place upward pressure on the pound's value.

   The international capital flow forces will place downward pressure on the pound's value, while the international trade flow forces will place upward pressure on the pound's value. Since the international capital flows are thought by Mesa to have a larger effect, Mesa expects that the net effect will be a decline in the pound's value.

3. Mesa believes international capital flows shift in response to changing interest rate differentials. Is there any reason why the changing interest rate differentials in this example will not necessarily cause international capital flows to change significantly? Explain.

   ANSWER: Given the potential upward pressure placed on the pound by the potential balance of trade adjustment, some investors may anticipate that the pound could appreciate. This may discourage British investors from attempting to capitalize on the higher U.S. interest rates (if the U.S. interest rates do rise as expected). If the uncertainty about the future exchange rate discourages British capital flows to the U.S., there is no reason to expect the pound to depreciate.

4. Based on your answer to Question 2, how would Mesa's cash flows be affected by the expected exchange rate movements? Explain.

   ANSWER: Mesa's cash flows would be adversely affected, because the pounds received by Mesa would convert to a smaller amount of dollars if the pound weakens.

5. Based on your answer to Question 4, should Mesa consider hedging its exchange rate risk? If so, explain how it could hedge using forward contracts, futures contracts, and currency options.

   ANSWER: Mesa should consider hedging exchange rate risk. It could use forward contracts to sell pounds forward (for future dates in which pounds will be received). Second, it could use currency futures contracts to sell pounds at the first available settlement date following the receipt of pounds. Third, it could purchase currency put options to hedge its pound receivables, as these options lock in the price at which Mesa could exchange pounds for dollars.

Chapter 6

Government Influence on Exchange Rates

Lecture Outline

Exchange Rate Systems

Fixed
Freely Floating
Managed Float
Pegged
Classification of Exchange Rate Arrangements

Exchange Rate Mechanism (ERM) Crisis

Government Intervention in the Foreign Exchange Market

Reasons for Intervention
Direct Intervention
Indirect Intervention

Exchange Rate Target Zones

Intervention as a Policy Tool

Chapter Theme

This chapter introduces the various exchange rate systems. In addition, it stresses the manner by which governments can influence exchange rates. These topics do not normally receive a full chapter in other textbooks. In fact, given a time constraint, some professors may skip this chapter. Yet, since exchange rate movements are critical to an MNC's performance, and the government has much influence over these exchange rates, the MNC should seriously consider the topics addressed in this chapter.

Topics to Stimulate Class Discussion

1. If you were elected to choose between a fixed, freely floating, or a dirty float exchange rate system, which would you choose for your home country? Why?

2. Assume that both the U.S. and Germany experience high unemployment. How can the U.S. central bank attempt to adjust the dollar value to reduce this problem? Is the German central bank likely to go along with the U.S. central bank's strategy, or retaliate? Why?

Answers to End of Chapter Questions

1. Compare and contrast the fixed, free float, and managed float exchange rate systems.

   ANSWER: Under a fixed exchange rate system, the governments attempted to maintain exchange rates within 1% of the initially set value (slightly widening the bands in 1971). Under a freely floating system, government intervention would be non-existent. Under a managed-float system, governments will allow exchange rates move according to market forces; however, they will intervene when they believe it is necessary.

2. What are some advantages and disadvantages of a freely floating exchange rate system versus a fixed exchange rate system?

   ANSWER: A freely floating system may help correct balance of trade deficits since the currency will adjust according to market forces. Also, countries are more insulated from problems of foreign countries under a freely floating exchange rate system. However, a disadvantage of freely floating exchange rates is that firms have to manage their exposure to exchange rate risk. Also, floating rates still can often have a significant adverse impact on a country's unemployment or inflation.

3. Describe the background of the European Monetary System (EMS).

   ANSWER: Under the EMS, exchange rates of member countries are tied to the European Currency Unit (ECU) and are maintained within limits. This is thought to stabilize trading patterns among these European nations.

4. How can a central bank use direct intervention to change the value of a currency?

   ANSWER: Central banks can use their currency reserves to buy up a specific currency in the foreign exchange market in order to place upward pressure on that currency. Central banks can also attempt to force currency depreciation by flooding the market with that specific currency (selling that currency in the foreign exchange market in exchange for other currencies).

5. How can a central bank use indirect intervention to change the value of a currency?

   ANSWER: To increase the value of its home currency, a central bank could attempt to increase interest rates, thereby attracting a foreign demand for the home currency to buy high-yield securities.

   To decrease the value of its home currency, a central bank could attempt to lower interest rates in order to reduce demand for the home currency by foreign investors.

6. The media frequently reports that "the dollar's value strengthened against many currencies in response to the Federal Reserve's plan to increase interest rates." Explain why the dollar's value may change even before the Federal Reserve affects interest rates.

   ANSWER: Foreign exchange market participants may anticipate that once the Fed increases interest rates, there will be an increased demand for dollars, which will result in a stronger dollar. Consequently, they may take positions in dollars immediately, which could place upward pressure on the dollar even before interest rates are affected.

7. Assume there is concern that the United States may experience a recession. Provide recommendations to the Federal Reserve regarding how it should attempt to directly influence the dollar to prevent a recession. How might U.S. exporters react to this policy (favorably or unfavorably)? What about U.S. importing firms?

   ANSWER: The Federal Reserve would normally consider a loose money policy to stimulate the economy. However, to the extent that the policy puts upward pressure on economic growth and inflation, it could weaken the dollar. A weak dollar is expected to favorably affect U.S. exporting firms and adversely affect U.S. importing firms. If the U.S. interest rates rise in response to the possible increase in economic growth and inflation in the U.S., this could offset the downward pressure on the U.S. dollar. In this case, U.S. exporting and importing firms would not be affected as much.

8. What is the impact of a weak home currency on the home economy, other things being equal?

   ANSWER: A weak home currency tends to increase a country's exports and decrease its imports, thereby lowering its unemployment. However, it also can cause higher inflation since there is a reduction in foreign competition (because a weak home currency is not worth much in foreign countries). Thus, local producers can more easily increase prices without concern about pricing themselves out of the market.

9. What is the impact of a strong home currency on the home economy, other things equal?

   ANSWER: A strong home currency can keep inflation in the home country low, since it encourages consumers to buy abroad. Local producers must maintain low prices to remain competitive. Also, foreign supplies can be obtained cheaply. This also helps to maintain low inflation. However, a strong home currency can increase unemployment in the home country. This is due to the increase in imports and decrease in exports often associated with a strong home currency (imports become cheaper to that country but the country's exports become more expensive to foreign customers).

10. Explain the potential feedback effects of a currency's changing value on inflation.

    ANSWER: A weak home currency can cause inflation since it tends to reduce foreign competition within any given industry. Higher inflation can weaken the currency further since it encourages consumers to purchase goods abroad (where prices are not inflated).

    A strong home currency can reduce inflation since it reduces the prices of foreign goods, and forces home producers to offer competitive prices. Low inflation, in turn, places upward pressure on the home currency.

11. Explain why a central bank may desire to smooth exchange rate movements.

    ANSWER: Abrupt movements in a home currency's value would cause more volatile business cycles, and many cause more concern in financial markets (and therefore more volatility in these markets). Central bank intervention used to smooth exchange rate movements may stabilize the economy and financial markets.

12. Why do foreign market participants attempt to monitor the Fed's direct intervention efforts? How does the Fed attempt to hide its intervention actions?

    ANSWER: Foreign market participants make investment and borrowing decisions that can be influenced by anticipated exchange rate movements and therefore by the Fed's direct intervention efforts. Thus, they may attempt to obtain information from commercial banks about the Fed's intervention actions. The Fed may attempt to disguise its actions by requesting bid and ask quotes on exchange rates, and even mixing some buy orders with sell orders, or vice versa.

13. In the fall of 1992, France was experiencing a relatively high unemployment rate. During this period, Great Britain and Italy suspended their participation in the exchange rate mechanism (ERM), but France continued to participate. Some analysts stated that France "paid a high price" for its continued participation in the ERM during this period. Interpret this statement.

    ANSWER: German interest rates had risen, and French interest rates were essentially forced to increase as well, because capital flowed from France to Germany, until interest rates were realigned. The French government would have preferred to reduce French interest rates to stimulate its economy. Instead, the increase in French interest rates had the opposite effect on the economy.

14. In the fall of 1992, the interest rates of several European countries moved in tandem with the rise in German interest rates. Yet, U.S. interest rates were not moving in tandem with German interest rates. Explain why German interest rate movements tend to have a stronger effect on interest rates of other European countries than on U.S. interest rates.

    ANSWER: When European currencies are tied through the ERM, capital will flow to the European country where the interest rate is highest, causing a realignment in all European interest rates. However, U.S. investors must consider the exchange rate risk when investing in a European country, because the dollar is not tied to the European currencies. Some U.S. investors may attempt to capitalize on higher German interest rates, but the potential gains are subject to more uncertainty because of greater exchange rate risk.

15. In January, 1992, the Fed used direct intervention by selling dollars in exchange for Japanese yen. Some analysts suggested that this action was politically motivated. Given the timing of this intervention, explain why this intervention may be perceived to be politically motivated.

    ANSWER: a weaker dollar could reduce the large balance of trade deficit with Japan, and stimulate the U.S. economy. In January 1992, the U.S. was experiencing a recession, and the presidential election was ten months away.

16. Assume that the currency of South Korea is tied to the dollar. How would the following trade patterns be affected by the dollar's depreciation against the Japanese yen: (a) South Korean exports to Japan and (b) South Korean exports to the United States? Explain.

ANSWER:

a. South Korea exports to Japan should increase because dollar depreciation against the yen implies that the South Korean currency must also depreciate against the yen. Therefore, South Korean goods will be less expensive to Japanese importers.

b. South Korean exports to the U.S. should increase because Japanese goods become more expensive to U.S. importers as a result of dollar depreciation. Therefore, some U.S. importers may find that even though the exchange rate between the dollar and South Korean currency is unchanged, the South Korean prices are now lower than Japanese prices (from a U.S. perspective).

This answer assumes that Japanese exporters did not reduce their prices to compensate U.S. importers for the weaker dollar. If Japanese exporters do reduce their prices, to fully offset the effect of the weaker dollar, there would be less of a shift to South Korean goods.

17. Assuming that U.S. bond prices are normally inversely related to U.S. inflation, offer your opinion on why expectations of a weak dollar can reduce bond prices, other things being equal.

ANSWER: Expectations of a weak dollar can cause expectations of higher inflation, because a weak dollar places upward pressure on U.S. prices for reasons mentioned in the chapter. Higher inflation tends to place upward pressure on interest rates. Because there is an inverse relationship between interest rates and bond prices, bond prices would be expected to decline. Such an expectation causes bond portfolio managers to liquidate some of their bond holdings, thereby causing bond prices to decline immediately.

18. When it was announced on June 2, 1987, that Paul Volcker would resign as chairman of the Federal Reserve, the dollar weakened substantially. Why?

ANSWER: Volcker was respected for his ability to keep inflation low. The announced resignation ignited inflationary fears. Since high U.S. inflation places downward pressure on the dollar's value, the announcement created expectations of a weaker dollar. These expectations caused some market participants to react immediately by liquidating dollar-denominated securities (shifting their investments into securities expected to strengthen). These activities caused the dollar to depreciate immediately.

19. Explain the meaning of target zones and how they would be implemented. What are their limitations?

ANSWER: Target zones would serve as boundaries for exchange rates. Whenever an exchange rate approached an upper or lower boundary, control banks would need to intervene to maintain the rate within the target zone. However, the limitations of target zones are that (1) countries may not agree on the appropriate zone for each currency, and (2) some central banks may be unwilling to maintain their home currency within a target zone under some conditions.

20. Explain the difference between sterilized and nonsterilized intervention.

    ANSWER: Sterlized intervention is conducted to ensure no change in the money supply while nonsterilized intervention is conducted without concern about maintaining the same money supply.

Solution to WSJ Case: Central Bank Intervention in Europe

1. Explain why Europe's weaker currencies increased in value following a cut in German interest rates by Bundesbank (the German central bank).

   ANSWER: Exchange rates in Europe (and elsewhere) are partially driven by relative interest rates of the countries of concern. When Germany's interest rates decline, there is a smaller flow of funds to be exchanged into German marks because the interest rate is not as attractive to European investors.

2. How does the widening of Europe's Exchange Rate Mechanism (ERM) affect the degree of central bank intervention?

   ANSWER: Central banks have more flexibility because there is more room for exchange rates to float before they hit the upper or lower limit. Therefore, central banks may not need to intervene as much.

3. At the time, France and Denmark had low inflation and weak economies. Explain how the central banks would be likely to adjust interest rates in these countries, and how their currencies (French franc and Danish krone) would respond to the central bank intervention.

   ANSWER: The central banks would likely attempt to lower interest rates, which causes the currency to weaken. A weaker currency and lower interest rates can stimulate the economy.

Solution to Case Problem: Hull Importing Company

a) When the pound is tied to the mark (indirectly through the ECU), the pound's movements against the dollar will coincide with the mark's movements against the dollar. The effects on Hull will be more pronounced when each currency has the same effect. Since the pound is no longer tied to the mark, the movements in the pound's value would not coincide with movements in the mark's value. Therefore, the overall effects on Hull's business would not be as pronounced.

b) If the German mark's value is increased, Hull's expenses are increased, causing an adverse effect. The effect would be smaller after the pound's value was no longer tied to the ECU because the pound would not be indirectly tied to the mark. Thus, an increase in the value of the mark against the dollar would not force an increase in the value of the pound against the dollar When the pound was tied to the ECU, the pound would have been forced to appreciate against the dollar if the mark appreciated. Thus, effects would have been more pronounced at that time.

Project

1. Review the Wall Street Journal for the last few weeks (ignoring the weekend). Summarize any central bank intervention in the table below.

Date	Identify the central banks that intervened	Was the intervention intended to strengthen or weaken the dollar?	Describe movements of the dollar on that day

This project forces students to monitor central bank intervention, so that they will realize that intervention is common, but does not always have a major effect on a currency.

Chapter 7

International Arbitrage and Interest Rate Parity

Lecture Outline

International Arbitrage

- Locational Arbitrage
- Triangular Arbitrage
- Covered Interest Arbitrage

Interest Rate Parity

- Derivation of Interest Rate Parity
- Numerical Example of Interest Rate Parity
- Graphic Analysis of Interest Rate Parity
- How to Test Whether Interest Rate Parity Exists
- Does Interest Rate Parity Hold?
- Considerations When Assessing Interest Rate Parity

Chapter Theme

This chapter illustrates how three types of arbitrage (locational, triangular, and covered interest) are executed. An effort must be made to emphasize that the key to arbitrage from an MNC's perspective is not the potential profits, but the relationships that should exist due to arbitrage. The linkage between covered interest arbitrage and interest rate parity is critical.

Topics to Stimulate Class Discussion

1. Why are quoted spot rates very similar across all banks?

2. Why don't arbitrage opportunities exist for long periods of time?

3. Present a scenario and ask whether any type of international arbitrage is possible. If so, how would it be executed and how would market forces be affected?

4. Provide current interest rates of two countries and ask students to determine the forward rate that would be expected according to interest rate parity.

Answers to End of Chapter Questions

1. Explain the concept of locational arbitrage and the scenario necessary for it to be plausible.

   ANSWER: Locational arbitrage can occur when the spot rate of a given currency varies among locations. Specifically, the ask rate at one location must be lower than the bid rate at another location. The disparity in rates can occur since information is not always immediately available to all banks. If a disparity does exist, locational arbitrage is possible; as it occurs, the spot rates among locations should become realigned.

2. Assume the following information:

	Bank X	Bank Y
Bid price of Swiss francs	$.401	$.398
Ask price of Swiss francs	$.404	$.400

Given this information, is locational arbitrage possible? If so, explain the steps that would reflect locational arbitrage and compute the profit from this arbitrage if you had $1,000,000 to use.

ANSWER: Yes! One could purchase francs at Bank Y for $.40 and sell them to Bank X for $.401. With $1 million available, 2.5 million francs could be purchased at bank Y. These francs could then be sold to Bank X for $1,002,500, thereby generating a profit of $2,500.

3. Based on the information in the previous question, what market forces would occur to eliminate any further possibilities of locational arbitrage?

   ANSWER: The large demand for francs at Bank Y will force this bank's ask price on francs to increase. The large sales of francs to Bank X will force its bid price down. Once the ask price of Bank Y is no longer less than the bid price of Bank X, locational arbitrage will no longer be beneficial.

4. Explain the concept of triangular arbitrage and the scenario necessary for it to be plausible.

   ANSWER: Triangular arbitrage is possible when the actual cross exchange rate between two currencies differs from what it should be. The appropriate cross rate can be determined given the values of the two currencies with respect to some other currency.

5. Assume the following information for a particular bank:

	Quoted Price
Value of Canadian dollar in U.S. dollars	$ .90
Value of German marks in U.S. dollars	$ .30
Value of Canadian dollar in German marks	DM3.02

   Given this information, is triangular arbitrage possible? If so, explain the steps that would reflect triangular arbitrage, and compute the profit from this strategy if you had $1,000,000 to use.

   ANSWER: Yes. The appropriate cross exchange rate should be 1 Canadian dollar = 3 German marks. Thus, the actual value of the Canadian dollars in terms of marks is more than what it should be. One could obtain Canadian dollars with U.S. dollars, sell the Canadian dollars for marks and then exchange marks for U.S. dollars. With $1,000,000, this strategy would generate $1,006,667 thereby representing a profit of $6,667.

   [$1,000,000/$.90 = C$1,111,111 x 3.02 = DM3,355,556 x $.30 = $1,006,667]

6. Based on the information in the previous question, what market forces would occur to eliminate any further possibilities of triangular arbitrage?

   ANSWER: The value of the Canadian dollar with respect to the U.S. dollar would rise. The value of the Canadian dollar with respect to German marks would decline. The value of German marks with respect to the U.S. dollar would fall.

7. Explain the concept of covered interest arbitrage, and the scenario necessary for it to be plausible.

   ANSWER: Covered interest arbitrage involves the short-term investment in a foreign currency which is covered by a forward contract to sell that currency when the investment matures. Covered interest arbitrage is plausible when the forward premium does not reflect the interest rate differential between two countries specified by the interest rate parity formula. If transactions costs or other considerations are involved, the excess profit from covered interest arbitrage must more than offset these other considerations for covered interest arbitrage to be plausible.

8. Assume the following information:

	Quoted Price
Spot rate of Canadian dollar	$.80
90-day Forward rate of Canadian dollar	$.79
90-day Canadian interest rate	4%
90-day U.S. interest rate	2.5%

   Given this information, what would be the yield (percentage return) to a U.S. investor who used covered interest arbitrage? (Assume the investor invests $1,000,000).

ANSWER:

$1,027,000 - $1,000,000/$1,000,000 =
$1,000,000/$.80 = C$1,250,000 x (1.04)
= C$1,300,000 x $.79
= $1,027,000

Yield = 2.7%, which exceeds the yield in the U.S. over the 90-day period. [See P. 184-185]

9. Based on the information in the previous question, what market forces would occur to eliminate any further possibilities of covered interest arbitrage?

   ANSWER: The Canadian dollar's spot rate should rise, and its forward rate should fall; in addition, the Canadian interest rate may fall and the U.S. interest rate may rise.

10. Assume the following information:

Spot rate of French franc	= $.100
180-day Forward rate of the French franc	= $.098
180-day French interest rate	= 6%
180-day U.S. interest rate	= 5%

   Given this information, is covered interest arbitrage worthwhile for French investors? Explain your answer.

   ANSWER: To answer this question, begin with an assumed amount of francs and determine the yield to French investors who attempt covered interest arbitrage. Using FF1,000,000 as the initial investment:

   FF1,000,000 x $.100 = $100,000 x (1.05) = $105,000/$.098
   = FF1,071,429

   French investors would generate a yield of about 7.1% which exceeds their domestic yield. Thus, it is worthwhile for them.

11. Explain the concept of interest rate parity. Provide a rationale for its possible existence.

   ANSWER: Interest rate parity states that the forward rate premium (or discount) of a currency should reflect the differential in interest rates between the two countries. If interest rate parity didn't exist, covered interest arbitrage could occur (in the absence of transactions costs, and foreign risk), which should cause market forces to move back toward conditions which reflect interest rate parity. The exact formula is provided in the chapter.

12. Describe a method for testing whether interest rate parity exists.

   ANSWER: At any point in time, identify the interest rates of the U.S. versus some foreign country. Then determine the forward rate premium (or discount) which should exist according to interest rate parity. The determine whether this computed forward rate premium (or discount) is different from the actual premium (or discount).

13. Why are transactions costs, currency restrictions, and differential tax laws important when evaluating whether covered interest arbitrage can be beneficial?

    ANSWER: Even if interest rate parity does not hold, covered interest arbitrage could be of no benefit if transactions costs or tax laws offset any excess gain. In addition, currency restrictions enforced by a foreign government may disrupt the act of covered interest arbitrage.

14. Assume that the existing U.S. one-year interest rate is 10 percent and the Canadian one-year interest rate is 11 percent. Also assume that interest rate parity exists. Should the forward rate of the Canadian dollar exhibit a discount or a premium? If U.S. investors attempted covered interest arbitrage, what would be their return? If Canadian investors attempted covered interest arbitrage, what would be their return?

    ANSWER: The Canadian dollar's forward rate should exhibit a discount because its interest rate exceeds the U.S. interest rate.

    U.S. investors would earn a return of 10 percent using covered interest arbitrage, the same as what they would earn in the U.S.

    Canadian investors would earn a return of 11 percent using covered interest arbitrage, they would earn a return of 11 percent, the same as what they would earn in Canada.

15. Why would investors consider covered interest arbitrage in a foreign country where interest rate is lower than their home interest rate?

    ANSWER: If the forward premium on a foreign currency more than offsets its lower interest rate, investors could benefit use covered interest arbitrage by investing in that currency and achieve higher returns than in their own country.

16. Consider investors that invest in either U.S. or British one-year Treasury bills. Assume zero transaction costs and taxes.

    a. If interest rate parity exists, then the return for U.S. investors who use covered interest arbitrage would be the same as the return for U.S. investors who invest in U.S. Treasury bills. Is this statement true or false? If false, correct the statement.

    ANSWER: True

b. If interest rate parity exists, then the return for British investors who use covered interest arbitrage would be the same as the return for British investors who invest in British Treasury bills. Is this statement true or false? If false, correct the statement.

ANSWER: True

17. Assume that the Swiss forward rate presently exhibits a premium of 6 percent, and that interest rate parity exists. How will this premium change if U.S. interest rates decrease, in order for interest rate parity to be maintained. Why might we expect the premium to change?

ANSWER: The premium will decrease in order to maintain IRP, because the difference between the interest rates is reduced.

We would expect the premium to change because as U.S. interest rates decrease, U.S. investors could benefit from covered interest arbitrage if the forward premium stays the same. The return earned by U.S. investors that use covered interest arbitrage would not be any higher than before, but the return would now exceed the interest rate earned in the U.S. Thus, there is downward pressure on the forward premium.

18. In the early 1980s the forward rate premiums of several currencies were higher than they are now. What does this imply about interest rate differentials between the United States and foreign countries today compared to those in the early 1980s.

ANSWER: The interest rate differentials are generally smaller now than they were in the early 1980s. Consequently, the forward premiums of low interest rate currencies such as the German mark, Japanese yen and Swiss franc are now smaller.

19. If the relationship that is specified by interest rate parity does not exist at any period, but does exist on average, then covered interest arbitrage should not be considered by U.S. firms. Do you agree or disagree with this statement? Explain.

ANSWER: Disagree. If at any point in time, interest rate parity does not exist, covered interest arbitrage could earn excess returns (unless transactions costs, tax differences, etc. offset the excess returns).

20. The one-year Swiss interest rate is 6 percent. The one-year U.S. interest rate is 10 percent. The spot rate of the Swiss franc is $50. The forward rate of the Swiss franc is $.54. Is covered interest arbitrage feasible for U.S. investors? Is it feasible for Swiss investors? Explain why each of these opportunities for covered interest arbitrage is or is not feasible.

To determine the yield from covered interest arbitrage by U.S. investors, start with an assumed initial investment, such as $1,000,000:

ANSWER:

$1,000,000/$.50 = SF2,000,000 x (1.06)

= SF2,120,000 x $.54 = $1,144,800

Yield = ($1,144,800 - $1,000,000/$1,000,000 = 14.48%

Thus, U.S. investors can benefit from covered interest arbitrage because this yield exceeds the U.S. interest rate of 10 percent.

To determine the yield from covered interest arbitrage by Swiss investors, start with an assumed initial investment, such as SF1,000,000:

SF1,000,000 x $.50 = $500,000 x (1.10)

= $550,000/$.54 = SF1,018,519

Yield = (SF1,018,519 - SF1,000,000)/SF1,000,000 = 1.85%

Thus, Swiss investors would not benefit from covered interest arbitrage since the yield of 1.85% is less than the 6% that they could receive from investing their funds in Switzerland.

21. Assume that the one-year U.S. interest rate is 11 percent, while the one-year interest rate in a specific less developed country (LDC) is 40 percent. Assume that a U.S. bank is willing to purchase the currency of that country from you one year from now at a discount of 13 percent. Would covered interest arbitrage be worth considering? Is there any reason why you should not attempt covered interest arbitrage in this situation? (Ignore tax effects.)

ANSWER: Covered interest arbitrage would be worth considering since the return would be 21.8 percent, which is much higher than the U.S. interest rate. However, the funds would be invested in an LDC, which could cause some currency about default risk or government restrictions on convertibility of the currency back to dollars.

22. Why do you think currencies of countries with high inflation rates tend to have forward discounts?

    ANSWER: These currencies have high interest rates, which cause forward rates to have discounts as a result of interest rate parity.

23. In 1989 and 1990 the German economy expanded significantly in response to European integration and the reunification of West and East Germany. How might these conditions affect that forward discount of the German mark?

    ANSWER: Expansion in Germany creates a demand for loanable funds, which places upward pressure on German interest rates, which increases the forward discount on the German mark (or reduces the premium).

24. Assume that the thirty-day forward premium of the Canadian dollar was -1 percent annualized, while the ninety-day forward premium of the Canadian dollar was 2 percent annualized. Explain the likely interest rate conditions that would cause these conditions. Does this ensure that covered interest arbitrage is worthwhile?

    ANSWER: The scenario would occur when the Canadian thirty-day interest rate is above the U.S. thirty-day interest rate, but the Canadian ninety-day interest rate is below the U.S. ninety-day interest rate. Covered interest arbitrage is not necessarily worthwhile, since interest rate parity may still hold.

Solution to WSJ Case: Arbitrage Within Europe's Exchange Rate Mechanism (ERM)

1. The bands of Europe's exchange rate mechanism (ERM) can restrict currency movements. Attempt to create a scenario in which a European firm could engage in arbitrage by investing in other European currencies to achieve high interest earnings, even without covering the position in the forward market. Such a strategy can be feasible when exchange rates are restricted.

   ANSWER: If a European currency is already at the bottom of the ERM band (it cannot weaken any further against the other European currencies) and has a high interest rate, European firms could invest in that currency and are guaranteed that it will not depreciate (unless the band is adjusted).

2. Refer back to your answer to the previous question. Could U.S. firms benefit from arbitrage in the same manner as European firms? Explain.

ANSWER: The bands restrict exchange rates between European currency movements against other European currencies, not against the dollar. Thus, the bands do not create an automatic arbitrage opportunity for U.S. firms.

3. Before the ERM bands had widened, the spot and forward exchange rates between any two European currencies were almost identical. When the ERM bands were widened, there was a wider gap between the spot and forward exchange rates. Explain why this would occur, using interest rate parity in your explanation.

   ANSWER: When ERM bands were narrow, European interest rates were very similar. As the ERM bands were widened, European countries began to adjust their interest rates without aligning them with other European interest rates. Thus, interest rate parity forced the forward rate of one European currency (relative to another European currency) to adjust as the interest rate in one European country deviated from the other.

Solution to Case Problem: Zuber, Inc.

a) The expected value of the yield on investing funds in this country would be 14 percent, versus only 9 percent in the U.S. However, there is much uncertainty about the foreign yield. If the currency depreciates by a large amount, it will wipe out some of the principal invested. Given that Zuber did not want to target these funds for a speculative purpose, it would not be wise to invest these funds in the country without covering.

b) Covered interest arbitrage would involve exchanging dollars for the currency today, investing the currency in the country's Treasury securities, and negotiating a forward contract to sell the currency in one year in exchange for dollars.

   Given that $10 million is available, this amount would be converted into 25 million units of the foreign currency, which would accumulate to 28.5 million units (at 14 percent) by the end of the year, and be converted into $11,115,000 at the time (based on a forward rate of $.39.) This reflects a return of 11.15 percent.

c) The risks of covered interest arbitrage are as follows:

   - The Treasury of the country could default on its securities issued.

   - The bank may not fulfill its obligation on the forward contract (the bank was just recently privatized and does not have a track record as a privatized institution).

- The government could restrict funds from being converted into dollars. (Since the country has only allowed foreign investments recently, it does not have a track record. There is some uncertainty about its future laws on international finance.)

d) While covered interest arbitrage would be expected to achieve a yield of 11.15 percent (versus only 9 percent in the U.S.), the risks are significant, especially considering that the country is still experimenting with cross-border transactions. Since some students will probably suggest going for the higher returns, this question may allow for an interesting class discussion.

Projects

1. Look up the spot rate and one-year forward rate of the British pound in a recent *Wall Street Journal*. Also, look up (in the Money Rates section) U.S. and British one-year interest rates. Assume these rates were applicable for investors and reflected investments with equal risk. Determine whether a U.S. investor would benefit from utilizing covered interest arbitrage.

   This project provides students with experience in determining whether covered interest arbitrage is possible. They will begin to realize that the forward rate truly does tend to reflect interest rate differentials in the real world.

2. Using a recent *Wall Street Journal*, fill in the following blanks: (assume that cross exchange rates are properly aligned so that triangular arbitrage is not profitable)

   Spot rate of British pound in $ = $ ____________________

   Spot rate of Swiss franc in $ = $ ____________________

   Spot rate of Japanese yen in $ = $ ____________________

   Spot rate of British pound in Swiss francs = SF ____________________

   Spot rate of British pound in yen = Y ____________________

   Spot rate of Swiss franc in yen = Y ____________________

   This project provides students with experience in computing cross exchange rates.

3. Determine whether covered interest arbitrage would have been profitable from a U.S. perspective, using data from the back of this text on a country of your choice. Assess several historical points in time.

   This project allows students to determine whether covered interest arbitrage is feasible. It should be realized that the quotes provided in the data bank were not instantaneous, so deviations from interest rate parity may be partially due to data limitations.

Chapter 8

Relationships Between Inflation, Interest Rates, and Exchange Rates

Lecture Outline

Purchasing Power Parity (PPP)

Derivation of PPP
Numerical Examples of PPP
Rationale Behind PPP
Using PPP to Forecast
Graphic Analysis of PPP
Testing the PPP Theory
Why PPP Does Not Occur
Limitation in Tests of PPP

International Fisher Effect

Derivation of the IFE
Graphic Analysis of the IFE
Tests of the IFE
Why the IFE Does Not Occur

Comparison of IRP, PPP, and IFE Theories

Chapter Theme

This chapter discusses the relationship between inflation and exchange rates according to the purchasing power parity (PPP) theory. Since this is one of the most popular subjects in international finance, it is covered thoroughly. While PPP is a relevant theory, it should be emphasized that PPP will not always hold in reality. It does however, provide a foundation in understanding how inflation can affect exchange rates. The international Fisher effect (IFE) is also discussed in this chapter. This theory is also very important. Yet, it should again be emphasized that this theory does not always hold. If the PPP and IFE theories held consistently, decision-making by MNCs would be much easier. Because these theories do not hold consistently, an MNC's decision-making is very challenging.

Topics to Stimulate Class Discussion

1. Provide reasoning for why highly inflated countries such as Argentina tend to have weak home currencies.

2. Identify the inflation rate of your home country and some well-known foreign country. Then, identify the percentage change of your home currency with respect to that foreign country. Did the currency change in the direction and by the magnitude that you would have expected according to PPP. If not, offer possible reasons for this discrepancy.

3. Identify the quoted one-year interest rates in your home country and in a well-known foreign country as of one year ago. Also determine how your home currency changed relative to this foreign currency over the last year. Did the currency change according to the IFE theory? If not, does this information disprove IFE? Elaborate.

4. Provide a simple explanation of the difference between interest rate parity (from the previous chapter), PPP (from this chapter), and IFE (from this chapter).

Answers to End of Chapter Questions

1. Explain the theory of purchasing power parity (PPP). Based on this theory, what is a general forecast of the values of currencies in highly inflated countries?

   ANSWER: PPP suggests that the purchasing power of a consumer will be similar when purchasing goods in a foreign country or in the home country. If inflation in a foreign country differs from inflation in the home country, the exchange rate will adjust to maintain equal purchasing power.

Currencies in highly-inflated countries will be weak according to PPP, causing the purchasing power of goods in the home country versus these countries to be similar.

2. Explain the rationale behind purchasing power parity?

   ANSWER: When inflation is high in a particular country, foreign demand for goods in that country will decrease. In addition, that country's demand for foreign goods should increase. Thus, the home currency of that country will weaken; this tendency should continue until the currency has weakened to the extent that a foreign country's goods are no more attractive than the home country's goods. Inflation differentials are offset by exchange rate changes.

3. Explain how you could determine whether purchasing power parity exists.

   ANSWER: One method is to choose two countries and compare the inflation differential to the exchange rate change for several different periods. Then, determine whether the exchange rate changes were similar to what would have been expected under PPP theory.

   A second method is to choose a variety of countries and compare the inflation differential of each foreign country relative to the home country for a given period. Then, determine whether the exchange rate changes of each foreign currency were what would have been expected based on the inflation differentials under PPP theory.

4. Inflation differentials between the U.S. and industrialized countries have typically been a few percentage points in any given year. Yet, there have been many years in which annual exchange rates between the corresponding currencies have changed by 10 percent or more. What does this information suggest about purchasing power parity (PPP)?

   ANSWER: The information suggests that there are other factors besides inflation differentials that influence exchange rate movements. Thus, the exchange rate movements will not necessarily conform to inflation differentials, and therefore PPP will not necessarily hold.

5. Explain why purchasing power parity does not hold.

   ANSWER: PPP does not consistently hold because there are other factors besides inflation that influences exchange rates. Thus, exchange rates will not move in perfect tandem with inflation differentials. In addition, there may not be substitutes for traded goods. Therefore, even when a country's inflation increases, the foreign demand for its products will not necessarily decrease (in the manner suggested by PPP) if substitutes are not available.

6. Describe a limitation in testing whether purchasing power parity holds.

ANSWER: A limitation is that the results will vary with the base period chosen. The base period should reflect an equilibrium position, but it is difficult to determine when such a period exists.

7. Explain the International Fisher Effect (IFE). What are the implications of IFE to firms with excess cash that consistently invest in foreign Treasury bills?

   ANSWER: The IFE suggests that a currency's value will adjust in accordance with the differential in interest rates between two countries. Consequently, a firm that consistently purchases foreign Treasury bills will on <u>average</u> earn a similar return as domestic Treasury bills.

8. What is the rationale for the existence of the international Fisher effect?

   ANSWER: If a particular currency exhibits a high nominal interest rate, this may reflect a high anticipated inflation. Thus, the inflation will place downward pressure on the currency's value if it occurs.

9. Assume U.S. interest rates are generally above foreign interest rates. What does this suggest about the future strength or weakness of the dollar based on the international Fisher effect? Explain.

   ANSWER: The IFE would suggest that the U.S. dollar will depreciate over time if U.S. interest rates are currently higher than foreign interest rates. Consequently, foreign investors who purchased U.S. securities would on average receive a similar yield as what they receive in their own country, and U.S. investors that purchased foreign securities would on average receive a yield similar to U.S. rates.

10. Compare and contrast interest rate parity (discussed in the previous chapter), purchasing power parity (PPP), and the international Fisher effect (IFE).

    ANSWER: Interest rate parity can be evaluated using data at any one point in time, to determine the relationship between the interest rate differential of two countries and the forward premium (or discount). PPP suggests a relationship between the inflation differential of two countries and the percentage change in the spot exchange rate over time. IFE suggests a relationship between the interest rate differential of two countries and the percentage change in the spot exchange rate over time. IFE is based on nominal interest rate differentials, which are influenced by expected inflation. Thus, the IFE is closely related to PPP.

11. One assumption made in developing the international Fisher effect is that all investors in all countries require the same real return. What does this mean?

ANSWER: The real return is the nominal return minus the inflation rate. If all investors require the same real return, then the differentials in nominal interest rates should be solely due to differentials in anticipated inflation among countries.

12. How could you use regression analysis to determine whether the relationship specified by purchasing power parity (PPP) exists on average? Specify the model, and describe how you would assess the regression results to determine if there is *significant* difference from the relationship suggested by PPP.

ANSWER: A regression model could be applied to historical data to test PPP. The model is specified as:

$$e_f = a_0 + a_1 \left[\frac{(1 + I_{U.S.})}{1 + I_f} - 1 \right] + u$$

where E_f is the percentage change in the foreign currency's exchange rate, $I_{U.S.}$ and I_f are U.S. and foreign inflation rates, a_0 is a constant, a_1 is the slope coefficient, and u is an error term. If PPP holds, a_0 should equal zero, and a_1 should equal 1. A t-test on a_0 and a_1 is shown below.

$$\text{t-test for } a_0\text{: } t = \frac{a_0 - 0}{\text{s.e. of } a_0}$$

$$\text{t-test for } a_1\text{: } t = \frac{a_1 - 1}{\text{s.e. of } a_1}$$

The t-statistic can be compared to the critical level (from a t-table) to determine whether the values of a_0 and a_1, differ significantly from their hypothesized values.

13. Describe a statistical test for the international Fisher effect.

ANSWER: A regression model could be applied to historical data to test IFE. The model is specified as:

$$e_f = a_0 + a_1 \left[\frac{(1 + I_{U.S.})}{1 + I_f} - 1 \right] + u$$

where E_f is the percentage change in the foreign currency's exchange rate, i_{US} and i_f are U.S. and foreign interest rates, a_0 is a constant, a_1 is the slope coefficient, and u is an error term. If IFE holds, a_0 should equal zero and a_1 should equal 1. A t-test on a_0 and a_1 is shown below:

$$\text{t-test for } a_0\text{: } t = \frac{a_0 - 0}{\text{s.e. of } a_0}$$

$$\text{t-test for } a_1\text{: } t = \frac{a_1 - 1}{\text{s.e. of } a_1}$$

The t-statistic can be compared to the critical level from a t-table) to determine whether the values of a_0 and a_1 differ significantly from their hypothesized values.

14. If investors in the United States and Canada required the same real return, and the nominal rate of interest was 2 percent higher in Canada, what would this imply about expectations of U.S. inflation and Canadian inflation? What do these inflationary expectations suggest about future exchange rates?

    ANSWER: Expected inflation in Canada is 2 percent above expected inflation in the U.S. If these inflationary expectations come true, PPP would suggest that the value of the Canadian dollar should depreciate by 2 percent against the U.S. dollar.

15. Some countries with high inflation rates tend to have high interest rates. Why?

    ANSWER: If investors among countries require the same real (inflation-adjusted) return, they will require a high nominal interest rate when inflation is expected to be high.

16. Currencies of some Latin American countries, such as Brazil and Argentina, consistently weaken against most other currencies. What concept in this chapter would explain this occurrence?

    ANSWER: Latin American countries typically have very high inflation, such as 200 percent or more. PPP theory would suggest that currencies of these countries will depreciate against the U.S. dollar (and other major currencies) in order to retain purchasing power across countries. The high inflation discourages demand for Latin American imports and places downward pressure in their Latin American currencies. Depreciation of the currencies offsets the increased prices on Latin American goods, from the perspective of importers in other countries.

17. Japan has typically had lower inflation than the United States. How would one expect this to affect the Japanese yen's value? Why has this expected relationship not always occurred?

    ANSWER: Japan's low inflation should place upward pressure in the yen's value. Yet, other factors can sometimes offset this pressure. For example, Japan had heavily invested in U.S. securities during the early 1980s, which placed downward pressure on the yen's value.

18. Assume that the nominal interest rate in Mexico is 48 percent and the interest rate in the United States is 8 percent for one-year securities that are free from default risk. What would the Fisher effect suggest about the differential in expected inflation in these two countries? Using this information and purchasing power parity, describe the expected nominal return to U.S. investors who invest in Mexico.

    ANSWER: If investors from the U.S. and Mexico required the same real (inflation-adjusted) return, then any difference is nominal interest rates is due to differences in expected inflation. Thus, the inflation rate in Mexico is expected to be 40 percentage points above the U.S. inflation rate.

    According to PPP, the Mexican peso should depreciate by the amount of the differential between U.S. and Mexican inflation rates. Using a 40 percent differential, the Mexican peso should depreciate by about 40 percent. Given a 48 percent nominal interest rate in Mexico and expected depreciation of the peso of 40 percent, U.S. investors will earn about 8 percent. (This answer used the inexact formula, since the concept is stressed here more than precision.)

19. Shouldn't the international Fisher effect discourage investors from attempting to capitalize on higher foreign interest rates? Why do some investors continue to invest overseas, even when they have no other transactions overseas?

    ANSWER: According to the IFE, higher foreign interest rates should not attract investors because these rates imply high expected inflation rates, which in turn imply potential depreciation of these currencies. Yet, some investors still invest in foreign countries where nominal interest rates are high. This may suggest that some investors believe that (1) the anticipated inflation rate embedded in a high nominal interest rate is overestimated, or (2) the potentially high inflation will not cause substantial depreciation of the foreign currency (which could occur if adequate substitute products were not available elsewhere), or (3) there are other factors that can offset the possible impact of inflation on the foreign currency's value.

20. Assume that the inflation rate in France is expected to increase substantially. How would this affect French nominal interest rates and the French exchange rate? If the international Fisher effect holds, how would the nominal return to U.S. investors who invest in France be affected by the higher inflation in France? Explain.

ANSWER: The French nominal interest rate would likely increase to maintain the real return required by French investors. The French franc would be expected to depreciate according to the IFE. If the IFE holds, the return to U.S. investors who invest in France would not be affected. Even though they now earn a higher nominal interest rate, the expected decline in the franc offsets the additional interest to be earned.

21. How is it possible for purchasing power parity to hold, if the international Fisher effect does not?

ANSWER: For the IFE to hold, the following conditions are necessary:

(1) investors across countries require the same real returns,
(2) the expected inflation rate embedded in the nominal interest rate occurs,
(3) the exchange rate adjusts to the inflation rate differential according to PPP.

If conditions (1) or (2) do not hold, PPP may still hold, but investors may achieve consistently higher returns when investing in a foreign country's securities. Thus, IFE would be refuted.

22. Explain why the international Fisher effect may not hold.

ANSWER: Exchange rate movements react to other factors in addition to interest rate differentials. Therefore, an exchange rate will not necessarily adjust in accordance with the nominal interest rate differentials, so that IFE may not hold.

23. Assume that the spot exchange rate of the British pound is $1.73. How would this spot rate adjust according to purchasing power parity if Great Britain experiences an inflation rate of 7 percent while the United States experiences an inflation rate of 2 percent?

ANSWER: $1.73 [1 + (-.02)] = $1.6435

24. Assume the spot exchange rate of the Swiss franc is $.70. The one-year interest rate is 11 percent in the United States and 7 percent in Switzerland. What would be the spot rate in one year according to the international Fisher effect? (You may use the approximate formula to answer this question.)

ANSWER: $.70 (1 + .04) = $.728

25. As of today, assume the following information is available:

	U.S.	France
Real rate of interest required by investors	2%	2%
Normal interest rate	11%	15%
Spot rate	_____	\$.20
One-year forward rate	_____	\$.19

a. Use the forward rate to forecast the percentage change in the French franc over the next year.

ANSWER: (.19 - \$.20)/\$.20 = -.05, or -5%

b. Use the differential in expected inflation to forecast the percentage change in the French franc over the next year.

ANSWER: 11%-15% = -4%; the negative sign represents depreciation of the franc

c. Use the spot rate to forecast the percentage change in the French franc over the next year.

ANSWER: zero percent change

26. During February 1990 interest rates of the German mark rose to their highest level in seven years. The increase was mostly attributed to the strong demand for funds in West Germany as a result of the reunification effort with East Germany. Explain how the forward premium of the German mark would likely be affected by this event. How would the forecast of the percentage change in the mark be affected by the increased German interest rates according to the international Fisher effect?

ANSWER: The forward premium should decline if German interest rates rise while U.S. interest rates do not. As German interest rates rise to approach U.S. rates, the magnitude of expected appreciation in the mark would now be smaller than before (when using the IFE). If German interest rates are above U.S. rates, IFE would suggest that the mark should depreciate.

27. Would PPP be more likely to hold between the United States and Hungary if trade barriers were completely removed and if Hungary's currency were allowed to float without any goverment intervention? Explain.

ANSWER: Changes in international trade result from inflation differences, and affects the exchange rate (by affecting the demand for the currency and the supply of the currency for sale). The effect on the exchange rate is more likely to occur if (a) free trade is allowed, and (b) the currency's exchange rate is allowed to fluctuate without any government intervention.

28. Would IFE be more likely to hold between the United States and Hungary if trade barriers were completely removed and if Hungary's currency were allowed to float without any government intervention? Explain.

ANSWER: The underlying force of IFE is the differential in expected inflation between two countries, which can affect trade and capital flows. The effects on the exchange rate are more likely to occur if (a) free trade is allowed, and (b) the currency's exchange rate is allowed to fluctuate without government intervention.

Solution to WSJ Case: Inflation and Exchange Rates in Russia

1. Explain why the Russian inflation of about 800 percent was placing severe pressure on the value of the Russian ruble.

   ANSWER: As Russian prices were increasing, the purchasing power of Russian consumers was declining. This would encourage them to purchase goods in the U.S. and elsewhere, which results in a large supply of rubles for sale. Given the high Russian inflation, foreign demand for rubles to purchase Russian goods would be low. Thus, the ruble's value should depreciate against the dollar, and against other currencies.

2. Does the effect of Russian inflation on the decline of the ruble's value support the theory of purchasing power parity (PPP)? How might the relationship be distorted by political conditions in Russia?

   ANSWER: The general relationship suggested by PPP is supported, but the ruble's value will not normally move exactly as specified by PPP. The political conditions that could restrict trade or currency convertibility can prevent Russian consumers from shifting to foreign goods. Thus, the ruble may not decline by the full degree to offset the inflation differential between Russia and the U.S. Furthermore, the government may not allow the ruble to float freely to its proper equilibrium level.

3. Does it appear that the prices of Russian goods will be equal to the prices of U.S. goods from the perspective of Russian consumers (after considering exchange rates)? Explain.

   ANSWER: Russian prices will likely be higher than U.S. prices, even after considering exchange rates, because the ruble will not depreciate enough to fully offset the Russian inflation of 800 percent. The exchange rate cannot fully adjust if there are no barriers on trade or currency convertibility.

4. Given the 800 percent inflation and the decline in the ruble, will the effects offset each other for U.S. importers? That is, how will U.S. importers of Russian goods be affected by the conditions?

   ANSWER: U.S. importers will likely experience higher prices, because the Russian inflation will not be completely offset by the decline in the ruble's value. This may cause a reduction in the U.S. demand for Russian goods.

Solution to Case Problem: Flame Fixtures, Inc.

a) If the peso depreciates by more than the inflation differential, then the dollar cost to Flame will be even lower than expected.

b) If the peso depreciates by less than the inflation differential, then the dollar cost to Flame will be even higher than expected. Consider a scenario in which the Mexican inflation rate is 80 percent or so, causing the bill in pesos to be 80 percent higher. Yet, if the peso depreciated by a relatively small amount over this period (say 20 percent or so), the dollar cost to Flame will increase substantially. Since there are other factors in addition to inflation that also affect the peso's exchange rate, the peso will not necessarily depreciate by an amount that fully offsets the high inflation.

c) Stable dollar payments would only occur if the peso depreciated by an amount that offset its high inflation rate. It is unlikely that there will be a perfect offset in any given period. Therefore, Flame's dollar payments would be unstable, and so would its profits.

d) The risk would increase, because its payments for parts would now be more volatile, and so would its profits. Given that it does not have much liquidity, it will suffer a cash squeeze if the peso does not depreciate much while Mexican inflation is high. Over the long run, there may be periods in which this happens. Flame would be locked into this arrangement with Coron for ten years, and therefore cannot back out, even if the peso's depreciation does not offset the inflation differential.

Project

1. Use data from the back of this text to determine whether a U.S. investor could have earned a higher return (on average) on consecutive investments in the United Kingdom than in the U.S. Assess several historical periods. What do your results imply about the international Fisher effect?

   This project forces students to determine exchange rate adjusted returns to U.S. investors who invested in British securities. Students will realize the impact exchange rate movements have had on the returns. They will realize that these returns often deviate substantially from U.S. returns, but are not consistently above or below U.S. returns.

Integrative Problem for Part II

Exchange Rate Behavior

1. As an employee of the foreign exchange department for a large company, you have been given the following information.

Beginning of Year	End of Year
Spot rate of £ = \$1.596	£ = \$1.6758
Spot rate of SF = \$.70	SF = \$.73
Cross Exchange rate: £1 = SF2.28	£1 = SF2.295
One-year Forward rate of SF = \$.71	
One-year Forward rate of £ = \$1.58004	
One-year U.S. interest rate = 8.00%	
One-year British interest rate = 9.09%	
One-year Swiss interest rate = 7.00%	

1. Determine whether triangular arbitrage is feasible, and if so, how it would be conducted to make a profit.

   ANSWER: Triangular arbitrage is not feasible because the cross exchange rate between £ and SF is properly specified:

$$\text{Proper Cross exchange rate} = \frac{\text{Spot rate of £}}{\text{Spot rate of SF}} = \frac{\$1.596}{\$.7} = 2.28\ ;$$

2. Using the information in Question 1, determine whether covered interest arbitrage is feasible, and if so, how it would be conducted to make a profit.

ANSWER: Covered interest arbitrage is only feasible when interest rate parity does not exist. To text whether interest rate parity exists, determine the forward premium that should exist for the pound and for the Swiss franc.

Currency	Forward Premium that Should Exist	Actual Forward Premium
Pound (£)	$p = \frac{(1+i_h)}{(1+i_f)} - 1$	$p = \frac{F - S}{S}$
	$= \frac{(1.08)}{(1.0909)} - 1$	$= \frac{\$1.58004 - \$1.596}{\$1.596}$
	= -.01	= -.01
Swiss franc (SF)	$p = \frac{(1+i_h)}{(1+i_f)} - 1$	$p = \frac{F - S}{S}$
	$= \frac{(1.08)}{1.07} - 1$	$= \frac{.71 - \$.70}{\$.70}$
	= .0093	= .01428

Interest rate parity exists for the British pound. However, interest rate parity does not exist for the SF. The actual forward premium is higher than it should be. U.S. investors could benefit from the discrepancy by using covered interest arbitrage. The forward premium they would receive when selling SF at the end of one year more than offsets the interest rate differential. While the U.S. investors receive 1 percent less interest on the Swiss investment, they receive 1.428 percent more when selling SF than what they initially pay for SF.

3. Based on the information in Question 1 for the beginning of the year, use the international Fisher effect (IFE) theory to forecast the annual percentage change in the British pound's value over the year.

ANSWER: The IFE suggest that given two currencies, the currency with a higher interest rate reflects higher expected inflation, which will place downward pressure on the value of that currency (based on purchasing power parity). The currency adjustment will offset the differential in interest rates.

$$e_f = \frac{(1 + i_h)}{(1 + i_f)} - 1$$

$$= \frac{(1 + .08)}{(1 + .0909)} - 1$$

$$\approx -.01 \text{ or } -1\%$$

Thus, the pound was expected to depreciate by 1 percent over the year, based on the IFE.

4. Assume that at the beginning of the year, the pound's value is in equilibrium. Assume that over the year, the British inflation rate is 6 percent while the U.S. inflation rate is 4 percent. Assume that any change in the pound's value due to the inflation differential has occurred by the end of the year. Using this information and the information provided in Question 1, determine how the pound's value changed over the year in accordance with purchasing power parity (PPP).

ANSWER: If PPP held, the pound would have changed by:

$$e_p = \frac{(1 + I_h)}{1 + I_f} - 1$$

$$= \frac{1.04}{1.06} - 1$$

$$\approx .0189 \text{ or } -1.89\%$$

5. Assume that the pound's depreciation over the year was attributed directly to central bank intervention. Explain the type of direct intervention that would place downward pressure on the value of the pound.

   ANSWER: If central banks used pounds to purchase dollars in the foreign exchange market, they would place downward pressure on the pound's value.

Chapter 9

Forecasting Exchange Rates

Lecture Outline

Why Multinational Firms Forecast Exchange Rates

Forecasting Techniques

Technical Forecasting
Fundamental Forecasting
Market-Based Forecasting
Mixed Forecasting

Further Examination of the Forward Rate as a Predictor

How to Evaluate Exchange Rate Forecasting Accuracy

Forecast Accuracy Over Time
Forecast Accuracy Among Currencies
Search for Forecast Bias

Graphic Evaluation of Forecasting Performance

Comparison of Forecasting Techniques

Forecasting Performance and Market Efficiency

Chapter Theme

This chapter stresses the value of reliable forecasts, but suggests that reliable forecasts can't always be obtained. Because no single forecast technique has been singled out as superior, various techniques are mentioned. Whatever techniques the MNC chooses, it should monitor performance over time. This chapter illustrates how this evaluation can be accomplished.

Topics to Stimulate Class Discussion

1. Which forecast technique would you use if you were hired by an MNC to forecast exchange rates?

2. Do you think there will ever be a published technical forecasting model which you could use in the future to most accurately forecast exchange rates? Why or why not?

3. Recall the theories of purchasing power parity (PPP) and international Fisher effect (IFE) in Chapter 7. If these theories were used to forecast exchange rates, which techniques would they be classified as? Why?

4. Suppose that I told you that I have a regression model which was able to identify the factors which affected exchange rate movements in a recent four-year period. Also, suppose that the sensitivity of the exchange rate's movements to each factor was precisely quantified. Is there any reason not to expect superior forecasting results from this method in the future? Elaborate!

5. What is the use of detecting a forecast bias?

Answers to End of Chapter Questions

1. Explain corporate motives for forecasting exchange rates.

   ANSWER: Several decisions of MNCs require an assessment of the future. Future exchange rates will affect all critical characteristics of the firm such as costs and revenues. To be more specific, various operations of MNCs use exchange rate projections, including hedging, short-term financing and investing, capital budgeting decisions, long-term financing, and earnings assessment. Such operations will be more effective of exchange rates are forecasted accurately.

2. Explain the technical technique for forecasting exchange rates.

   ANSWER: Technical forecasting involves the review of historical exchange rates to search for a repetitive pattern which may occur in the future. This pattern would be the basis for future exchange rate movements.

3. Explain the fundamental technique for forecasting exchange rates.

   ANSWER: Fundamental forecasting is based on underlying relationships which are believed to exist between one or more variables and a currency's value. Given these relationships, a change in one or more of these variables (or a forecasted change in them) will lead to a forecast of the currency's value.

4. Explain the market-based technique for forecasting exchange rates.

   ANSWER: The market determines the spot exchange rate and forward exchange rate. These market-based rates can be used to forecast since if they were not good indicators of the future rates, speculators would take positions. This speculative movement would force the rates to gravitate toward the expectation of the future spot rate.

5. Explain the mixed technique for forecasting exchange rates.

   ANSWER: Mixed forecasting involves a combination of two or more techniques. The specific combination can differ in terms of techniques included and the weight of importance assigned to each technique.

6. What are some limitations of using technical forecasting to predict exchange rates?

   ANSWER: Even if a technical forecasting model turns out to be valuable, it will no longer be valuable once other market participants use it. This is because their actions in the market due to the model's forecast will cause the currency values to move as suggested by the model immediately instead of in the future.

   Also, MNCs often prefer long-term forecasts. Technical forecasting is typically conducted for short time horizons.

7. What are some limitations of using a fundamental technique to forecast exchange rates?

ANSWER: Even if a fundamental relationship exists, it is difficult to accurately quantify that relationship in a form applicable to forecasting. Even if the relationship could be quantified, there is no guarantee that the historical relationship will persist in the future. It is difficult to determine the lagged impact of some variables. It is also difficult to incorporate some qualitative factors into the model.

8. What is the rationale for using market-based forecasts?

ANSWER: Market-based forecasts should reflect an expectation of the market on future rates. If the market's expectation differed from existing rates, then the market participants should react by taking positions in various currencies until the current rates do reflect an expectation of the future.

9. Explain how to assess performance in forecasting exchange rates.

ANSWER: Performance can be evaluated by computing the absolute forecast error as a percent of the realized value for all periods where a forecast was necessary. Then an average of this type of error can be computed. This average can be compared among all currencies or among all forecasting models.

10. Explain how to detect a bias in forecasting exchange rates.

ANSWER: A forecast bias exists from consistently underestimating or overestimating exchange rates. The bias can be detected graphically by comparing forecasted exchange rates to realized exchange rates as shown in Exhibit 8.7. If the majority of points are above the 45 degree perfect forecast line, then the forecasts generally underestimate the realized values. If the majority of points are below the 45 degree perfect forecast line, then the forecasts generally overestimate the realized values.

11. You are hired as a consultant to assess a firm's ability to forecast. The firm has developed a point forecast for two different currencies. It wants to determine which currency was forecast with greater accuracy. The information is provided.

Period	Yen Forecast	Actual Yen Value	Pound Forecast	Actual Pound Value
1	$.0050	$.0051	$1.50	$1.51
2	.0048	.0052	1.53	1.50
3	.0053	.0052	1.55	1.58
4	.0055	.0056	1.49	1.52

ANSWER: Absolute Forecast Error as a Percentage of the Realigned Value

Period	Yen Forecast	Pound Forecast
1	1.96%	.66%
2	7.69	2.00
3	1.92	1.89
4	1.78	1.97
Mean	3.34%	1.63%

Because the mean absolute forecast error of the pound is lower than that of the yen, the pound was forecasted with greater accuracy.

12. You are hired as a consultant to determine whether there is a bias from forecasting the percentage change in the Dutch guilder (DG). A set of 200 data points was used to develop the following regression equation.

Actual %
change in = $a_0 + a_1$ (Forecasted % change
DG over in DG over Period t)
Period t

The regression results are as follows:

Coefficient	Standard error
$a_0 = .006$	.011
$a_1 = .800$	.05

Based on these results, is there a bias in the forecast? Verify your conclusion. If there is a bias, explain whether it is an overestimate or an underestimate.

ANSWER: This question is appropriate for students with a background in regression analysis. If there is no bias, a_0 is hypothesized to equal zero and a_1 is hypothesized to equal one. The t-statistics are estimated below:

$$t = \frac{a_0 - 0}{\text{s.e. of } a_0}$$

$$= \frac{.006}{.011}$$

$$= .54$$

t-statistic for a_1 =

$$t = \frac{a_1 - 1}{\text{s.e. of } a_1}$$

$$= \frac{80 - 1}{.05}$$

$$= \frac{-.20}{.05}$$

$$= -4.0$$

The results suggest that while a_0 is not significantly different from its hypothesized value of zero, a_1 is significantly below its hypothesized value of 1. This implies that the realized spot rate is significantly below the forecasted rate. Thus, the forecast contains an upward bias, because it is overestimating the future spot rate.

13. Syracuse Corporation believes that future real interest rate movements will affect exchange rates, and has applied regression analysis to historical data in order to assess the relationship. It will use the regression coefficient derived from this analysis along with forecasted real interest rate movements in order to predict exchange rates in the future. Explain at least three limitations of this method.

ANSWER: First, the timing of the impact of real interest rates on exchange rates may differ from what is specified by the model.

Second, the forecasted real interest rates may be inaccurate, causing inaccurate forecasts of the exchange rate.

Third, the sensitivity of exchange rates to real interest rate movements may change in the future (differ from what was determined when using historical data).

Fourth, the model has ignored other factors that also influence exchange rates.

14. Lexington Company is a U.S.-based MNC with subsidiaries in most major countries. Each subsidiary is responsible for forecasting the future exchange rate of its local currency, relative to the U.S. dollar. Comment on this policy. How might Lexington Company assure consistent forecasts among the different subsidiaries?

ANSWER: If each subsidiary uses its own data and techniques to forecast its local currency's exchange rate, its forecast may be inconsistent with forecasts of other currencies by other subsidiaries. Subsidiary forecasts could be consistent if forecasts for all currencies were based on complete information from all subsidiaries (its beta).

15. Assume that the following regression model was applied to historical quarterly data:

$$e_t = a_0 + a_1 INT_t + a_2 INF_{t-1} + \mu_t$$

where e_t = percentage change in the exchange rate of the franc in period t

INT_t = average real interest rate differential (U.S. interest rate minus French interest rate) over period t

INF_{t-1} = inflation differential (U.S. inflation rate minus French inflation rate) in the previous period

a_0, a_1, a_2 = regression coefficients

μ_t = error term

Assume that the regression coefficients were estimated as follows:

$a_0 = 0.0$
$a_1 = .9$
$a_2 = .8$

Also assume that the inflation differential in the most recent period was 3 percent. The real interest rate differential in the upcoming period is forecasted as follows:

Interest rate Differential	Probability
0%	30%
1	60
2	10

If Stillwater Inc. uses this information to forecast the French franc's exchange rate, what will be the probability distribution of the franc's percentage change over the upcoming period?

ANSWER:

Forecast of interest rate differential	Forecast of the percentage change in the French franc	Probability
0%	.9(0%) + .8(3%) = 2.4%	30%
1%	.9(1%) + .8(3%) = 3.3%	60%
2%	.9(2%) + .8(3%) = 4.2%	10%

16 Assume that the four-year annualized interest rate in the United States is 9 percent and the four-year interest rate in Switzerland is 6 percent. Assume interest rate parity holds for a four-year horizon. Assume that the spot rate of the Swiss franc is $.60. If the forward rate is used to forecast exchange rates, what will be the forecast for the Swiss franc's spot rate in four years? What percentage appreciation or depreciation does this forecast imply over the four-year period.

Country	Four-year compounded return
U.S.	$(1.09)^4 - 1 = 41\%$
Switzerland	$(1.06)^4 - 1 = 26\%$

$$\frac{\text{Premium on a Swiss - franc}}{\text{four - year forward rate}} = \frac{1.41}{1.26} - 1$$

$$= 11.9\%$$

ANSWER: Thus, the four-year forward rate should contain an 11.9% premium above today's spot rate of \$.60, which means the forward rate is \$.60(1 + .119) = \$.6714. The forecast for the Swiss franc's spot rate in four years is \$.6714, which represents 11.9% appreciation over the four-year period.

17. Assume that foreign exchange markets were found to be weak-form efficient. Does this suggest anything about utilizing technical analysis to speculate in the foreign exchange markets?

    ANSWER: Technical analysis should not be able to achieve excess profits if foreign exchange markets are weak-form efficient.

18. If MNCs believed that foreign exchange markets are strong-form efficient, why would they develop their own forecasts of future exchange rates? Why wouldn't they simply use today's quoted rates as indicators about future rates? After all, today's quoted rates should reflect all relevant information.

    ANSWER: Today's rates do not provide information about the range of possible outcomes. MNCs may desire to assess the range of possible outcomes.

19. Most foreign currencies appreciated substantially against the dollar during the 1985-1987 period. Would market-based forecasts have overestimated or underestimated the realized values over this period? Explain.

    ANSWER: They would have underestimated the realized values over this period because the actual values were above the spot rates and forward rates quoted earlier.

20. The director of currency forecasting at Champaign-Urbana Corporation made the statement, "The most critical task of forecasting exchange rates is not to derive a point estimate of a future exchange rate, but to assess how wrong our estimate might be." What does this statement mean?

    ANSWER: Point estimate forecasts of exchange rates are not likely to be perfectly accurate. MNCs that develop point estimate forecasts recognize this, but would like to determine how far off the forecast may be. They will have more confidence in the forecasts of currencies that have been forecasted with only minor errors. For other currencies in which forecast errors have been large, they would be very careful when basing policy decisions on forecasts of these currencies.

21. Assume that in the 1990s, some countries in East Europe allow the exchange rates of their currencies to fluctuate against the dollar. Would the use of the fundamental technique (using historical relationships) be useful for forecasting future exchange rates of these currencies? Explain.

    ANSWER: Fundamental forecasting typically relies on historical relationships between economic factors and exchange rate movements. However, if exchange rates were not allowed to move in the past, historical relationships would not help predict future exchange rates of these currencies.

22. Royce Company is a U.S. firm with future receivables one year from now in Canadian dollars and British pounds. Its pound receivables are known with certainty, while its estimated Canadian dollar receivables are subject to a 2 percent error in either direction. The dollar values of both types of receivables are similar. There is no chance of default by the customers involved. The treasurer of Royce stated that the estimate of dollar cash flows to be generated from the British pound receivables is subject to greater uncertainty than that of the Canadian dollar receivables. Explain the rationale for such a statement.

    ANSWER: The British pound's future spot rate is more difficult to predict because of the pound's volatility. Therefore, the dollar revenues from the pound receivables are more uncertain.

23. In the early months of 1991, most major currencies declined substantially against the dollar. Do you think the 30-day forward rates of major currencies were unbiased predictors of their respective future spot rates over these months? Explain.

    ANSWER: Since the spot rate declined significantly, the realized spot rates would be less than the forward rate quoted 30 days earlier (during early 1991). Therefore, the forward rates overestimated the future spot rates then.

24. Assume that you obtain a quote for a one-year forward rate on the Mexican peso. Over the next year, the peso depreciates by 12 percent. Do you think forward rate overestimated the spot rate one year ahead in this example? Explain.

    ANSWER: A quoted forward rate for the Mexican peso would contain a large discount because of the high interest rate in Mexico relative to the U.S. Assuming that the discount exceeds 12 percent, the forward rate would have actually <u>underestimated</u> the future spot rate in this example. (This answer may surprise many students; it deserves a little attention in class.)

25. The treasurer of Glencoe, Inc. detected a forecast bias when using the 30-day forward rate to forecast future spot rates over various periods. He believed he could use such information to determine whether imports ordered every week should be hedged (payment is made 30 days

after each order). The president of Glencoe stated that in the long run, the forward rate is unbiased and suggested that the treasurer should not waste time trying to "beat the forward rate," but should just hedge all orders. Who is correct?

ANSWER: Even if the forward rate is unbiased over the long run, Glencoe could save money if it could effectively detect a forward bias (assuming that the bias would continue after being detected). Glencoe may decide to hedge only when the forward rate is expected to be less than the future spot rate. The Treasurer is correct if the bias continues beyond the point at which it is detected.

Solution to WSJ Case: Using Economic Information to Forecast Exchange Rates

1. During the ERM crisis, Germany's interest rates increased, while U.S. interest rates declined. How did this affect the market's "bullish" opinion about the dollar?

   ANSWER: The market changed its opinion as the interest rate movements caused the mark to strengthen against the dollar.

2. What is meant by the statement that "the dollar is also poised to rise from a technical standpoint?"

   ANSWER: This means that the dollar is expected to appreciate based on recent movements in its value.

3. What fundamental factors are given attention by the analysts that offered forecasts of the dollar's value? Explain each factor.

   ANSWER: Interest rates are given attention because they affect international financial flows, which influence the supply and demand for a currency. The strength of the country's economy is also considered, mainly because of its potential effects on interest rates. The political stability is considered, as money tends to flow to more politically stable countries. Inflation is considered, because it affects purchasing power, and can change international trade patterns.

Solution to Case Problem: Whaler Publishing Co.

1. The exchange rate data for this case were compiled from 1975 through 1990. So this case could simulate an actual example as of the beginning of 1991.

The first step is to measure the standard deviation of the percentage change in each exchange rate, which can most easily be done with a spreadsheet. This information can then be used along with today's spot exchange rate to derive the confidence intervals for each exchange rate.

Currency	Approximate Standard Deviation	68 Percent Confidence Interval	95 Percent Confidence Interval
Australian $	9.26%	$.6960 to $.8381	$.6250 to $.9092
Canadian $	4.92	$.8200 to $.9049	$.7775 to $.9474
New Zealand $	11.62	$.5289 to $.6681	$.4594 to $.7376
British pound	15.84	$1.6311 to $2.2453	$1.3241 to $2.5524

Using the intervals described above and the number of foreign currency units to be received from each country, the range of forecasted U.S. dollar revenues (in thousands) from each country is disclosed below:

Currency	68 Percent Confidence Interval	95 Percent Confidence Interval
Australian $	$26,450 to $31,850	$23,751 to $34,550
Canadian $	$28,702 to $31,674	$27,214 to $33,158
New Zealand $	$17,455 to $22,046	$15,159 to $24,342
British pound	$55,457 to $76,340	$45,016 to $86,782

The numbers here may differ slightly from those of students due to rounding. The standard deviations estimated above suggest that the Canadian dollar is the most stable currency so the U.S. dollar revenues coming from Canada are more predictable. Conversely, the standard deviation of the British pound has been most volatile, so that the U.S. dollar revenues coming from the United Kingdom are less predictable. The above comparison of predictability of U.S. dollar revenues from various countries assumes that the foreign currency revenues in each country is known. In other words, the reason for the uncertainty in dollar revenues is the exchange rate, not the demand for textbooks by each given country.

Notice that the estimates were not pooled in any way to derive a confidence interval about the overall dollar revenues. This would require an assumption that each exchange rate moves independently of the others. If some of these currencies were positively correlated, such an assumption would cause one to underestimate the dispersion in the confidence interval when combining estimates from individual countries. If time permits, you may wish to challenge the students by asking them whether combining the individual country results would be appropriate. The case problem in the following chapter focuses on this issue, and is an extension of this case problem.

Project

1. Assess the forecasting accuracy of the forward rate using a currency of your choice and the data in the back of this text. Use a procedure similar to that used within this chapter on the British pound. Is the forward rate of your currency more accurate than the forward rate of the pound (based on results shown in this chapter)? Did your forward rate exhibit a consistent upward or downward bias in any periods? Explain.

   This project provides students with experience in assessing forecasting accuracy and detecting a forecast bias. Students should recognize that a bias will exist in periods when this currency consistently appreciates or consistently depreciates against the dollar.

Chapter 10

Measuring Exposure to Exchange Rate Fluctuations

Lecture Outline

Is Exchange Rate Risk Relevant?

Transaction Exposure

Transaction Exposure to "Net" Cash Flows
Transaction Exposure Based on Currency Variability
Transaction Exposure Based on Currency Correlations
Assessing Transaction Exposure: An Example

Economic Exposure

Economic Exposure to Local Currency Appreciation
Economic Exposure to Local Currency Depreciation
Indirect Economic Exposure
Economic Exposure of Domestic Firms
Economic Exposure of MNCs
Measuring Economic Exposure

Translation Exposure

Does Translation Exposure Matter?
Determinants of Translation Exposure
Example of Translation Exposure

Chapter Theme

This chapter distinguishes between three forms by which MNCs are exposed to exchange rate risk: (1) transaction exposure, (2) economic exposure, and (3) translation exposure. It should be emphasized that a firm sometimes benefits due to exposure. Yet, it typically would prefer to control its own destiny and therefore be insulated from exposure. Each firm differs in degree of exposure. A firm should be able to measure its degree of each type of exposure as described in this chapter. Then, it can decide how to cover that exposure using methods described in the following two chapters.

Topics to Stimulate Class Discussion

1. Describe in general terms how you would measure the transaction exposure of a particular MNC.

2. What is the relationship between transaction exposure and economic exposure?

3. Firm "X" is a small firm in New York City that produces various metals and sells them to local manufacturers. It has no foreign sales and purchases all supplies and materials locally. Does transaction exposure exist for this firm? Does economic exposure exist for this firm?

Answers to End of Chapter Questions

1. Why would an MNC consider examining only its "net" cash flows in each currency when assessing its transaction exposure?

   ANSWER: Consideration of all cash flows in a particular currency is not necessary when some inflows and outflows offset each other. Only net cash flows are necessary.

2. Your employer, a large MNC, has asked you to assess its transaction exposure. Its projected cash flows are as follows for the next year:

Currency	Total Inflow	Total Outflow	Current Exchange Rate in U.S. Dollars
French francs (FF)	FF 4,000,000	FF 2,000,000	$.15
British pounds (BP)	BP 2,000,000	BP 1,000,000	$1.50
German marks (DM)	DM 3,000,000	DM 4,000,000	$.30

Provide your assessment as to your firm's degree of economic exposure (as to whether the exposure is high or low). Substantiate your answer. Use any background data available to you in order to answer your question.

ANSWER: The net exposure to each currency in U.S. dollars is derived below:

Foreign Currency	Net Inflows in Foreign Currency	Current Exchange Rate	Value of Exposure
French franc (FF)	+FF 2,000,000	$ .15	$ 300,000
British pound (BP)	+BP 1,000,000	$1.50	$ 1,500,000
German marks (DM)	DM 1,000,000	$ .30	$-3,000,000

The franc and mark values typically move in tandem against the dollar. Their dollar value of exposure is the same but the franc exposure shows positive net inflows while the mark exposure shows negative net inflows. Thus, their exposure should be offset if their exchange rates against the U.S. dollar continue to be highly correlated. The firm's main concern about exposure should therefore be the British pound net inflows.

3. What factors affect a firm's degree of transaction exposure? For each factor, explain the desirable characteristics that would reduce transaction exposure.

   ANSWER: Currency variability - low level is desirable.

   Currency correlations - low level is desirable for currencies which are net inflows, while a high level is desirable for pairs of currencies in which one currency shows future net inflows while the other currency shows future net outflows.

4. Are currency correlations perfectly stable over time? What does your answer imply about using past data on correlations as an indicator for the future?

   ANSWER: No! Thus, past correlations will not serve as perfect forecasts of future correlations. Yet, historical data may still be useful if the general ranking of correlations is somewhat stable.

5. If a firm has net receivables in several currencies which are highly correlated with each other, what does this imply about the firm's overall degree of transaction exposure?

   ANSWER: Its exposure is high since all currencies move in tandem-- no offsetting effect is likely. If one of these currencies depreciates substantially against the firm's local currency, all others will as well, and this reduces the value of these net receivables.

6. Compare and contrast transaction exposure and economic exposure.

   ANSWER: Transaction exposure is due only to international transactions by a firm. Economic exposure includes any form by which the firm's cash flow will be affected. Foreign competition may increase due to currency fluctuations. This could affect the firm's cash flow, but did not affect the value of any ongoing transactions. Thus, it represents a form of economic exposure but not transaction exposure. Transaction exposure is a subset of economic exposure.

7. How should appreciation of a firm's home currency generally affect its cash inflows? Why?

   ANSWER: It should reduce inflows since the foreign demand for the firm's goods is reduced and foreign competition is increased.

8. How should depreciation of a firm's home currency generally affect its cash outflows? Why?

   ANSWER: It should increase inflows since it will likely increase foreign demand for the firm's goods and reduce foreign competition.

9. Assume that Firm Z is in the exporting business and that it obtains its supplies and borrowed funds locally. How would depreciation of this firm's local currency likely affect its net cash flows? Why?

   ANSWER: It would help Firm Z. Its cash outflows should not be affected much since the outflows are normally local anyway. Yet, the inflows would increase since foreign demand for the firm's goods should increase.

10. Why are even the cash flows of purely domestic firms exposed to exchange rate fluctuations?

    ANSWER: If the firm competes with foreign firms that also sell in a given market, then the consumers may switch to foreign products if the local currency strengthens.

11. Assume that an MNC hires you as a consultant to assess its degree of economic exposure to exchange rate fluctuations. How would you handle this task? Be specific.

    ANSWER: Regression analysis can be used to determine the relationship between the firm's value and exchange rate fluctuations. Stock returns can be used as a proxy for the change in firm's value. The time period can be segmented into two subperiods so that regression analysis can be run for each subperiod. The sign and magnitude of the regression coefficient will imply how the firm's value is influenced by each currency. Also, the coefficients can be compared among subperiods for each currency to determine how the impact of a currency is changing over time. This concept is discussed in the appendix.

12. a. In using regression analysis to assess a firm's degree of economic exposure to exchange rate movements, what is the use of breaking the data base into subperiods? (See Appendix 10A.)

ANSWER: It enables one to understand how the impact of the currency is changing over time.

b. Assume that the regression coefficients based on assessing economic exposure were much higher in this second subperiod than in the first subperiod. What does this tell you about the firm's degree of economic exposure over time? Why might such results occur? (See Appendix 10A.)

ANSWER: It suggests that the firm is more exposed to change in currency values. This could occur if the firm hedges currency positions less, or is simply increasing its degree of foreign business.

13. a. Present an argument for why translation exposure is relevant to an MNC.

ANSWER: It affects consolidated financial statements, which are often used by shareholders to assess the performance of the MNC.

b. Present an argument for why translation exposure is not relevant to an MNC.

ANSWER: It does not affect cash flow, since it simply reflects the impact of exchange rate fluctuation on consolidated financial statements.

14. What factors affect the firm's degree of translation exposure? Explain how each factor influences translation exposure.

ANSWER: The greater the percentage of business conducted by subsidiaries, the greater is the translation exposure. The greater the variability of each relevant foreign currency relative to the headquarters home (reporting) currency, the greater is the translation exposure. The type of accounting method employed can also affect translation exposure.

15. How have MNCs changed over time (based in surveys) with respect to their attitude about the importance of transaction exposure versus translation exposure?

ANSWER: They now believe transaction exposure is more important than translation exposure.

16. How does FASB-52 differ from FASB-8? (See Appendix 10C.)

ANSWER: A key difference is that FASB-52 does not account for translation gains and losses within the income statement. Also, some items such as inventory are translated at the current rate under FASB-52 versus the historical rate under FASB-8.

17. Consider a period in which the U.S. dollar weakens against most foreign currencies. How will this affect the reported earnings of a U.S.-based MNC with subsidiaries all over the world?

ANSWER: The consolidated earnings will be increased due to the strength of the subsidiaries' local currencies.

18. Consider a period in which the U.S. dollar strengthens against most foreign currencies. How will this affect the reported earnings of a U.S. based MNC with subsidiaries all over the world?

ANSWER: The consolidated earnings will be reduced due to the weakness of the subsidiaries' local currencies.

19. Walt Disney World decided to build an amusement park in France that opened in 1992. How do you think this project will affect Disney's overall economic exposure to exchange rate movements? Explain.

ANSWER: This is a good question for class discussion. The typical first reaction is that Walt Disney World's exposure may increase, since this new park would generate revenues in French francs, which may someday be converted to dollars. If the franc weakens against the dollar, the revenues will be converted to fewer dollars.

However, keep in mind that Walt Disney was already affected by movements in the French franc and other major currencies before this park was built. When major currencies weaken against the dollar, foreign tourism decreases and Walt Disney's business in the U.S. declines. By having a European amusement park, it may be able to offset the declining U.S. business during strong dollar cycles, since more European tourists may go to the Disney park in France during the periods. Overall, Disney may become less exposed to exchange rate movements because of the park.

20. Using the following cost and revenue information for DeKalb Inc., determine how the costs, revenues, and earnings items would be affected by three possible exchange rate scenarios: (1) DM = \$.50, (2) DM = \$.55, (3) DM = \$.60. (Assume U.S. sales will be unaffected by the exchange rate.) Assume that DM earnings will be remitted to the U.S. at the end of the period.

Revenue and Cost Estimates: DeKalb Company
(in millions of U.S. dollars and German marks)

	U.S. Business	German Business
Sales	\$800	DM 800
Cost of goods sold	\$500	DM 100
Gross profit	\$300	DM 700
Operating expenses	\$300	
Earnings before interest and taxes	0	DM 700
Interest expense	\$100	0
Earnings before taxes	-\$100	DM 700

(Figures are in millions)

	DM=$.50	DM=$.55	DM=$.60
Sales			
U.S.	$800	$800	$800
German	DM800 = $400	DM800 = $440	DM800 = $480
Total	$1,200	$1,240	$1,280
Cost of goods sold			
U.S.	$500	$500	$500
German	DM100 = $ 50	DM100 = $ 55	DM100 = $ 60
Total	$550	$555	$560
Gross profit	$650	$685	$720
Operating expenses	$300	$300	$300
EBIT	$350	$385	$420
Interest expenses	$100	$100	$100
Earnings after taxes	$250	$285	$320

ANSWER: The preceding table shows that DeKalb Inc. is adversely affected by a weaker mark value. This should not be surprising since the German business has relatively high DM revenues compared to DM expenses. This analysis assumes that the DM received are converted to dollars at the end of the period.

21. Aggie Company produces chemicals. It is a major exporter to Germany, where its main competition is from other U.S. exporters. All of these companies invoice the products in U.S. dollars. Is Aggie's transaction exposure likely to be significantly affected if the mark strengthens or weakens? Explain. If the mark weakened for several years, can you think of any change that might occur within the global chemicals market?

    ANSWER: If the mark strengthens, German customers can purchase Aggie's goods with fewer marks. Since Aggie's competitors also invoice their exports in dollars, Aggie Company will not gain a competitive advantage. Nevertheless, the overall demand for the product could increase because it is now less expensive to German customers.

    If the mark weakens, German customers will need to pay more marks to purchase Aggie's goods. Since Aggie's competitors also invoice their exports in dollars, Aggie Company may not necessarily lose some of its market share. However, the overall German demand for chemicals could decline because the prices they pay for them have increased.

If the dollar remained weak for several years, some companies in West Germany may begin to produce the chemicals, so that customers could avoid purchasing dollars with weak marks. That is, the U.S. exporters could be priced out of the German market over time if the mark continually weakened.

22. Longhorn Company produces hospital equipment. Most of its revenues are in the United States. About half of its expenses require outflows in German marks (to pay for German materials). Most of Longhorn's competition is from U.S. firms that have no international business at all. How will Longhorn Company be affected if the mark strengthens?

    ANSWER: If the mark strengthens, Longhorn will incur higher expenses when paying for the German materials. Because its competition is not affected in a similar manner, Longhorn Company is at a competitive disadvantage when the mark strengthens.

23. Lubbock Inc. produces furniture and has no international business. Its major competitors import most of their furniture from Switzerland, then sell it out of retail stores in the United States. How will Lubbock Inc. be affected if the Swiss franc strengthens over time?

    ANSWER: If the Swiss franc strengthens, U.S. retail stores will likely have to pay higher prices for the furniture from Switzerland, and may pass some or all of the higher cost on to customers. Consequently, some customers may shift to furniture produced by Lubbock Inc. Thus, Lubbock Inc. is expected to be favorably affected by a strong Swiss franc.

24. Sooner Company is a U.S. wholesale company that imports expensive high-quality luggage and sells it to retail stores around the United States. Its main competitors also import high-quality luggage and sell it to retail stores. None of these competitors hedge their exposure to exchange rate movements. The treasurer of Sooner Company told the board of directors that the firm's performance would be more volatile over time if it hedged its exchange rate exposure. How could a firm's cash flows be more stable as a result of such high exposure to exchange rate fluctuations?

    ANSWER: If Sooner Company hedged its imports, then it would have an advantage over the competition when the dollar weakened (since its competitors would pay higher prices for the luggage), and could possibly gain market share or would have a higher profit margin. It would be at a disadvantage relative to the competition when the dollar strengthened and may lose market share or be forced to accept a lower profit margin.

    When Sooner Company does not hedge, the amount paid for imports would depend on exchange rate movements, but this is also true for all of its competitors. Thus, Sooner is more likely to retain its existing market share.

25. Boulder Inc. exports chairs to Germany (invoiced in U.S. dollars) and competes against local German companies. If purchasing power parity exists, why would Boulder not benefit from a stronger mark?

    ANSWER: If purchasing power parity exists, a stronger mark would occur only because the U.S. inflation is higher than German inflation. Thus, the German demand for Boulder's chairs may not be affected much since the inflated prices of U.S.-made chairs would have offset the German's ability to obtain cheaper dollars. The German consumer's purchasing power of German chairs versus U.S. chairs is not affected by the change in the mark's value.

26. Toyota Motor Corporation measures the sensitivity of exports to the yen exchange rate (relative to the U.S. dollar). Explain how regression analysis could be used for such a task. Identify the expected sign of the regression coefficient if Toyota primarily exported to the United States. If Toyota established plants in the United States, how might the regression coefficient on the exchange rate variable change?

    ANSWER: The dependent variable is a percentage change (from one period to the next) in Toyota's export volume to the U.S. The independent variables are (1) the percentage change in the yen's value with respect to the dollar, (2) a measure of the strength of the U.S. economy, and (3) any other factors that could affect the volume of Toyota's exports. The regression coefficient related to the exchange rate variable (as defined here) would be negative, since a decrease in the yen's value is likely to cause an increase in the U.S. demand for Toyotas built in Japan.

    If Toyota established plants in the U.S., dealers do not need to purchase Toyotas in Japan. Thus, the demand for Toyotas is less sensitive to the exchange rate, which should cause the regression coefficient for the exchange rate variable to decrease.

27. How can a U.S. company use regression analysis to assess its economic exposure to fluctuations in the British pound?

    ANSWER: A U.S. company could quantify its performance by measuring the percentage change in earnings, or stock price, or some other variable, to be used as the dependent variable. The independent variable is percentage change in the British pound. Lagged exchange rate variables could also be included as additional independent variables to capture any lagged impact of the pound's movements on the firm.

28. Cornhusker Company is an exporter of products to France. It wants to know how its stock price is affected by changes in the franc's exchange rate. It believes that the impact may occur with a lag of one to three quarters. How could regression analysis be used to assess the impact?

ANSWER: A possible regression model for this task is to regress percentage change in its stock price over quarter t (PSP_t) against (1) the percentage change in the French franc (PFF) in the three previous quarters, as shown below:

$$PSP_t = a_0 + a_1PFF_{t-1} + a_2PFF_{t-2} + a_3PFF_{t-3} + u_t$$

where u_t is an error term.

29. Vegas Corporation is a U.S. firm that exports most of its products to Germany. It historically invoiced its products in German marks to accommodate the importers. However, it was adversely affected during the first quarter of 1989, when the mark weakened against the dollar. Since Vegas did not hedge, its mark receivables were converted into a relatively small amount of dollars. After a few more years of continual concern about possible exchange rate movements, Vegas called its customers and requested that they pay for future orders with dollars instead of marks. At this time, the mark was valued at $.51. The customers decided to oblige, since the number of marks to be converted to dollars when importing the goods from Vegas was still slightly smaller than the number of marks that would be needed to buy the product from a German manufacturer. Based on this situation, has transaction exposure changed for Vegas Corporation? Has economic exposure changed? Explain.

    ANSWER: Transaction exposure is reduced since Vegas will have less receivables in marks. However, the economic exposure will not necessarily be reduced because a weak mark could cause a lower demand for its exports, and will still affect cash flows.

30. Saab, the Swedish automobile manufacturer, purchases many of its components from Germany. It exports many of its automobiles to the United States. Recently, the Swedish kronor depreciated against the German mark and appreciated against the U.S. dollar. Holding other factors constant, how would Saab's performance be affected by these currency movements?

    ANSWER: Saab was adversely affected. As evidence, its chief financial officer stated that the kronor's depreciation against the mark cost Saab the equivalent of $6 million, and the kronor's appreciation against the dollar cost Saab the equivalent of $30 million.

31. A German company called Bonz Company has heavy exposure in French francs as a result of importing French supplies denominated in French francs. Stark Company, also German, has heavy exposure in Canadian dollars as a result of importing Canadian supplies denominated in Canadian dollars. Both firms receive German mark cash flows on all their products sold. Neither firm hedges payments on imports. Assume that the values of imported supplies ordered by the firms are about the same. Also assume that other characteristics of the firms are similar. Which firm will likely experience more volatile profit streams over time? Why?

ANSWER: Stark Company will experience more volatile profit streams because the Canadian dollar value is more volatile than the French franc value from a German perspective. The French franc value is somewhat stable against the mark, while the Canadian dollar is volatile against the mark. Some students will initially offer the wrong answer if they simply apply what they know about exchange rate volatility from a U.S. perspective. They need to recognize that a currency's volatility will be affected by the country perspective.

32. The French franc appreciated against most other European currencies in the 1992-1993 period. How would you expect this to affect EuroDisney's business?

    ANSWER: The strength of the French franc discouraged tourism from other parts of Europe, and adversely affected the cash flows of EuroDisney. In the fourth quarter of 1993, EuroDisney experienced a large loss, which was partially attributed to the French franc's strength.

Solution to WSJ Case: Dow Chemical's Exchange Rate Exposure

1. Why might Dow Chemical benefit from pricing all of its European products in German marks?

   ANSWER: Dow Chemical will avoid receiving cash inflows denominated in some other European currency that has weakened. In this way, it limits its exchange rate risk.

2. Dow Chemical's strategy (of pricing all of its European products in German marks) was announced shortly after the exchange rate mechanism (ERM) was adjusted to allow much wider bands around the exchange rates between European currencies. Explain why the ERM adjustment may have caused Dow Chemical to implement the strategy.

   ANSWER: When the ERM was adjusted to allow for wider bands, the exchange rates between European currencies became more volatile. Thus, some European currencies were more likely to weaken, and would not be as protected by central banks. This would have affected Dow Chemical to a greater degree.

3. Why might Dow Chemical's cash flows be adversely affected by its strategy of pricing European products in marks?

   ANSWER: European customers must pay their bills in marks. If the mark strengthens against other European currencies, this will increase the cost to European customers. Thus, the European customers may consider purchasing their goods from other firms in Europe that accept payment in other currencies, so that they can avoid the exchange rate risk.

Solution to Case Problem: Whaler Publishing Company

a) Using the exchange rate data from the case problem in the previous chapter, scenarios for the percentage change in each exchange rate and the forecasted spot rate in one year are determined. Then, for each scenario, the forecasted spot rate is multiplied by the number of foreign currency units to be received; estimate the U.S. dollar revenues to be generated from each country. These revenues are then aggregated across the four countries to estimate total dollar revenues.

Year Used to Create a Scenario	U.S. Dollar Revenues From All Countries in Aggregate (in Thousands)
1	$129,010
2	153,443
3	148,241
4	148,957
5	150,588
6	127,897
7	127,785
8	133,492
9	122,130
10	155,426
11	147,028
12	174,021
13	148,228
14	133,270
15	160,220

Since each scenario has an equal probability of occurring, the expected value of U.S. dollar revenues from all countries in aggregate is the average of these numbers, $143,982,000. The standard deviation of the U.S. dollar revenues from all countries in aggregate is $14,018,000. Thus, the 68 percent confidence interval is $143,982,000 ± $14,018,000 or from $129,964,000 to $158,000,000. The 95 percent confidence interval is $115,946,000 to $172,018,000.

b) There is some evidence of positive correlation between all currencies. The correlation coefficient matrix is filled in below:

	A$	C$	N$	Pound
A$	1.00			
C$	.35	1.00		
N$	.41	.39	1.00	
Pound	.30	.17	.82	1.00

Based on this evidence, the aggregate dollar cash flows received by Whaler is more uncertain than if the exchange rate movements were completely independent. If one currency declines in value, the other currencies would probably decline as well, which is not accounted for by the assumption of independent exchange rate movements.

c) The executive's approach may be slightly easier to use, but is normally less reliable. Whaler does not use past exchange rate data to simulate those actual exchange rates, but to simulate the annual percentage changes in those exchange rates. For example, it may not expect the Canadian dollar's value to be what it was 12 years ago. The historical data are used to simulate the comovements in exchange rates over time, in order to capture these dependencies when developing a distribution of aggregate U.S. dollar cash flows to be received.

Projects

1. Select an MNC and assess the sensitivity of its stock returns to historical exchange rate movements, using the procedure described in Appendix A. Several software packages including *LOTUS* have a regression package that can perform regression analysis.

   This project allows students to assess an MNC's exposure. Some major currencies can have a significant impact on an MNC's returns.

2. Review the annual report on an MNC, and summarize how the MNC was affected by recent changes in the U.S. dollar's value. Explain why an MNC was favorably or unfavorably affected by the dollar's recent movement. Summarize the MNC's translation exposure and the effect of the dollar's recent movements on consolidated earnings.

   Many annual reports of U.S.-based MNCs will suggest that they are favorably affected by a weak dollar because of (1) increased demand for their imports, (2) reduced foreign competition, and (3) the favorable translation effect on reported earnings. During a strong dollar period, MNCs are more likely to suggest that their foreign subsidiary earnings are underestimated by translation at a low exchange rate.

3. Using the data bank in the back of the text, estimate the standard deviation of:

   a) percentage changes in the British pound over the last 20 quarters.
   b) percentage changes in the German mark over the last 20 quarters.
   c) percentage changes in the Japanese yen over the last 20 quarters.
   d) percentage changes in an equally weighted portfolio of these three currencies; that is, the percentage change in the portfolio is equal to (1/3 x % Δ in pound) + (1/3 x % Δ in mark) + (1/3 x % Δ in yen).

   Compare the standard deviation of the portfolio to those of the individual currencies. Explain why the portfolio's standard deviation is lower. See Appendix 10B for related information.

   This project will demonstrate how volatile currencies are, and that a portfolio can exhibit less volatility than each individual component (which relates to diversification benefits).

Chapter 11

Managing Transaction Exposure

Lecture Outline

Transaction Exposure
- Identifying Net Transaction Exposure
- Adjusting the Invoice Policy to Reduce Transaction Exposure

Hedging Techniques
- Futures Contract Hedge
- Forward Contract Hedge
- Money Market Hedge
- Implications of IRP: Comparing the Forward and Money Market Hedge
- Currency Option Hedge
- Summary of Hedging Techniques

Limitation of Repeated Short-Term Hedging Over Time

Hedging Long-Term Transaction Exposure
- Long-term Forward Contracts
- Currency Swap
- Parallel Loan

Techniques to Reduce Transaction Exposure
- Leading and Lagging
- Cross-Hedging
- Currency Diversification

Chapter Theme

A primary objective of the chapter is to provide an overview of hedging techniques. Yet, transaction exposure cannot always be hedged in all cases. Even when it can be hedged, the firm must decide whether a hedge is feasible. While a firm will only know for sure whether hedging is worthwhile after the period of concern, it can incorporate its expectations about future exchange rates, future inflows and outflows, as well as its degree of risk aversion to make hedging decisions.

Topics to Stimulate Class Discussion

1. Is transaction exposure relevant?

2. Why should a firm bother identifying net transaction exposure?

3. Should management of transaction exposure be conducted at the subsidiary level or at the centralized level? Why?

4. Assume that you decided to hedge future payables of 1 million Swiss francs using the forward hedge. Go through the specific steps required for you to use the forward hedge of 1 million francs.

5. Assume that you decided to hedge future receivables of 1 million Canadian dollars using currency options. Go through the specific steps required for you to use currency options to hedge this position.

Answers to End of Chapter Questions

1. Quincy Corporation estimates the following cash flows in 90 days at its subsidiaries:

	Net Position in Each Currency Measured in the Parent's Currency (in 1000s of Units)		
Subsidiary	Currency 1	Currency 2	Currency 3
A	+200	-300	-100
B	+100	- 40	- 10
C	-180	+200	- 40

Determine the consolidated net exposure of the MNC to each currency.

ANSWER: The net exposure to Currency 1 is $120,000; the net exposure to Currency 2 is -$140,000; the net exposure to Currency 3 is -$150,000.

2. Assume that Stevens Point Company has net receivables of 100,000 Swiss francs in 90 days. The spot rate of the franc is $.50, and the Swiss interest rate is 2% over 90 days. Suggest how the U.S. firm could implement a money market hedge. Be precise.

   ANSWER: The firm could borrow the amount of Swiss francs such that 100,000 francs to be received could be used to pay off the loan. This amounts to (100,000/1.02) = about SF98,039, which could be converted to about $49,020 and invested. The borrowing of francs has offset the transaction exposure due to the future receivables in francs.

3. Assume that Vermont Company has net payables of 200,000 French francs in 180 days. The French interest rate is 7% over 180 days, and the spot rate of the French franc is $.10. Suggest how the U.S. firm could implement a money market hedge. Be precise.

   ANSWER: If the firm deposited FF186,916 (computed as FF200,000/1.07) into a French bank earning 7% over 6 months, the deposit would be worth 200,000 francs at the end of the six-month period. This amount would then be used to take care of the net payables. To make the initial deposit of 186,916 francs, the firm would need about $18,692 (computed as 186,916 x $.10). It could borrow these funds.

4. Assume that Citadel Company purchases some goods in West Germany that are denominated in marks. It also sells goods denominated in U.S. dollars to some German firms. At the end of each month, it has a large net payables position in German marks. How can it use an invoicing strategy to reduce this transaction exposure? List any limitations on the effectiveness of this strategy.

   ANSWER: It could invoice its exports to West Germany in marks; the marks received would then be used to make payment on the imports from West Germany firms. One limitation is that the German firms may not agree to this (although they likely would); if they are willing, limitations of the invoicing strategy occur if (1) the timing does not perfectly match up, or (2) the amounts received versus paid do not perfectly match up.

5. Explain how a U.S. corporation could hedge net receivables in British pounds with futures contracts.

   ANSWER: The U.S. corporation could agree to a futures contract to sell pounds at a specified date in the future and at a specified price. This locks in the exchange rate at which the pounds could be sold.

6. Explain how a U.S. corporation could hedge net payables in Japanese yen with futures contracts.

   ANSWER: The U.S. corporation could purchase yen futures contracts which provide for yen to be received in exchange for dollars at a specified future date and at a specified price. The firm has locked in the rate at which it will exchange dollars for yen.

7. Explain how a U.S. corporation could hedge net receivables in French francs with a forward contract.

   ANSWER: The U.S. corporation could sell francs forward using a forward contract. This is accomplished by negotiating with a bank to provide the bank francs in exchange for dollars at a specified exchange rate (the forward rate) for a specified future date.

8. Explain how a U.S. corporation could hedge payables in Canadian dollars with a forward contract.

   ANSWER: The U.S. corporation could purchase Canadian dollars forward using a forward contract. This is accomplished by negotiating with a bank to provide the bank U.S. dollars in exchange for Canadian dollars at a specified exchange rate (the forward rate) for a specified future date.

9. Assume that Loras Corporation needs 100,000 Swiss francs 180 days from now. It is trying to determine whether or not to hedge this position. It has developed the following probability distribution for the Swiss franc:

Possible Value of Swiss Franc in 180 Days	Probability
$.40	5%
.45	10%
.48	30%
.50	30%
.53	20%
.55	5%

   The 180 day forward rate of the Swiss franc is $.52. The spot rate of the Swiss franc is $.49. Develop a table showing a feasibility analysis for hedging. That is, determine the possible differences between the costs of hedging versus no hedging. What is the probability that hedging will be more costly to the firm not hedging?

Possible Spot Rate of Swiss Franc	Probability	Nominal Cost of Hedging 100,000 Francs	Amount of U.S. Dollars Needed to Buy 100,000 Francs if Firm Remains Unhedged	Real Cost of Hedging
$.40	5%	$52,000	$40,000	$12,000
$.40	10%	$52,000	$45,000	$7,000
$.48	30%	$52,000	$48,000	$4,000

ANSWER: There is 75% probability that hedging will be more costly than no hedge.

10. Using the information in Question 9, determine the expected value of the additional cost of hedging?

ANSWER:

5%($12,000) + 10%($7,000) + 30%($4,000) + 30%($2,000)
+ 20%(-$1,000) + 5%(-$3,000)

= $600 + $700 + $1200 + $600 - $200 - $150

= $2,750

11. If hedging is expected to be more costly than not hedging, why would a firm even consider hedging?

ANSWER: Firms often prefer knowing what their future cash flows will be as opposed to the uncertainty involved with an open position in a foreign currency. Thus, they may be willing to hedge even if they expect that the real cost of hedging will be positive.

12. Assume that Suffolk Company negotiated a forward contract to purchase 200,000 British pounds in 90 days. The 90-day forward rate was $1.40 per British pound. The pounds to be purchased were to be used to purchase British supplies. On the day the pounds were delivered in accordance with the forward contract, the spot rate of the British pound was $1.44. What was the real cost of hedging the payables for this U.S. firm?

ANSWER: The U.S. dollars paid when hedging = $1.40(200,000) = $280,000. The dollars received if unhedged = \$1.44(200,000) = \$288,000. The real cost of hedging payables = \$280,000 - \$288,000 = -\$8,000.

13. Repeat Question 12, except assume that the spot rate of the British pound was \$1.34 on the day the pounds were delivered in accordance with the forward contract. What was the real cost of hedging the payables in this example?

    ANSWER: The U.S. dollars paid when hedging = \$1.40(200,000) = \$280,000. The dollars paid if unhedged = \$1.34(200,000) = \$268,000. The real cost of hedging payables = \$280,000 - \$268,000 = \$12,000.

14. Assume that Bentley Corporation negotiated a forward contract to sell 100,000 Canadian dollars in one year. The one year forward rate on the Canadian dollar was \$.80. This strategy was designed to hedge receivables in Canadian dollars. On the day the Canadian dollars were to be sold off in accordance with the forward contract, the spot rate of the Canadian dollar was \$.83. What was the real cost of hedging receivables for this U.S. firm?

    ANSWER: The nominal amount of hedged receivables = \$.80(100,000) = \$80,000. The nominal amount of receivables if unhedged = \$.83(100,000) = \$83,000. The real cost of hedging receivables = \$83,000 - \$80,000 = \$3,000.

15. Repeat Question 14, except assume that the spot rate of the Canadian dollar was \$.75 on the day the Canadian dollars were to be sold off in accordance with the forward contract. What was the real cost of hedging receivables in this example?

    ANSWER: The nominal amount of hedged receivables = \$.80(100,000) = \$80,000. The nominal amount of receivables if unhedged = \$.75(100,000) = \$75,000. The real cost of hedging receivables is \$75,000 - \$80,000 = -\$5,000.

16. Assume the following information:

    90-day U.S. interest rate = 4%
    90-day German interest rate = 3%
    90-day forward rate of German mark = \$.400
    Spot rate of German mark = \$.404

    Assume that Santa Barbara Company from the U.S. will need 300,000 marks in 90 days. It wishes to hedge this payables position. Would it be better off using forward hedge or money market hedge? Substantiate your answer with estimated costs for each type of hedge.

    ANSWER: If the firm uses the forward hedge, it will pay out 300,000(\$.400) = \$120,000 in 90 days.

number of U.S. dollars to be borrowed now is (291,262 x $.404) = $117,670. If this amount is borrowed today, Firm Z will need $122,377 to repay the loan in 90 days (computed as $117,670 x 1.04 = $122,377).
In comparison, the firm will pay out $120,000 in 90 days if it uses the forward hedge and $122,377 if it uses the money market hedge. Thus, it should use the forward hedge.

17. Assume the following information:

    180-day U.S. interest rate = 8%
    180-day British interest rate = 9%
    180-day forward rate of British pound = $1.50
    Spot rate of British pound = $1.48

    Assume that Riverside Corporation from the U.S. will receive 400,000 pounds in 180 days. Would it be better off using a forward hedge or a money market hedge? Substantiate your answer with estimated revenues for each type of hedge.

    ANSWER: If the firm uses a forward hedge, it will receive 400,000($1.50) = $600,000 in 180 days.

    If the firm uses a money market hedge, it will borrow (400,000/1.09) = $366,972 pounds, to be converted to U.S. dollars and invested in the U.S. The 400,000 pounds received in 180 days will pay off this loan. The 366,972 pounds borrowed convert to about $543,119 (computed as 366,972 x $1.48) which when invested at 8% interest will accumulate to be worth about $586,569.

    In comparison, the firm will receive $600,000 in 180 days using the forward hedge, or about $586,569 in 180 days using the money market hedge. Thus, it should use the forward hedge.

18. Why would a firm consider hedging net payables or net receivables with currency options rather than forward contracts? What are disadvantages of hedging with currency options as opposed to forward contracts?

    ANSWER: Currency options not only provide a hedge, but they provide flexibility since they do not require a commitment to buy or sell a currency (whereas the forward contract does).

    A disadvantage of currency options is that a price (premium) is paid for the option itself. The only payment by a firm using a forward contract is the exchange of a currency as specified in the contract.

19. Relate the use of currency options to hedging net payables and receivables. That is, when should currency puts be purchased, and when should currency calls be purchased?

ANSWER: Currency call options should be purchased to hedge net payables. €urrency put options should be purchased to hedge net receivables.

20. Can an MNC determine whether currency options will be more or less expensive than a forward hedge when considering both hedging techniques to cover net payables? Why or why not?

ANSWER: No. The amount paid out when using a forward contract is known with certainty. However, the amount paid out when using currency options is not known until the period is over (since the firm has the flexibility to exercise the option only if it is feasible). Thus, the MNC cannot determine whether currency options will be more or less expensive than forward contracts when hedging net payables.

21. How can a firm hedge long-term currency positions? Elaborate on each method.

ANSWER: Long-term forward contracts are available to cover positions of 5 years or longer in some cases (for major currencies).

Currency swaps are available whereby an arrangement is made for two firms to swap currencies for a specified future time period at a specified exchange rate. Banks often act as middlemen linking up two firms who can help each other out (each firm will have what the other firm will need).

Parallel loans can be used to exchange currencies, and re-exchange the currencies at a specified future exchange rate and date.

22. Under what conditions would an MNC's subsidiary consider use of a "leading" strategy to reduce transaction exposure?

ANSWER: If a subsidiary expected its currency to depreciate against an invoice currency on goods it imported, it may "lead" its payments (make payments early).

23. Under what conditions would an MNC's subsidiary consider use of a "lagging" strategy to reduce transaction exposure?

ANSWER: If a subsidiary expected its currency to appreciate against an invoice currency on goods it imported, it may "lag" its payments (make a late payment).

24. Explain how cross-hedging can be used by a firm to reduce transaction exposure.

ANSWER: If a firm cannot hedge a specific currency, it can use a forward contract on a currency that is highly correlated with the currency of concern.

25. Explain how currency diversification can be used by a firm to reduce transaction exposure.

ANSWER: If a firm has net inflows in a variety of currencies which are not highly correlated with each other, exposure is not as great as if the equivalent amount of funds were denominated in a single currency. This is because not all currencies will depreciate against the firm's home currency simultaneously by the same degree. There may be a partial offsetting effect due to a diversified set of inflow currencies.

If the firm has net outflows in a variety of currencies, the same argument would apply.

26 a. Assume that Carbondale Company expects to receive SF500,000 in one year. The existing spot rate of the Swiss franc is $.60. The one-year forward rate of the Swiss franc is $.62. Carbondale created a probability distribution for the future spot rate in one year as follows:

Future Spot Rate	Probability
$.61	20%
.63	50
.67	30

Assume that one-year put options on francs are available, with an exercise price of $.63 and a premium of $.04 per unit. One-year call options on francs are available with an exercise price of $.60 and a premium of $.03 per unit. Assume the following money market rates:

	U.S.	Switzerland
Deposit rate	8%	5%
Borrowing rate	9	6

Given this information, determine whether a forward hedge, money market hedge, or a currency options hedge would be most appropriate. Then compare the most appropriate hedge to an unhedged strategy, and decide whether Carbondale should hedge its payables position.

ANSWER:

Forward hedge
Sell SF500,000 x $.62 = $310,000

Money market hedge

1. Borrow SF471,698 (SF500,000/1.06 = SF471,698)
2. Convert SF471,698 to $283,019 (at $.60 per SF)
3. Invest the $283,019 at 8% to earn $305,660 by the end of the year.

Put option hedge (Exercise price = $.63; premium = $.04)

Possible Spot Rate	Option Premium per Unit	Exercise	Amount Received per Unit (also accounting for premium)	Total Amount Received for SF 500,000	Probability
$.61	$.04	Yes	$.59	$295,000	20%
$.63	$.04	Yes or No	$.59	$295,000	50%
$.67	$.04	No	$.63	$315,000	30%

The forward hedge is superior to the money market hedge, and has a 70% chance of outperforming the put option hedge. Therefore, the forward hedge is the optimal hedge.

Unhedged Strategy

Possible Spot Rate	Total Amount Received for SF 500,000	Probability
$.61	$305,000	20%
$.63	$315,000	50%
$.67	$335,000	30%

When comparing the optimal hedge (the forward hedge) to no hedge, the unhedged strategy has an 80% chance of outperforming the forward hedge. Therefore, the firm may desire to remain unhedged.

b. Assume that Baton Rouge, Inc. expects to need SF1 million in one year. Using any relevant information in Part (a), determine whether a forward hedge, money market hedge, or a currency options hedge would be most appropriate. Then, compare the most appropriate hedge to an unhedged strategy, and decide whether Baton Rouge should hedge its receivables position.

ANSWER:

Forward hedge

Purchase SF1,000,000 one year forward:
SF1,000,000 x \$.62 = \$620,000

Money market hedge

1. Need to invest SF952,381
   (SF1,000,000/1.05 = SF952,381)
2. Need to borrow \$571,429
   (SF952,381 x \$.60 = \$571,429)
3. Will need \$622,857 to repay the loan in one year (\$571,429 x 1.09 = \$622,857)

Call option hedge (Exercise price = \$.60; premium = \$.03)

Possible spot rate	Option premium per unit	Exercise option?	Amount paid per unit (including the premium)	Total amount paid for SF1,000,000	Probability
\$.61	\$.03	Yes	\$.63	\$630,000	20%
.63	.03	Yes	.63	630,000	50
.67	.03	Yes	.63	630,000	30

The optimal hedge is the forward hedge.

Unhedged Strategy

Possible spot rate	Total amount paid for SF500,000	Probability
\$.61	\$610,000	20%
.63	630,000	50
.67	670,000	30

The forward hedge is preferable to the unhedged strategy because there is an 80 percent chance that it will outperform the unhedged strategy and may save the firm as much as \$50,000.

27. SMU Corporation has future receivables on DM4,000,000 in one year. It must decide whether to use options or a money market hedge to hedge this position. Use any of the following information to make the decision. Verify your answer by determining the estimate (or probability distribution) of dollar revenues to be received in one year for each type of hedge.

Spot rate of DM = $.54
One-year call option: exercise price = $.50; premium = $.07
One-year put option: exercise price = $.52; premium = $.03

	U.S.	Germany
One-year deposit rate	9%	6%
One-year borrowing rate	11	8

	Rate	Probability
Forecasted DM spot rate in 1 year	$.50	20%
	.51	50
	.53	30

ANSWER:

Put option hedge (Exercise price = $.52; premium = $.03)

Possible Spot Rate	Put Option Premium	Exercise Option?	Amount per Unit Received Accounting for Premium	Total Amount Received for DM 4,000,000	Probability
$.50	$.03	Yes	$.49	$1,960,000	20%
$.51	$.03	Yes	$.49	$1,960,000	50%
$.53	$.03	No	$.50	$2,000,000	30%

Money market hedge

1. Borrow DM3,703,704 (DM4,000,000/1.08 = DM3,703,704)

2: Convert DM3,703,704 to $2,000,000 (at $.54 per mark)

3: Invest $2,000,000 to accumulate $2,180,000 at the end of one year ($2,000,000 x 1.09 = $2,180,000)

The money market hedge is superior to the put option hedge.

28. As treasurer of Tucson Corporation, you must decide how to hedge (if at all) future receivables of 250,000 marks 90 days from now. Put options are available for a premium of \$.03 per unit and an exercise price of \$.49 per mark. The forecasted spot rate of the mark in 90 days follows:

Future Spot Rate	Probability
\$.44	30%
\$.40	50
.38	20

Given that you hedge you position with options, create a probability distribution for dollars to be received in 90 days.

ANSWER:

Possible Spot Rate	Put Option Premium	Exercise Option?	Amount per Unit Received Accounting for Premium	Total Amount Received for DM 250,000	Probability
\$.44	\$.03	Yes	\$.46	\$115,000	30%
\$.40	\$.03	Yes	\$.46	\$115,000	50%
\$.38	\$.03	Yes	\$.46	\$115,000	20%

The probability distribution represents a 100% probability of receiving \$115,000, based on the forecasts of the future spot rate of the mark.

29. As treasurer of Tempe Corporation, you are confronted with the following problem. Assume the one-year forward rate of the British pound is \$1.59. You plan to receive 1 million pounds in one year. There is a one-year put option available. It has an exercise price of \$1.61. The spot rate as of today is \$1.62, and the option premium is \$.04 per unit. Your forecast of the percentage change in the spot rate was determined from the following regression model:

$$e_t = a_0 + a_1 DINF_{t-1} + DINT_t + u$$

where e_t = percentage change in British pound value over period t

$DINF_{t-1}$ = differential in inflation between the United States and the United Kingdom in period t-1

$DINT_t$ = average differential between the United States interest rate and British interest rate over period t

a_0, a_1, and a_2 = regression coefficients

u = error term

The regression model was applied to historical annual data, and the regression coefficients were estimated as follows:

a_0 = 0
a_1 = 1.1
a_2 = .6

Assume last year's inflation rates were 3 percent for the United States and 8 percent for the United Kingdom. Also assume that the interest rate differential ($DINT_t$) is forecasted as follows for this year:

Forecast of $DINT_t$	Probability
1%	40%
2	50
3	10

Using any of the available information, should the treasurer choose the forward hedge or the put option hedge? Show your work.

ANSWER:

Forecast of $DINT_t$	Forecast of e_t	Probability
1%	1.1(-5%) + .6(1%) = -4.9%	40%
2%	1.1(-5%) + .6(2%) = -4.3%	50%
3%	1.1(-5%) + .6(3%) = -3.7%	10%

Forecast of e_t (derived above)	Approximate Forecasted spot rate of pound in one year	Probability
-4.9%	1.62 x [1 + (-4.9%)] = $1.54	40%
-4.3	1.62 x [1 + (-4.3%)] = $1.55	50%
-3.7	1.62 x [1 + (-3.7%)] = $1.56	10%

Put option hedge (Exercise price = $1.61; premium = $.04)

Possible spot rate of pound in one year (derived above)	Put option premium	Exercise option?	Amount received per unit (accounting for premium)	Total amount received for 1 million pounds	Probability
$1.54	$.04	Yes	$1.57	$1,570,000	40%
1.55	.04	Yes	$1.57	1,570,000	50
1.56	.04	Yes	$1.57	1,570,000	10

Forward hedge
Sell 1,000,000 pounds one year forward:
1,000,000 pounds x $1.59 = $1,590,000

ANSWER: The forward hedge is preferable to the put option hedge.

30. Would a U.S. firm's real cost of hedging Swiss franc payables every 90 days have been positive, negative, or about zero on average over a period in which the dollar weakened consistently? What does this imply about the forward rate as an unbiased predictor of the future spot rate? Explain.

ANSWER: The nominal cost when hedging Swiss franc payables would have been below the nominal cost of payables on an unhedged basis during the weak dollar period, because the franc substantially appreciated during this period. Thus, the real cost of hedging would have been negative during the period. This implies that the franc's forward rate consistently underestimated the franc's future spot rate during the period, and was therefore biased.

31. If interest rate parity exists, would a forward hedge be more favorable, equally favorable, or less favorable than a money market hedge on French franc payables? Explain.

ANSWER: It would be equally favorable (assuming no transactions costs). If IRP exists, the forward premium on the forward rate would reflect the interest rate differential The hedging of future payables with a forward purchase provides the same results as borrowing at the home interest rate and investing at the foreign interest rate to hedge payables.

32. Would a U.S. firm's real cost of hedging Japanese yen receivables have been positive, negative, or about zero on average over a period in which the dollar weakened consistently? Explain.

ANSWER: During the weak dollar period, the yen appreciated substantially against the dollar. Thus, the dollars received from hedging yen receivables would have been less than the dollars received if the yen receivables were not hedged. This implies that the real cost of hedging yen receivables would have been positive during the weak dollar period.

33. If you are a U.S. importer of German goods, and you believe that today's forward rate of the mark is a very accurate estimate of the future spot rate, do you think German mark call options would be a more appropriate hedge than the forward hedge? Explain.

    ANSWER: If the forward rate is close to or exceeds today's spot rate, the forward hedge would be preferable because the call option hedge would require a premium to achieve about the same locked-in exchange rate. If the forward rate was much lower than today's spot rate, the call option could be preferable because the firm could let the option expire and would be better off.

34. You are an exporter of goods to the United Kingdom, and you believe that today's forward rate of the British pound substantially underestimates the future spot rate. Company policy requires you to hedge your British pound receivables in some way. Would a forward hedge or a put option hedge be more appropriate? Explain.

    ANSWER: A put option would be preferable because it gives you the flexibility to exchange pounds for dollars at the prevailing spot rate when receiving payment.

35. Explain how a French firm can use the forward market to hedge periodic purchases of U.S. goods denominated in U.S. dollars.

    ANSWER: A French firm can purchase dollars forward with francs, which locks in the exchange rate at which it trades its francs for dollars.

36. Explain how a German firm can use the forward market to hedge periodic sales of goods sold to the U.S. that are invoiced in dollars.

    ANSWER: The German firm could purchase marks forward with dollars.

37. Explain how a French firm can use the forward market to hedge periodic purchases of Japanese goods denominated in yen.

    ANSWER: The French firm can negotiate a forward contract with a bank to exchange francs for yen at a future point in time.

38. Cornell Company purchases computer chips denominated in yen on a monthly basis from a Japanese supplier. To hedge its exchange rate risk, this U.S. firm negotiates a three-month forward contract

three months before the next order will arrive. In other words, Cornell is always covered for the next three monthly shipments. Because Cornell consistently hedges in this manner, it is not concerned with exchange rate movements. Is Cornell insulated from exchange rate movements? Explain.

ANSWER: No! Cornell is exposed to exchange rate risk over time because the forward rate changes over time. If the yen appreciates, the forward rate of the yen will likely rise over time, which increases the necessary payment by Cornell.

39. Malibu Inc. is a U.S. company that imports British goods. It plans to use call options to hedge payables of 100,000 pounds in 90 days. Three call options are available which have an expiration date 90 days from now. Fill in the number of dollars needed to pay for the payables (including the option premium paid) for each option available under each possible scenario.

Scenario	Spot Rate of Pound 90 days from now	Exercise Price = $1.74; Premium = $.06	Exercise Price = $1.76; Premium = $.05	Exercise Price = $1.79; Premium = $.03
1	$1.65			
2	1.70			
3	1.75			
4	1.80			
5	1.85			

If each of the five scenarios had an equal probability of occurrence, which option would you choose? Explain.

ANSWER:

Scenario	Spot Rate of Pound 90 days from now	Exercise Price = $1.74; Premium = $.06	Exercise Price = $1.76; Premium = $.05	Exercise Price = $1.79; Premium = $.03
1	$1.65	$171,000	$170,000	$168,000
2	.70	176,000	175,000	173,000
3	1.75	180,000	180,000	178,000
4	1.80	180,000	181,000	182,000
5	1.85	180,000	181,000	182,000

The option with the $.03 premium is slightly better than the other two options on average.

Solution to WSJ Case: How U.S. Firms are Managing Exchange Rate Risks

1. Does Wedco's strategy of pricing its materials for European customers in dollars avoid economic exposure? Explain.

   ANSWER: Wedco avoids transaction exposure, but not economic exposure. If the European currencies weaken against the dollar, European customers would have to pay more for Wedco's materials. This may encourage the customers to purchase their materials from other firms.

2. Explain why Circon Corporation negotiates a very short term of payment when selling products overseas.

   ANSWER: The exchange rate may not fluctuate as much over a short period of time, so that Circon's exchange rate risk over the period is limited.

3. Explain why the earnings of Telematics International, Inc. were affected by changes in the value of the pound. Why would Telematics leave its exposure unhedged?

ANSWER: Telematics International, Inc. has sales to European customers, some of which are denominated in British pounds. Since Telematics did not hedge its exposure, its pound receivables converted to a relatively small amount of dollars when the pound depreciated.

Telemantics probably expected the pound to appreciate, which would have increased its dollar cash flows as the pound receivables were converted to dollars.

Solution to Case Problem: Blackhawk Company

The data used for this example were compiled over the 1986-1990 period. This case uses actual data to show how inaccurate forecasts can be.

a) Using the regression model in which FSR is the dependent variable and FR is the independent variable, the slope coefficient is about .857 and the standard error of the coefficient is .0825. Therefore, the t-statistic in testing for a bias is:

$$t = \frac{.857 - 1}{.0825}$$

$$= -1.733$$

Using a .05 level of significance, the bias is not significant.

b) There appears to be a bias, in that the use of the forward rate resulted in negative forecast errors (overestimation) over seven of the first nine quarters and then positive forecast errors (under-estimation) over seven of the next 11 quarters.

c) The average absolute forecast error when using the forward rate is .02963.

d) Using the regression model in which FSR is the dependent variable and SR is the independent variable, the slope coefficient is about .8635 and the standard error of the coefficient is about .081. Therefore, the t-statistic in testing for a bias is:

$$t = \frac{.8635 - 1}{.081}$$

$$= -1.685$$

Using a .05 level of significance, the bias is not significant.

e) There appears to be a bias, in that the use of the spot rate resulted in negative forecast errors (overestimation) over the first nine quarters and then positive forecast errors (under-estimation) over seven of the next 11 quarters.

f) The average absolute forecast error when using the spot rate is .029815. The forward rate was slightly better, based on a lower absolute forecast error.

g) Using regression analysis, $b_0 = .791$ and $b_1 = 4.333$. It should be mentioned that the forecast based on regression analysis is prone to error, as the inflation differential did not explain much of the variation in PDM over the 20 quarters. Since DIFF is assumed to be 2%, then the forecast of PDM using the regression coefficients is:

$$PDM = b_0 + b_1\ DIFF$$

$$= .791\% + 4.333\ (2\%)$$

$$= 9.457\%$$

If the DM rises by 9.457%, the FSR will be $.589 (1.09457) = about $.645.

h) The probability distribution for FSR is:

Probability	FSR
40%	$.6450
40%	$.5878
20%	$.5890

i) The probability distribution for payments if Blackhawk does not hedge is:

Probability	$ Amount Needed
40%	$516,000
40%	$470,240
20%	$471,200

j) The probability distribution for the real cost of hedging is determined below:

Probability	$ Amount Needed if Hedged	$ Amount Needed if Unhedged	Real Cost of Hedging
40%	$470,240	$516,000	-$45,760
40%	$470,240	$470,240	$0
20%	$470,240	$471,200	$-960

k) The probability distribution of payments when owning a call option is shown below:

Probability	FSR	Exercise Option?	$ Needed (Incl. Prem.)
40%	.6450	Yes	$488,000
40%	.5878	No	$478,240
20%	.5890	No	$479,200

l) Money market hedge

Amount of DM to invest = $\frac{\text{DM}800{,}000}{(1.021)}$

= DM783,545

Amount of $ to borrow = DM783,545 x $.589

= $461,508

Amount of $ needed to
repay loan = $461,508 x (1.025) = $473,046

The dollars that would be needed when using the forward hedge is DM800,000 x $.5878 = $470,420. This amount is less than the amount that would be needed when using the money market hedge.

m) The forward hedge would be preferable to the call option hedge because it would be cheaper, for any of the three FSR scenarios.

n) The forward hedge is preferable to not hedging because it does as well or better than not hedging in all three FSR scenarios.

Projects

1. Assume that your company needed 100,000 units of a foreign currency every quarter to purchase foreign supplies. Use the data in the back of the text to determine the real cost of hedging with that currency. (Choose a currency.) Identify periods in which the real cost of hedging was typically positive. Was the dollar strengthening or weakening in those periods? Explain. (This exercise could easily be set up on a spreadsheet first to reduce your computational time.)

   This project shows students the significant differences in dollars paid when hedging versus not hedging payables. It demonstrates the importance of the hedge versus no-hedge decision.

2. Repeat this project, except assume that you will receive 100,000 units of a foreign currency every quarter.

   This project shows students the significant difference in dollars received when hedging versus not hedging receivables. It demonstrates the importance of the hedge versus no-hedge decision.

Chapter 12

Managing Economic Exposure and Translation Exposure

Lecture Outline

Managing Economic Exposure
Example of Managing Economic Exposure
Effect of Restructured Operations on Economic Exposure

Managing Translation Exposure
Example Using Forward Contracts
Limitations of Hedging Translation Exposure

Chapter Theme

This chapter shows how an MNC can restructure its operations to reduce economic exposure. Such a strategy is related to the firm's long-run operations, unlike transaction exposure.
This chapter also briefly describes how translation exposure can be reduced. Yet, it is advised that the limitations of hedging translation exposure receive as much attention as the hedging strategy itself.

Topics to Stimulate Class Discussion

1. Identify the economic exposure of a small business that you are aware of.
2. Even if you believe translation exposure is relevant, is it worthwhile to hedge it? Explain.
3. Compare the degree of translation exposure between a small firm whose foreign subsidiary generates 50% of its business versus a huge exporting company with no subsidiaries.

Answers to End of Chapter Questions

1. St. Paul Company does business in the United States and Germany. It is attempting to assess its economic exposure and has compiled the following information.

   a. Its U.S. sales are somewhat affected by the German mark's value, because it faces competition from German exporters. It forecasts the U.S. sales based on the following three exchange rate scenarios.

Exchange Rate of Mark	Revenue from U.S. Business (in millions)
DM = $.48	$100
DM = .50	105
DM = .54	110

   b. Its German mark revenues on sales to Germany invoiced in marks are expected to be DM600 million.

   c. Its anticipated cost of goods sold is estimated at $200 million from the purchase of U.S. materials and DM100 million from the purchase of German materials.

   d. Fixed operating expenses are estimated at $30 million.

   e. Variable operating expenses are estimated at 20 percent of total sales (after including German sales, translated to a dollar amount).

f. Interest expense is estimated at $20 million on existing U.S. loans, and the company has no existing German loans.

Create a forecasted income statement for St. Paul Company under each of the three exchange rate scenarios. Explain how St. Paul's projected earnings before taxes are affected by possible exchange rate movements. Explain how it can restructure its operations to reduce the sensitivity of its earnings to exchange rate movements, without reducing its volume of business in Germany.

ANSWER:

Forecasted Income Statements for St. Paul Company
(Figures are in millions)

	DM = $.48	DM = $.50	DM = $.54
Sales			
U.S.	$100	$105	$110
German	DM600 = $288	DM600 = $300	DM600 = $324
Total	$388	$405	$434
Cost of goods sold			
U.S.	$200	$200	$200
German	DM100 = $ 48	DM100 = $ 50	DM100 = $ 54
Total	$248	$250	$254
Gross profit	$140	$155	$180
Operating expenses			
U.S.: Fixed	$ 30	$ 30	$ 30
U.S.: Variable (20% of total sales)	$ 78	$ 81	$ 87
Total	$108	$111	$117
Earnings before interest and taxes	$ 32	$ 44	$ 63
Interest expense			
U.S.	$ 20	$ 20	$ 20
German	DM0 = $ 0	DM0 = $ 0	DM0 = $ 0
Total	$ 20	$ 20	$ 20
Earnings before taxes	$ 12	$ 24	$ 43

ANSWER: The forecasted income statements show that St. Paul Company is favorably affected by a strong mark (since its mark inflow payments exceed its mark outflow payments). St. Paul Company could reduce its economic exposure without reducing its German revenues by shifting expenses from the U.S. to Germany. In this way, its mark outflow payments would be more similar to its mark inflow payments.

2. Baltimore Inc. is a U.S.-based MNC that obtains 10 percent of its supplies from European manufacturers. Sixty percent of its revenues are due to exports in Europe, where its product is invoiced in European currencies. Explain how Baltimore Inc. could attempt to reduce its economic exposure to exchange rate fluctuations.

   ANSWER: Baltimore Inc. could reduce its economic exposure by shifting some of its U.S. expenses to Europe. This may involve shifting its sources of materials or even part of its production process to Europe. It could also reduce its European revenues but this is probably not desirable.

3. UVA Company is a U.S.-based MNC that obtains 40 percent of its foreign supplies from Switzerland. It also borrows Swiss francs from Swiss banks and converts the francs to dollars to support U.S. operations. It presently receives about 10 percent of its revenues from Swiss customers. Its sales to Swiss customers are denominated in francs. Explain how UVA Company can reduce its economic exposure to exchange rate fluctuations.

   ANSWER: UVA Company has periodic outflow payments in Swiss francs that are substantially more than its Swiss francs inflow payments. UVA could reduce its economic exposure by attempting to increase sales in Switzerland, which would generate additional Swiss franc inflows.

4. Albany Corporation is a U.S.-based MNC that has a large government contract with Germany. The contract will continue for several years and generates more than half of Albany's total sales volume. The German government pays Albany in German marks. About 10 percent of Albany's operating expenses are in German marks; all other expenses are in U.S. dollars. Explain how Albany Company can reduce its economic exposure to exchange rate fluctuations.

   ANSWER: Albany may ask the German government to provide payment in dollars. Alternatively, Albany could attempt to shift some of its expenses to Germany, by either purchasing German supplies or shifting part of the production process to Germany. These strategies will increase German mark outflows, so that the mark inflows and outflows are more balanced.

5. When an MNC restructures its operations to reduce its economic exposure, it may sometimes forgo economies of scale. Explain.

ANSWER: An MNC may attempt to use several production plants. The production could be increased in countries whose home currency is weak (since demand for products in those countries would be higher). However, to have such flexibility requires that production plants are scattered. Consequently, the firm foregoes the economies of scale that may be achieved by establishing one large production plant.

6. Explain how a U.S.-based MNC's consolidated earnings are affected if the dollar weakens against most foreign currencies.

   ANSWER: A U.S.-based MNC's consolidated earnings are enhanced by the translation effect when the dollar is weak. Foreign earnings are translated at the average exchange rate over the fiscal year. The average exchange rates of foreign currencies will be relatively high if the dollar has weakened.

7. Explain how a firm can hedge its translation exposure.

   ANSWER: A firm can hedge translation exposure by selling forward the currency of the firm's foreign subsidiary. Thus, if the foreign currency depreciates, the translation loss will be somewhat offset by the gain on the short position created by the forward contract.

8. Explain some limitations of hedging translation exposure.

   ANSWER: The limitations are as follows. First, the firm needs to forecast its foreign subsidiary earnings, and may forecast inaccurately. Thus, it will hedge against a level of foreign earnings that differ from actual foreign earnings.

   Second, forward contracts are not available for all currencies.

   Third, translation losses are not tax-deductible, while gains on forward contracts used to hedge translation exposure are taxed.

   Fourth, transaction exposure may be increased as a result of hedging translation exposure.

9. Would a more established MNC or a less established MNC be more capable of effectively hedging its given level of translation exposure? Why?

   ANSWER: This question is intended to stimulate class discussion. There is no perfect answer. One opinion is that a more established MNC can better predict its level of foreign earnings, because its foreign business is stabilized. Therefore, it is more able to hedge the appropriate amount of foreign earnings.

10. If U.S.-based MNCs are concerned with how shareholders react to changes in consolidated earnings, but prefer not to hedge their translation exposure, how can they attempt to reduce shareholder reaction to a decline in consolidated earnings that results from a strengthened dollar?

    ANSWER: MNC's could emphasize in their annual reports how consolidated earnings were adversely influenced by the translation effect.

11. Carlton Company and Palmer Inc. are U.S.-based MNCs with subsidiaries in Germany that distribute medical supplies (produced in the United States) to customers throughout Europe. Both subsidiaries purchase the products at cost and sell the products at 90 percent markup. The other operating costs of the subsidiaries are very low. Carlton Company has a research and development center in the United States which focuses on improving its medical technology. Palmer Inc. has a similar center that is based in France. The parent of each firm subsidizes its respective research and development center on an annual basis. Which firm is subject to a higher degree of economic exposure? Explain.

    ANSWER: Carlton Co. is subject to a higher degree of economic exposure because it does not have much offsetting cost in Germany. Palmer Co. incurs costs in France for its research and development center. The French franc and German mark are highly correlated against the dollar. If the mark weakens, the value of the mark inflows is reduced. However, the franc would also weaken, so that the parent's cost of subsidizing the research and development center in France would be reduced.

12. Nelson Company is a U.S. firm with annual export sales of about DM800 million. Its main competitor is Mez Company, also based in the United States, with a subsidiary in Germany that generates about DM800 million in annual sales. Any earnings generated by the subsidiary are reinvested to support its operations. Based on the information provided, which firm is subject to a higher degree of translation exposure? Explain.

    ANSWER: Since Nelson Corporation does not have any subsidiaries, its exposure to exchange rate fluctuations would not be classified as translation exposure. Conversely, Mez Company is subject to translation exposure.

Solution to WSJ Case: Managing Economic Exposure Since the ERM Crisis

1. Explain why the establishment of several production sites across European countries by FMC Corporation can reduce exposure to exchange rate fluctuations.

    ANSWER: As exchange rates change, the prices to customers can change, allowing a site in one European country (where the currency is weak) to be cheaper. Thus, the demand for the firm's products will not be reduced by the movement in a single currency.

2. Peerless Manufacturing Company has subcontractors in France and in Germany. Explain how Peerless can manage its exposure to exchange rates better by having subcontractors in two different countries.

   ANSWER: The cost of paying a subcontractor in a foreign country is dependent on the exchange rate. If the German mark is relatively strong while the French franc is relatively weak, Peerless may avoid the German subcontractors in favor of the French subcontractors.

3. When Gillete has receivables in marks and payables in francs, it is concerned about its exchange rate risk. Why is this type of risk more pronounced since the widening of the Exchange Rate Mechanism (ERM) bands?

   ANSWER: When the bands were narrow, the mark and franc moved in tandem against the dollar (within narrow boundaries). When the bands were widened, there was more potential for the mark and franc to move by different degrees, so that the effects are not offsetting.

4. Explain how the widening of the ERM bands can increase the volatility of cash flows of Euro Disney (based in France).

   ANSWER: The widening of the ERM bands caused more volatility of each European currency against the French franc, which makes the demand more volatile, and therefore makes cash flows more volatile.

Solution to Case Problem: Madison, Inc.

a) While economic exposure adversely affected the firm's performance in a recent period, it should favorably affect the firm's performance in the future. A weak Canadian dollar (which has been forecasted) would favorably affect Madison, Inc. under the prevailing operational structure. If the structure is revised, Madison will be less exposed to the Canadian dollar's exchange rate movements. Therefore, it will not benefit as much from the weaker Canadian dollar. Economic exposure can be beneficial when currencies move in a particular direction. The shareholders would be better off if the firm remains exposed while the Canadian dollar is expected to weaken.

   One may argue that the Vice-president should also be better off if Madison remains exposed, based on the forecast of the Canadian dollar. However, a counter argument is that the Vice--president may be better off if economic exposure is reduced. If by chance the Canadian dollar unexpectedly continued to appreciate, Madison's earnings would be adversely affected, and the Vice-president could lose his job. This issue usually generates much classroom discussion. Students should attempt to put themselves in the place of the Vice-president. If the Vice-president does not receive a bonus tied to earnings, he may prefer a strategy that is least risky in order to preserve his job (even if this strategy conflicts with satisfying shareholders).

b) The prevailing operational structure allows the firm to benefit from a weaker Canadian dollar. Yet, if the Canadian dollar appreciates, the Vice-president could be fired. Thus, the Vice-president may choose a structure that reduces economic exposure, even though the expected earnings are reduced. Shareholders would have preferred that Madison remained exposed, since the expected return is higher, and do not suffer the same severe consequences as the Vice-president if the Canadian dollar appreciates.

   If the Vice-president's compensation was somewhat tied to earnings, there would be less chance of a conflict of interests. The Vice-president would be more encouraged to preserve the exposure because he would directly realize some of the benefits resulting from higher performance. In addition, the firm should have an implicit policy that does not place all the blame on the Vice-president if the policy of maintaining the prevailing structure backfires. If the Canadian dollar appreciates and earnings are adversely affected, is the poor performance the fault of the Vice-president? Is it the fault of the employees that developed the forecasts of the Canadian dollar? These issues generate interesting discussion. It should be emphasized that employees should not be fired any time they incorrectly forecast a currency to move in a particular direction. And the Vice-president should not be fired when his decision was based on input from others that he thought was reliable.

Project

1. Many annual reports of MNCs indicate where their operations are located. Use this information to suggest how the MNC could restructure its operations (without reducing its foreign business) to reduce exposure. Refer back to the chapter for an example. Your analysis may need to be more generalized than the example used in the chapter because you will not have specific details.

   This project is designed to let students realize how MNCs differ in their exposure. MNCs that emphasize exporting are affected by economic exposure differently than MNCs that have most of their production facilities overseas.

Integrative Problem for Part III

Exchange Rate Risk Management

1. Vogl Company is a U.S. firm conducting a financial plan for the next year. It has not foreign subsidiaries, but more than half of its sales are from exports. Its foreign cash inflows to be received from exporting and cash outflows to be paid for imported supplies over the next year are disclosed below:

Currency	Total Inflow	Total Outflow
Canadian dollars (C$)	C$32,000,000	C$ 2,000,000
German mark (DM)	DM5,000,000	DM1,000,000
French franc (FF)	FF11,000,000	FF10,000,000
Swiss franc (SF)	SF 4,000,000	SF 8,000,000

The spot rates and one-year forward rates as of today are:

Currency	Spot Rate	One-Year Forward Rate
C$	$ .90	$ .93
DM	.60	.59
FF	.18	.15
SF	.65	.64

Based on the information provided, determine the net exposure of each foreign currency in dollars.

ANSWER:

Currency	Net Inflow or Outflow	Spot Exchange Rate	Net Inflow or Outflow Measured in Dollars
Canadian dollars (C$)	C$30,000,000 Inflow	$.90	$27,000,000 Inflow
German mark (DM)	DM4,000,000 Inflow	.60	2,400,000 Inflow
French franc (FF)	FF1,000,000 Inflow	.18	180,000 Inflow
Swiss franc (SF)	SF4,000,000 Outflow	.65	2,600,000 Outflow

2. Assume that today's spot rate is used as a forecast of the future spot rate one year from now. The European currencies are expected to move in tandem against the dollar over the next year. The Canadian dollar movements are expected to be unrelated to movements of the

European currencies. Since exchange rates are difficult to predict, the forecasted net dollar cash flows per currency may be inaccurate. Do you anticipate any offsetting exchange rate effects from whatever exchange rate movements do occur? Explain.

ANSWER: The European currencies are expected to move in tandem. The dollar value of exposure on net inflows is about equal to the dollar value of exposure on net outflows for the European currencies. Thus, the exchange rate effects of the 2 European inflow currencies (DM and FF) should be offset by the effects of the one European outflow currency (SF).

3. Given the forecast of the Canadian dollar along with the forward rate of the Canadian dollar, what is the expected increase or decrease in dollar cash flows that would result from hedging the net cash flows in Canadian dollars? Would you hedge the Canadian dollar position?

   ANSWER: The expected dollar cash flows from hedging the net cash flows of C$30,000,000 (inflow) is C$30,000,000 x $.93 = $27,900,000. This is $900,000 more than the dollars that would be received without hedging (assuming that the forecasted spot rate for one year ahead is accurate). It is reasonable to hedge the Canadian dollar position based on the information given. However, if the amount of C$ to be received may be less than what is expected, the firm may want to hedge only a portion of the C$30,000,000 in expected net inflows.

4. Assume that the Canadian dollar net inflows may range from C$20,000,000 to C$40,000,000 over the next year. Explain the risk of hedging C$30,000,000 in net inflows. How can Vogl Company avoid such a risk? Is there any tradeoff resulting from your strategy to avoid that risk?

   ANSWER: If the C$ received is less than the amount to be sold by the firm as specified in the forward contract, the firm will have to purchase some C$ in the spot market. For example, if the firm receives only C$20,000,000 by the end of the year from exporting, and has negotiated a forward sale of C$30,000,000, it will need to obtain an additional C$10,000,000 to fulfill its forward contract. If the Canadian dollar appreciated over the year, the firm will be adversely affected because it much purchase C$ in the spot market for a higher price than the exchange rate specified in the forward contract.

   The firm can avoid this risk by only hedging the transaction amount that it knows will occur. However, this may prevent the firm from hedging the full transaction, which means it will not be completely covered. Using our example, if the firm hedges only C$20,000,000, it can be affected by depreciation in the C$ over the year if more than C$20,000,000 in net cash flows are received. This is a very common dilemma faced by firms. In many cases, firms attempt to only cover the minimum net cash flow amount expected (for reasons expressed above), which forces them to remain partially exposed to exchange rate risk.

5. Vogl Company recognizes that its year-to-year hedging strategy only hedges the risk over a given year, but does not insulate it from long-term trends in the C$ value. It has considered

establishing a subsidiary in Canada. The goods would be sent from the U.S. to the Canadian subsidiary and distributed by the subsidiary. The proceeds received would be reinvested by the Canadian subsidiary in Canada. In this way, Vogl Company would not have to convert C$ to dollars each year. Has Vogl eliminated its exposure to exchange rate risk by using this strategy? Explain.

ANSWER: Vogl may avoid the year-to-year hedging decision with this strategy, but is increasing its exposure to the C$ over time. It is essentially reinvesting the proceeds in the same currency, thereby compounding the exposure over time. Someday, the parent may need these funds, and the C$ may be even weaker by the time the funds are sent to the parent. In essence, this strategy defers the transaction exposure while the C$ build up over time, but the exposure becomes much larger in the future when the C$ are converted to dollars. Furthermore, by establishing a Canadian subsidiary, Vogl will be subject to translation exposure. That is, the annual consolidated earnings will be affected by movements in the C$ value even though the parent's dollar cash flows are insulated (at least temporarily) from these movements. Also, recognize that if the parent does not generate cash flows from its Canadian business, it must find other sources or funds to support the production and transportation costs incurred as a result of the Canadian business.

Chapter 13

Financing International Trade

Lecture Outline

Terms of Payment for International Trade

Prepayment
Letter of Credit
Drafts
Consignment
Open Account

Trade Finance Techniques

Accounts Receivable Financing
Factoring
Letter of Credit
Banker's Acceptance
Short-Term Bank Loans
Forfeiting
Countertrade

Agencies that Motivate International Trade

Export-Import Bank of the U.S.
Foreign Credit Insurance Association (FCIA)
Private Export Funding Corporation (PEFCO)
Overseas Private Investment Corporation (OPIC)

Chapter Theme

This chapter first suggests why international trade can be difficult. Then, it explains the various ways in which banking institutions can facilitate international trade by resolving problems faced by the exporter and importer.

Topics to Stimulate Class Discussion

1. Assume that you receive a call from an old friend who has set up a computer parts store. He says that he plans to begin exporting these parts soon. What potential complications should he consider?

2. Why do exporters sometimes sell off their banker's acceptances? Would they be better off obtaining a short-term loan instead? What information is necessary to answer this question?

3. What is the common role of a banking institution in international trade besides financing?

Answers to End of Chapter Questions

1. How can a banker's acceptance be beneficial to (1) an exporter? (2) an importer? (3) a bank?

   ANSWER: A banker's acceptance guarantees payment to the exporter so that credit risk of the importer is not worrisome. It allows the importers to import goods without being turned down due to uncertainty about their credit standing. It is a revenue generator for the bank since a fee is received by the bank for this service.

2. Why would an exporter provide financing for an importer? Is there much risk in this activity? Explain.

   ANSWER: An exporter could increase sales by allowing the importer to pay at a future date. There may be high credit risk incurred by the exporter here, especially if the importer is an unknown small firm.

3. What is the role of a factor within international trade transactions? How can a factor aid an exporter?

   ANSWER: A factor can relieve the exporter of the worry about the credit risk of the importer. In return, the factor is rewarded by being able to purchase the accounts receivables at a lower price than their cash value.

4. What is the role today of the Export-Import Bank of the U.S.?

   ANSWER: The role today is to finance and facilitate the export of American goods and to strengthen the competitiveness of U.S. industries involved in foreign trade.

5. What are bills of lading and how do they facilitate international trade transactions?

   ANSWER: Bills of lading provide a receipt for shipment, a summary of freight charges, and conveys title to the merchandise.

6. What is forfeiting? Specify the type of traded goods for which forfeiting is applied.

   ANSWER: A forfeiting transaction involves an importer that issues a promissory note to pay for the imported capital goods over a period of three to seven years or so. Notes are extended to the exporter who sells them at a discount to a forfeiting bank.

7. Briefly describe the role of PEFCO.

   ANSWER: PEFCO provides medium and long-term credit to importers of U.S. goods and services.

8. In this chapter, numerous forms of government insurance and guarantee programs are described. What motivates a government to establish so many programs?

   ANSWER: Governments may be able to boost exports by establishing policies that either protect the exporters from various types of risk, or encourage lenders to provide financing to the exporters.

9. Describe how the desirability for foreign trade would be affected if banks did not provide trade-related services.

   ANSWER: Foreign trade activity would decrease since exporters may not wish to accept the credit risk involved, or the financing in some cases.

10. What is countertrade?

    ANSWER: Countertrade involves the sale of goods to one country in exchange for goods from that country.

11. Briefly describe the Working Capital Guarantee Program administered by the Export-Import Bank.

    ANSWER: The Working Capital Guarantee Program allows exporters to obtain short-term loans from commercial banks that are guaranteed by the Eximbank. This protects the commercial banks against default risk of the exporter, and makes it easier for exporters to obtain loans.

12. Describe the Direct Loan Program that is administered by the Export-Import Bank.

    ANSWER: Under the Direct Loan Program, the Eximbank provides long-term loans to foreign buyers to purchase U.S. goods. The loan rates are channeled through banks, which serve as the intermediaries.

13. Describe the New-Export Policy.

    ANSWER: The New-Export Policy provides enhanced coverage against credit risk to new exporters.

14. Describe the role of the Overseas Private Investment Corporation (OPIC).

    ANSWER: The OPIC insures direct U.S. investments in foreign countries against the risks of currency inconvertibility, expropriation, and other potential risks; it also offers insurance coverage for exporters that bid on foreign contracts.

Solution to WSJ Case: Letters of Credit in Russia

1. Explain how the irrevocable letters of credit would normally facilitate the business transaction between the Russian importer and Ocean Traders of North America (the U.S. exporter.)

   ANSWER: The letter of credit was issued by a Russian bank to guarantee payment for the goods to be exported by the U.S. exporter.

2. Explain how the cancellation of the letter of credit could create a trade crisis between the U.S. and Russian firms.

   ANSWER: If exporting firms can not rely on letters of credit, they must resort to trusting the counterparty in the trade agreement. This will reduce trade, because exporters frequently do not know much about the counterparty.

3. Why do think situations like this (the cancellation of the letter of credit) are rare in industrialized countries?

   ANSWER: Governments or regulators have a vested interest in ensuring that banks follow through on letters of credit. Otherwise, there would be a reluctance to conduct trade in any country that does not back its guarantees.

4. Can you think of any other alternative strategy that the U.S. exporter could have used to protect itself more when dealing with a Russian importer?

   ANSWER: The U.S. exporter could have attempted to obtain a letter of credit from a U.S. bank, with the responsibility placed on the U.S. bank to guarantee payment. In this case, the U.S. bank would have been put in a position to demand payment from the Russian importer, or the importer's Russian bank.

Solution to Case Problem: Ryco Chemical Company

a) Ryco could attempt to work out a countertrade agreement. Ryco could provide chemicals that Concellos needs in exchange for the chemicals that Ryco normally purchases from Concellos. Ryco could benefit because its cost of importing some chemicals would no longer be tied to Brazilian inflation. Instead its cost would be tied to its own cost of producing the chemicals it must exchange for the imports. If Concellos would agree to the countertrade agreement, Ryco may be able to stabilize its cost of imports, which could reduce the uncertainty surrounding cash flows and profitability.

b) Concellos is exposed to the weak cruzeiro. If it purchases the chemicals used in production from Ryco, its cost will not be affected by the cruzeiro's exchange rate (as it could purchase the U.S. goods through a countertrade agreement). Thus, it may be able to stabilize its cost of imports in this matter.

c) Concellos' cost of obtaining imports is the cost of producing the chemicals it uses for exchange (based on the countertrade agreement). Given high inflation in Brazil, these production costs will rise. However, it may be able to raise its prices on its final products by the inflation rate to cover its higher costs of production. Overall, it will be able to offset these higher costs easier than offsetting the higher costs that would result from exchange rate effects. Since its competitors base their prices on local cost of production (as they are not exposed to a weak exchange rate risk), Concellos would now incur costs that are more similar to those of its competitors.

Chapter 14

Short-Term Financing

Lecture Outline

Sources of Short-Term Financing

International Financing by MNCs

Why MNCs Consider Foreign Financing
Foreign Financing to Offset Foreign Receivables
Foreign Financing to Reduce Costs

Determination of the Effective Financing Rate

Considerations When Financing in Foreign Currencies
Interest Rate Parity as a Criterion for the Financing Decision
The Forward Rate as a Criterion for the Financing Decision
Use of Exchange Rate Projections

Financing With a Portfolio of Currencies
Repeated Financing with a Currency Portfolio

Chapter Theme

This chapter explains short-term liability management of MNCs, a part of multinational management that is often neglected in other text books. From this chapter, students should learn that correct financing decisions can reduce the firm's costs. While foreign financing costs can not usually be perfectly forecasted, firms should evaluate the probability of reducing costs through foreign financing.

Topics to Stimulate Class Discussion

1. If a firm consistently exports to a country with low interest rates, and needs to consistently borrow funds, explain how it could coordinate its invoicing and financing to reduce its financing costs.

2. What is the risk of borrowing a low-interest rate currency?

3. Assume that foreign currencies X, Y, and Z are highly correlated. If a firm diversifies its financing among these three currencies, will it substantially reduce its exchange rate exposure (as opposed to borrowing all funds from one of these foreign currencies)? Explain.

Answers to End of Chapter Questions

1. Explain why an MNC parent would consider financing from its subsidiaries.

   ANSWER: A parent may obtain funds at a lower cost from its subsidiaries than from a bank, since a bank will maintain a spread between what it offers depositors and charges on loans.

2. Discuss the use of specifying a break-even point when financing in a foreign currency.

   ANSWER: A break-even exchange rate percentage change will indicate to a firm the amount by which a low-interest rate currency must appreciate to make its financing cost the same as a domestic currency.

3. Discuss the development of a probability distribution of "effective financing rates" when financing in a foreign currency. How is this distribution developed?

   ANSWER: First, a probability distribution of exchange rate changes is created. Using this along with the foreign currency's quoted interest rate, the probability distribution of effective financing rates can be developed.

4. Once the probability distribution of "effective financing rates" from financing in a foreign currency is developed, how can this distribution be used in deciding whether to finance in the foreign currency or the home currency?

   ANSWER: A distribution of effective financing rates can be used to determine the probability that foreign financing will be more costly than domestic financing. Then, the final decision will depend on the firm's degree of risk aversion.

5. How can a firm finance in a foreign currency and not necessarily be exposed to exchange rate risk?

   ANSWER: If the firm has future cash inflows in a foreign currency, it can use those inflows to pay off the loan in a foreign currency.

6. Explain how a firm's degree of risk aversion enters into its decision of whether to finance in a foreign currency or a local currency. What motivates the firm to even consider financing in a foreign currency?

   ANSWER: A very risk-averse firm may prefer to borrow domestically since it knows with certainty the cost of financing in advance. Yet, other firms may feel that the potential cost savings from foreign financing outweighs the risk (uncertainty); this may motivate them to consider financing in a foreign currency.

7. Assume that a U.S.-based MNC needs $3 million for a one-year period. Within one year, it will generate enough U.S. dollars to pay off the loan. It is considering three options: (1) borrowing U.S. dollars at an interest rate of 6%, (2) borrowing Swiss francs at an interest rate of 3%, or (3) borrowing German marks at an interest rate of 4%. The MNC has forecasted that the Swiss franc will appreciate by 1% over the next year, and that the German mark will appreciate by 3%. What is the expected "effective" financing rate for each of the three options? Which option appears to be most feasible? Why might the MNC not necessarily choose the option reflecting the lowest effective financing rate?

Interest Currency	Interest Rate	Expected Percentage Change in Currency	Expected Effective Financing Rate
Dollars	6%	--	6.00%
Swiss francs	3%	+1%	4.03%
German marks	4%	+3%	7.12%

   ANSWER: The Swiss franc option appears to be the most feasible option. Yet, the exchange rate percentage change is uncertain, which makes the effective financing rate uncertain. Thus, the MNC will not necessarily choose this option.

8. How is it possible for a firm to incur a negative effective financing rate?

   ANSWER: If the currency borrowed substantially depreciates against the firm's home currency (by at least the interest rate percentage as a rough approximation), the effective financing rate will be negative.

9. If interest rate parity does not hold, what strategy should a U.S. firm consider when it needs short-term financing? Assume that a U.S. firm needs dollars. It borrows German marks at a lower interest rate than that for dollars. If interest rate parity exists and if the forward rate of the mark is a reliable predictor of the future spot rate, what does this suggest about the feasibility of such a strategy? If the MNC expected the current spot rate to be a more reliable predictor of the future spot rate, what does this suggest about the feasibility of such a strategy?

   ANSWER: The firm could consider borrowing a foreign currency, and purchasing the currency forward to lock in its financing cost.

   If the forward rate is a reliable predictor, the effective financing rate on the foreign financing would be the same as the domestic financing. So foreign financing is not feasible.

   If the expected spot is more reliable, the foreign financing should be less costly then domestic financing, because this implies that the expected percentage change in the mark's value is zero, so that the German interest rate represents the expected effective financing rate when financing with marks.

10. A firm needs local currency. Assume that the local one-year loan rate is 15%, while a foreign one-year loan rate is 7%. By how much must the foreign currency appreciate to cause the foreign loan to be more costly than a local loan?

    ANSWER:

    $$\frac{(1.15)}{(1.07)} - 1 = 7.477\%$$

    The foreign currency must appreciate by about 7.477% in order to make the foreign loan as costly as a domestic loan.

11. A U.S.-based MNC decides to borrow Japanese yen for one year. The interest rate on the borrowed yen is 8 percent. The MNC has developed the following probability distribution for the yen's degree of fluctuation against the dollar:

Possible Degree of Fluctuation of Yen Against the Dollar	Percentage Probability
-4%	20%
-1%	30%
0%	10%
3%	40%

Given this information, what is the expected value of the effective financing rate of the Japanese yen from the U.S. corporation's perspective?

ANSWER:

Japanese Interest Rate	Possible % Change in Yen Value	Effective Financing Rate Based on that Change	Probability	Computation of Expected Value
8%	-4%	3.68%	20%	.736%
8%	-1%	6.92%	30%	2.076%
8%	0%	8.00%	10%	.800%
8%	3%	11.24%	40%	4.496%
				8.108%

Expected value = 8.108%

12. Assume that interest rate parity exists. If a firm believed that the forward rate was an unbiased predictor of the future spot rate, could it expect to achieve lower financing costs by consistently borrowing a foreign currency with a low interest rate?

ANSWER: No, because a foreign currency with a relatively low interest rate exhibits a forward premium that offsets the interest rate differential. Thus, if the forward rate is the expected future spot rate, this implies that the foreign currency will appreciate over the financing period by an amount that will offset the interest rate advantage.

13. Assume a U.S. firm considers obtaining 40 percent of its one-year financing in Canadian dollars and 60 percent in Swiss francs. The forecasts of appreciation in the Canadian dollar and Swiss franc for the next year are as follows:

Currency	Possible Percentage Change in the Spot Rate Over the Loan Life	Probability of That Percentage Change in the Spot Rate Occurring
Canadian dollar	4%	70%
Canadian dollar	7	30
Swiss franc	6	50
Swiss franc	9	50

The interest rate on the Canadian dollar is 9 percent, and the interest rate on the Swiss franc is 7 percent. Develop the possible effective financing rates of the overall portfolio and the probability of each possibility based on the use of joint probabilities.

ANSWER:

Currency	Interest Rate	Possible % Change	Effective Financing Rate Based on That Change	Probability
Canadian Dollar	9%	4%	13.36%	70%
Canadian Dollar	9	7	16.63	30
Swiss Francs	7	6	13.42	50
Swiss Francs	7	9	16.63	50

Possible Joint Effective Financing Rate		Joint Probability	Effective Financing Rate of Portfolio
C$	SF		
13.36%	13.42%	(70%)(50%)=35%	.4(13.36%)+.6(13.42%)=13.396%
13.36	16.63	(70%)(50%)=35%	.4(13.36%)+.6(16.63%)=15.322%
16.63	13.42	(30%)(50%)=15%	.4(16.63%)+.6(13.42%)=14.704%
16.63	16.63	(30%)(50%)=15%	.4(16.63%)+.6(16.63%)=16.630%

Thus, there is a 35% probability that the portfolio's effective financing rate will be 13.396%, and so on.

14. Why might a corporation attempt to borrow a portfolio of foreign currencies even when it needs to make payments in its local currency?

    ANSWER: A corporation may borrow foreign currencies since it can possibly reduce its financing cost; by borrowing a portfolio rather than a single foreign currency in order to reduce its exchange rate risk.

15. Does borrowing a portfolio of currencies offer any possible advantages over the borrowing of a single foreign currency?

    ANSWER: If a firm borrows a single foreign currency, it is especially vulnerable to that currency's exchange rate. The firm can lower its vulnerability to any single currency by borrowing a portfolio.

16. If a firm borrows a portfolio of currencies, what characteristics of the currencies will affect the potential variability of the portfolio's effective financing rate? What characteristics would be desirable from a borrowing firm's perspective?

    ANSWER: Currencies which are volatile and highly correlated with each other could cause the effective financing rate of the portfolio to be very volatile over time. Ideally, the currencies comprising the portfolio would have a low degree of volatility or negative correlations. This would reduce the exchange rate risk of the portfolio.

17. Boca Inc. needs $4 million for one year. It presently has no business in Germany but plans to borrow marks from a German bank, because the German interest rate is three percentage points lower than the U.S. rate. Assume that interest rate parity exists; also assume that Boca believes that the one-year forward rate of the mark exceeds the future spot rate one year from now. Will the expected effective financing rate be higher, lower, or the same as financing with dollars? Explain.

ANSWER: Since the forward rate is expected to overestimate the future spot rate, this implies that the mark will not appreciate to the level that would fully offset the interest rate differential. Therefore, the expected effective financing rate of the mark is lower than the U.S. financing rate.

18. Jacksonville Corporation is a U.S.-based firm that needs $600,000. It has no business in Switzerland but is considering one-year financing with Swiss francs, because the annual interest rate would be 5 percent versus 9 percent in the United States. The spot rate of the Swiss franc is presently $.62, while the forward rate is $.6436.

    a. Can Jacksonville benefit from borrowing Swiss francs and simultaneously purchasing francs one year forward to avoid exchange rate risk? Explain.

    ANSWER: If Jacksonville borrows francs and simultaneously purchases francs one year forward, it will pay a forward premium that will offset the interest rate differential. The premium is about 3.8%; thus the effective financing rate would be:

    (1 + 5%)(1 + 3.8%) - 1 = about 9%.

    b. Assume that Jacksonville does not cover its exposure and uses the forward rate to forecast the future spot rate. Determine the expected effective financing rate. Should Jacksonville finance with Swiss francs? Explain.

    ANSWER: If it does not cover the exposure, but uses the forward rate as a forecast, the expected percentage change in the Swiss franc's value is about 3.8 percent. Thus, the expected effective financing rate is 9%. Jacksonville should therefore finance with dollars rather than Swiss francs, since the expected cost of financing with dollars is no higher.

    c. Assume that Jacksonville does not cover its exposure and expects that the Swiss franc will appreciate by either 5 percent, 3 percent, or 2 percent, and with equal probability of each occurrence. Use this information to determine the probability distribution of the effective financing rate. Should Jacksonville finance with Swiss francs? Explain.

    ANSWER:

Possible % Change in Spot Rate of SF	Effective Financing Rate of SF if That Percentage Change Occurs	Probability
5%	(1.05)(1.05) - 1 = 10.25%	33.3%
3%	(1.05)(1.03) - 1 = 8.15	33.3%
2%	(1.05)(1.02) - 1 = 7.10	33.3%

Given the probability, there is about a 67 percent chance that financing with Swiss francs will be less costly than financing with dollars. The choice of financing with francs or dollars in this case is dependent on Jacksonville's degree of risk aversion.

19. Assume that the U.S. interest rate is 7 percent and the Swiss interest rate is 4 percent. Assume that the Swiss franc's forward rate has a premium of 4 percent. Is the following statement true? "Interest rate parity does not hold; therefore U.S. firms could lock in a lower financing cost by borrowing Swiss francs and purchasing francs forward for one year." Explain your answer.

    ANSWER: No. While interest rate parity does not hold, the financing with Swiss francs would result in an effective financing rate of:

$$(1 + 4\%)(1 + 4\%) - 1 = 8.16\%$$

    This exceeds the U.S. rate. For a U.S. firm to be able to lock in a lower financing cost by borrowing francs and purchasing francs forward, the premium on forward rate of the franc would have to be less than the interest rate differential.

20. Orlando Inc. is a U.S.-based MNC with a subsidiary in Mexico. Its Mexican subsidiary needs a one-year loan of 10 million pesos for operating expenses. Since the Mexican interest rate is 70 percent, it is considering borrowing dollars, which it would convert to pesos to cover the operating expenses. By how much would the dollar have to appreciate against the peso to cause such a strategy to backfire? (The one-year U.S. interest rate is 9%.)

    ANSWER:

$$\frac{1 + 70\%}{1 + 9\%} - 1 = 55.96\%$$

    The dollar would have to appreciate by more than 55.96 percent for the strategy to backfire.

21. Assume the following information. Raleigh Corporation needs to borrow funds for one year to finance an expenditure in the United States. The following interest rates are available:

	Borrowing Rate
U.S.	10%
Swiss	6%
Japan	5%

    The percentage change in the spot rates of the Swiss franc and Japanese yen over the next year are as follows:

Swiss Franc		Japanese Yen	
Probability	Percentage Change in Spot Rate	Probability	Percentage Change in Spot Rate
10%	5%	20%	6%
90%	2%	80%	1%

If Raleigh Corporation borrows a portfolio, 50 percent of funds from francs and 50 percent of funds from yen, determine the probability distribution of the effective financing rate of the portfolio. What is the probability that Raleigh will incur a higher effective financing rate from borrowing this portfolio than from borrowing dollars?

ANSWER:

Currency	Interest Rate	Possible % Change	Effective Financing Rate Based on That Change	Probability
Swiss franc	6%	5%	11.3%	10%
Swiss franc	6%	2%	8.12%	90%
Japanese yen	5%	6%	11.3%	20%
Japanese yen	5%	1%	6.05%	80%

Possible Joint Effective Financing Rate SF	JY	Joint Probability	Effective Financing Rate of Portfolio
11.3%	11.3%	(10%)(20%)=2%	.5(11.3%)+.5(11.3%)=11.3%
11.3	6.05	(10%)(80%)=8%	.5(11.3%)+.5(6.05%)=8.675%
8.12	11.3	(90%)(20%)=18%	.5(8.12%)+.5(11.3%)=9.71%
8.12	6.05	(90%)(80%)=72%	.5(8.12%)+.5(6.05%)=7.085%

There is a 2 percent chance that Raleigh will incur a higher effective financing rate from borrowing the portfolio.

Solution to WSJ Case: International Financing Since the ERM Crisis

1. Since interest rates across European currencies became more diverse and the Exchange Rate Mechanism (ERM) bands widened, explain how short-term financing decisions for European firms might change.

ANSWER: European firms may see more opportunities to achieve lower interest rates. For example, a German firm may attempt to borrow Swiss francs for use in Germany if the Swiss interest rate is lower. Of course, there is risk that the Swiss franc may appreciate against the mark over the financing period.

2. Consider an Italian firm that wishes to support its Italian operations with short-term funds. Given Italy's relatively high interest rates, the firm decides to borrow other European currencies (at lower interest rates) to support its Italian operations. The firm is somewhat concerned that the European currencies will appreciate substantially against the lira, which could more than offset the lower interest rate. Is this adverse scenario more likely now than it was before the ERM bands were widened? Explain.

   ANSWER: The wider bands allow more flexibility in exchange rates between European currencies. Thus, there is a higher probability that these currencies could appreciate substantially against the firm. Yet, keep in mind that it is the widening of the ERM bands that allows European interest rates to vary. The widening creates more opportunities for the Italian firm to obtain lower interest rates in Europe, but the firm must also realize that the currencies could appreciate against the firm to offset the interest rate advantage.

3. Consider a U.S. firm that frequently uses short-term financing in pounds to support its British operations. The interest expenses will depend on British interest rate levels over time. Do you think the firm's interest expenses over time will be more or less volatile since Great Britain removed itself from the ERM (meaning that it no longer ties its interest rates to other countries)?

   ANSWER: Open-ended question. One argument is that when a country is not linked to the others, its monetary policies will be directly focused on its conditions, and will not be tempered by the need to conform to other European country norms. This may cause the British interest rate to be more volatile, which would cause financing costs to be more volatile.

Solution to Case Problem: Flyer Company

a. The optimal portfolio is dependent on your degree of risk aversion. By converting the information in the table above into 4 bar charts (showing the probability distribution), one above another, you can review the risk-return tradeoff.

   By using a spreadsheet format, the percentage changes in exchange rates can be easily computed. Using these percentage changes along with the interest rates, the effective financing rate can be computed for each currency under each scenario. The effective financing rates are provided below for each scenario, along with the expected value of the effective financing rate (using the probabilities assigned to each scenario):

Currency	Strong $ Scenario	Somewhat Stable $ Scenario	Weak $ Scenario	Expected Value of Effective Financing Rate
Australian dollar	-0.56%	14.51%	28.07%	14.05%
British pound	4.56	14.48	21.10	13.49%
Canadian dollar	9.71	9.71	17.45	12.03%
French franc	-8.18	13.47	18.06	8.35%
German mark	-5.48	5.22	12.35	4.14%
Italian lira	2.2	10.60	20.40	11.02%
Japanese yen	-1.0	11.60	29.60	13.22%
Swedish krona	2.19	5.59	15.81	7.64%
Swiss franc	-7.44	3.01	16.45	3.91%
U.S. dollar	9.00	9.00	9.00	9.00%

Type of Portfolio	Percentage of Funds Borrowed From: A$	BP	C$	FF	DM	IL	JY	SK	SF	US$
Risk neutral	0	0	0	0	0	0	0	0	100	0
Balanced	0	0	0	25	25	0	0	25	25	0
Conservative	0	0	0	10	10	0	0	10	10	60
Ultra-conservative	0	0	0	0	0	0	0	0	0	100

Each portfolio's effective financing rates are determined as a sum of weighted effective financing rates under each scenario.

Portfolio	Portfolio's Effective Financing Rate Based on a Strong $ Scenario	Stable $ Scenario	Weak $ Scenario	Expected Value of Effective Financing Rate
Risk Neutral	-7.43%	3.01%	16.45%	3.91%
Balanced	-4.73	6.82	15.67	6.01
Conservative	3.51	8.13	11.67	7.80
Ultra-conservative	9.00	9.00	9.00	9.00

The decision of which portfolio to use would be based on your degree of risk aversion. By converting the table above into 4 bar charts, (showing the profitability distribution), one above another, you can review the tradeoff between lower financing costs and risk.

Project

1. Use the interest rate and exchange rate data in the back of the text to determine a U.S. firm's effective financing rate when borrowing German marks on a quarterly basis. Identify the periods in which this strategy would have resulted in very low effective financing rates. Was the dollar strengthening or weakening in those periods? (A computer spreadsheet could easily be created to reduce your computational time.)

   This project will demonstrate how the effective financing rate changes over quarterly periods in response to changing interest rates and exchange rates. The increase in effective financing rates during 1985-1987 will be obvious. This occurred because of the weak dollar.

Chapter 15

International Cash Management

Lecture Outline

Cash Flow Analysis: Subsidiary Perspective)

Cash Flow Analysis: Centralized Perspective

Techniques to Optimize Cash Flows
- Accelerating Cash Inflows
- Using Netting to Minimize Currency Conversion Costs
- Minimizing Tax on Cash Flow
- Managing Blocked Funds
- Inter-Subsidiary Cash Transfers

Common Complications In Optimizing Cash Flow
- Company-Related Characteristics
- Government Restrictions
- Characteristics of Banking Systems
- Perceived Irrelevance of Cash Flow Optimization
- Distorted Subsidiary Performance Due to Optimizing Cash Flow

Investing Excess Cash
- Centralized Cash Management
- Determining the Effective Yield from Foreign Investing
- IRP as a Criterion for Foreign Investing
- Forward Rate as a Criterion for Foreign Investing
- Diversifying Cash Across Currencies

Chapter Theme

This chapter emphasizes the decisions involved in the management of cash by an MNC. The additional opportunities and risks of cash management for an MNC versus a domestic firm should be stressed. There are actually three key components of the chapter. The first is distinguishing between subsidiary control over excess cash versus centralized control. An argument is made in favor of centralized control. The second component is optimizing cash flow. Several techniques are recommended to optimize cash flow. Finally, the decision of where to invest excess cash should be discussed with consideration of all factors that need to be incorporated for this decision.

Topics to Stimulate Class Discussion

1. Should international cash management be conducted at the subsidiary level or at the centralized level? Elaborate!

2. What is the use of netting to an MNC?

3. How can a firm deal with blocked funds?

4. Assume that as a treasurer of a U.S. corporation, you believe that the British pound's forward rate is an accurate forecast of the pound's future spot rate. What does this imply about your decision of whether to invest cash in the U.S. or in Great Britain?

Answers to End of Chapter Questions

1. Discuss the general functions involved in international cash management.

   ANSWER: The general functions of international cash management are optimizing cash flows and investing excess cash. These functions combined will lead to efficient usage of funds.

2. What is "netting" and how can it improve an MNC's performance?

   ANSWER: Netting is a centralized compilation of inter-subsidiary cash flows. It is designed to reduce currency conversion costs and processing costs associated with payments between subsidiaries. By specifying a single net payment to be made instead of all individual payments owed between subsidiaries, transactions costs are reduced and cash flows may be forecasted more accurately.

3. How can an MNC implement leading and lagging techniques to help subsidiaries in need of funds?

   ANSWER: A subsidiary in need of funds would receive cash inflows from another subsidiary sooner than is required. This early payment provides the necessary funds. If the subsidiary in need of funds is making payment, it may be allowed by the MNC parent or recipient subsidiary to delay on its payment.

4. Explain how the MNC's optimization of cash flow can distort the profits of each subsidiary.

   ANSWER: When subsidiaries adjust their cash transactions between each other to reduce taxes or financing costs, their individual performances are distorted. For example, a subsidiary which makes late payment to another subsidiary (due to its shortage of funds) benefits in that it avoided a short-term loan by delaying payment. The recipient subsidiary was hampered due to not receiving funds earlier (since the present value of the late payment is lower.

5. How can a centralized cash management system be beneficial to the MNC?

   ANSWER: A centralized cash management system is beneficial in that it allows for netting, which can reduce transactions costs and improve cash budgeting. In addition, it can increase yields on short-term investments by pooling excess cash of various subsidiaries.

6. Why would a firm consider investing short-term funds overseas?

   ANSWER: Interest rates may be higher on foreign short-term investments, or a foreign currency may have a high probability of appreciating.

7. Assume a U.S.-based MNC has $2,000,000 in cash available for 90 days. It is considering the use of covered interest arbitrage since the British 90-day interest rate is higher than the U.S. interest rate. What will determine whether this strategy is feasible?

   ANSWER: If interest rate parity exists, then the forward rate of the British pound contains a discount which sufficiently offsets the higher British interest rate. Consequently, the act of covered interest arbitrage would not be feasible.

8. Assume a U.S.-based MNC has $1,000,000 in cash available for 30 days. It can earn 1% on a 30-day investment in the U.S. Alternatively, if it converts the dollars to French francs, it can earn 1 1/2% on a French deposit. The spot rate of the French franc is $.12. The spot rate 30 days from now is expected to be $.10. Should this firm invest its cash in the U.S. or in France? Substantiate your answer.

ANSWER: If the firm invests in a French deposit, it will convert $1 million to 8,333,333 francs, which will accumulate to 8,458,333 francs after one month (due to the 1 1/2% interest rate). If the spot rate of the francs is $.10 after one month, the francs will be converted to $845,833, which is less than the amount of dollars the firm started with. Thus, the firm should invest its cash in the U.S.

9. Assume a U.S.-based MNC has $3,000,000 in cash available for 180 days. It can earn 7% on a U.S. Treasury bill or 9% on a British Treasury bill. The British investment does require conversion of dollars to British pounds. Assume that interest rate parity holds and that the MNC believes the 180 day forward rate is a reliable predictor of the spot rate to be realized 180 days from now. Would the British investment provide an effective yield which is below, above, or equal to the yield on the U.S. investment. Explain your answer.

   ANSWER: If the forward rate is an accurate forecast of the future spot rate, then the return on a foreign investment without covering the currency exposure will be the same as if it was covered. The uncovered foreign investment, like the act of covered interest arbitrage, will generate a return similar to the domestic return (given that interest rate parity exists).

10. Repeat Question 9, but this time assume that the firm expects the 180-day forward rate of the pound to substantially overestimate the spot rate to be realized in 180 days.

    ANSWER: In this case, the future spot rate will be less than the forward rate. If it was equal to the forward rate, the foreign return would have been similar to the domestic return for the U.S. firm (as explained in the answer to Question 9). If the future spot rate is lower than the forward rate, the U.S. firm will receive less when converting the pounds back to dollars. Thus, the foreign return is expected to be less than the domestic return.

11. Repeat Question 9, but this time assume that the firm expects the 180-day forward rate of the pound to substantially underestimate the spot rate to be realized in 180 days.

    ANSWER: In this case, the U.S. firm will receive more when converting the pounds back to dollars than the amount necessary to match the domestic return. Thus, the foreign return is expected to be greater than the domestic return.

12. Assume that the one-year U.S. interest rate is 10%, and the one-year Canadian interest rate is 13%. If a U.S. firm invests its funds in Canada, by what percentage will the Canadian dollar have to depreciate to make its effective yield the same as the U.S. interest rate from the U.S. firm's perspective?

    ANSWER:

$$\frac{(1 + 10\%)}{(1 + 13\%)} - 1 = \text{about } -2.65\%$$

13. A U.S.-based MNC plans to invest its excess cash in France for one year. The one-year French interest rate is 19%. The probability of the French franc's percentage change in value over the next year is shown below:

Possible Rate of Change in the French Franc Over The Life of the Investment	Probability of Occurrence
3%	20%
4%	50%
10%	30%

What is the expected value of the effective yield based on this information? Given that the U.S. interest rate for one year is 17%, what is the probability that a one-year investment in francs will generate a lower effective yield than could be generated if the U.S. firm simply invested domestically?

ANSWER:

Possible Rate of Change in Franc	Probability	Effective Yield if This Rate of Change in the Franc Does Occur
-3%	20%	(1.19)[1+(-3%)]-1=15.43%
4%	50%	(1.19)[1+(4%)]-1 =23.76%
10%	30%	(1.19)[1+(10%)]-1=30.90%

$$\begin{aligned} E(r) &= 20\%(15.43\%)+50\%(23.76\%)+30\%(30.90\%) \\ &= 3.086\% + 11.88\% + 9.27\% \\ &= 24.236\% \end{aligned}$$

There is a 20% probability that the franc's effective yield will be less than the domestic yield.

14. If a U.S. firm believes that the international Fisher effect holds, what are the implications regarding a strategy of continually attempting to generate high returns from investing in currencies with high interest rates?

ANSWER: High interest rate currencies will typically depreciate to offset their interest rate advantage (on average) according to the IFE. Therefore, this strategy will on average provide similar returns as a domestic investment, and the strategy is not worthwhile.

15. A U.S. firm considers placing 30% of its excess funds in a one-year French franc deposit and the remaining 70% of its funds in a one-year Canadian dollar deposit. The French one-year interest rate is 15%, while the Canadian one-year interest rate is 13%. The possible percentage changes in the two currencies over the next year are forecasted as follows:

Currency	Possible % Change in the Spot Rate Over % The Investment Horizon	Probability of That Change in the Spot Rate Occurring
French franc	-2%	20%
French franc	1%	60%
French franc	3%	20%
Canadian dollar	1%	50%
Canadian dollar	4%	40%
Canadian dollar	6%	10%

Given this information, determine the possible effective yields of the portfolio and the probability associated with each possible portfolio yield. Given a one-year U.S. interest rate of 16%, what is the probability that the portfolio's effective yield will be lower than the yield achieved from investing in the U.S.? (See Appendix 15.)

ANSWER:

Possible % Change in the Franc	Effective Yield Based on the % Change in the Franc
-2%	(1.15) [1 + (-2%)] - 1 = 12.7%
1%	(1.15) [1 + (1%)] - 1 = 16.15%
3%	(1.15) [1 + (3%)] - 1 = 18.45%

Possible % Change in the Canadian Dollar	Effective Yield Based on the % Change in the Canadian Dollar
1%	(1.13) [1 + (1%)] - 1 = 14.13%
4%	(1.13) [1 + (4%)] - 1 = 17.52%
6%	(1.13) [1 + (6%)] - 1 = 19.78%

Possible Joint Effective Yield French Franc	Possible Joint Effective Yield Canadian Dollar	Computation of Joint Probability	Computation of Effective Yield of Portfolio
12.7%	14.13%	(20%)(50%) = 10%	.3(12.7%)+.7(14.13%)=13.701%
12.7	17.52	(20%)(40%) = 8%	.3(12.7%)+.7(17.52%)=16.074%
12.7	19.78	(20%)(10%) = 2%	.3(12.7%)+.7(19.78%)=17.656%
16.15	14.13	(60%)(50%) = 30%	.3(16.15%)+.7(14.13%)=14.736%
16.15	17.52	(60%)(40%) = 24%	.3(16.15%)+.7(17.52%)=17.109%
16.15	19.78	(60%)(10%) = 6%	.3(16.15%)+.7(19.78%)=18.691%
18.45	14.13	(20%)(50%) = 10%	.3(18.45%)+.7(14.13%)=15.426%
18.45	17.52	(20%)(40%) = 8%	.3(18.45%)+.7(17.52%)=17.799%
18.45	19.78	(20%)(10%) = 2%	.3(18.45%)+.7(19.78%)=19.381%
		100%	

There is a 50% chance that the portfolio will generate a lower return than a U.S. investment (determined by the table above).

16. Why would a firm consider investing in a portfolio of foreign currencies instead of just a single foreign currency?

ANSWER: A portfolio of currencies reduces the probability of the foreign investment backfiring due to depreciation in the currencies denominating the investment. If all funds are in an investment denominated in a single foreign currency, risk of that currency substantially depreciating is relatively high (compared to an entire portfolio of currencies substantially depreciating).

17. Tallahassee Company has $2 million in excess cash that it has invested in Mexico at an annual interest rate of 60 percent. The U.S. interest rate is 9 percent. By how much would the Mexican peso have to depreciate to cause such a strategy to backfire?

$$\frac{1 + 9\%}{1 + 60\%} - 1 = -31.875\%$$

ANSWER: If the peso depreciates by more than 31.875 percent, the effective yield on the Mexican deposit will be less than the domestic yield.

18. San Antonio Corporation has several subsidiaries in less developed countries that trade goods and supplies with each other. Explain how transfer pricing could be used by San Antonio Corporation to reduce its overall tax payments.

    ANSWER: San Antonio Corporation's parent could request those subsidiaries in high-tax countries to reduce their prices charged on supplies sent to subsidiaries in relatively low-tax countries. This shifts taxable earnings from high-tax subsidiaries to low-tax subsidiaries.

19. Dallas Company has determined that the French interest rate is 16 percent while the U.S. interest rate is 11 percent for one-year Treasury bills. The one-year forward rate of the French franc has a discount of 7 percent. Does interest rate parity exist? Can Dallas Company achieve a higher effective yield by using covered interest arbitrage than by investing in U.S. Treasury bills? Explain.

    ANSWER: If interest rate parity (IRP) existed, the forward rate of the franc should have a discount reflecting the interest rate differential:

    $$\text{Forward discount} = \frac{(1 + 11\%)}{(1 + 16\%)} - 1 = -4.31\% \text{ (discount)}$$

    Since the French franc's actual discount exceeds that percentage, IRP does not exist. However, Dallas Company would achieve a lower effective yield if attempting covered interest arbitrage than if it invests in U.S. Treasury bills, because the franc's forward discount more than offsets the interest rate differential.

20. Corpus Company has a subsidiary in Country X that produces computer components and sells them to another subsidiary in Country Y, where the production process is completed. The tax rate in Country X is 50 percent, while the tax rate in Country Y is 20 percent. The pro forma income statements of the Corpus subsidiaries are shown in Exhibit A. Assume that Corpus headquarters adjusts its transfer pricing policy so that sales by Subsidiary X are reduced from $400,000 to $320,000 (this also affects the cost of goods sold at Subsidiary Y by the same amount). Determine the change in total tax payments of the consolidated subsidiaries as a result of this revised transfer pricing policy.

CORPUS COMPANY
PRO FORMA INCOME STATEMENTS FOR SUBSIDIARIES

	Subsidiary X	Subsidiary Y	Consolidated Subsidiaries
Sales	$400,000	$700,000	$1,100,000
Less: cost of goods sold	220,000	400,000	620,000
Gross profit	180,000	300,000	480,000
Less: operating exp	80,000	100,000	180,000
Earnings before interest and taxes	100,000	200,000	300,000
Interest expense	10,000	30,000	40,000
Earnings before taxes	90,000	170,000	260,000
Taxes (50% for Sub. X and 20% for Sub. Y)	45,000	34,000	79,000
Earnings after taxes	45,000	136,000	181,000

PRO FORMA INCOME STATEMENTS
BASED ON REVISED TRANSFER PRICING POLICY

	Subsidiary X	Subsidiary Y	Consolidated Subsidiaries
Sales	$320,000	$700,000	$1,020,000
Less: cost of goods sold	220,000	320,000	540,000
Gross profit	100,000	380,000	480,000
Less: operating exp.	80,000	100,000	180,000
Earnings before interest and taxes	20,000	280,000	300,000
Interest expense	10,000	30,000	40,000
Earnings before taxes	10,000	250,000	260,000
Taxes (50% for X and 20% for Y)	5,000	50,000	55,000
Earnings after taxes	5,000	200,000	205,000

The total tax payments have been reduced from $79,000 to $55,000 as a result of the revised transfer pricing policy.

Solution to WSJ Case: International Cash Management Since The ERM Crisis

Use the *Wall Street Journal* article in the case from the previous chapter as the article for this case. The article focuses on changes in the European Exchange Rate Mechanism (ERM), which have implications for international cash management.

1. As interest rates across European Currencies became more diverse, and the Exchange Rate Mechanism (ERM) bands widened, explain how international cash management for U.S. firms might change.

   ANSWER: U.S. firms will have more opportunities to capitalize on high interest rates or on the expected appreciation of a specific European currency through their international cash management. In the past, European interest rates and currency values were linked. Also, recognize that any one currency could experience wider swings because it is not restricted to move in tandem with the other European currencies.

2. Will diversifying cash among European currencies cause more or less stability in a U.S. firm's cash portfolio now, as opposed to previous years when the ERM band was tighter? That is, how have the benefits from diversification changed?

   ANSWER: The European currency movements are less correlated now, which causes greater diversification benefits for international cash management. In the past, the European currencies moved in tandem, so that if one of the currencies declined against the dollar, the others would as well by about the same degree.

3. Some MNCs have cash inflows in one European currency and cash outflows in others over any given month. A centralized division overseeing this situation may argue that if the dollar equivalent amounts of the cash inflows and outflows in European currencies are about equal, the firm's exposure is negligible. Explain how this view may have been affected since ERM bands were widened.

   ANSWER: The firm's exposure is probably not offset as well now, because European currency movements against the dollar are not as correlated as they were before the ERM band was widened. Thus, the effects of cash inflows in one European currency will not necessarily be offset by the effects of cash outflows (in the same dollar equivalent amount) in another European currency.

Solution to Case Problem: Islander Corporation

a) By using a spreadsheet format, the percentage changes in exchange rates can be easily computed for each scenario. Using these percentage changes along with the interest rates, the effective yield can be computed for each currency under each scenario. The effective yields are provided below for each scenario, along with the expected value of the effective yield (using the probabilities assigned to each scenario):

Currency	Strong $ Scenario	Somewhat Stable $ Scenario	Weak $ Scenario	Expected Value of Effective Yield
Australian dollar	-0.56%	14.51%	28.07%	14.05%
British pound	4.56	14.48	21.10	13.49
Canadian dollar	9.71	9.71	17.45	12.03
French franc	-8.18	13.47	18.06	8.35
German mark	-5.48	5.22	12.35	4.14
Italian lira	2.2	10.60	20.40	11.02
Japanese yen	-1.0	11.60	29.60	13.22
Swedish krona	2.19	5.59	15.81	7.64
Swiss franc	-7.44	3.01	16.45	3.91
U.S. dollar	9.00	9.00	9.00	9.00

Based on the expected values of effective yields for the currencies, the optimal composition of each portfolio is disclosed in the following table:

	Percentage of Funds Invested In:									
Type of Portfolio	A$	BP	C$	FF	DM	IL	JY	SK	SF	US$
Risk neutral	100	0	0	0	0	0	0	0	0	0
Balanced	25	25	25	0	0	0	25	0	0	0
Conservative	10	10	10	0	0	10	10	0	0	50
Ultra-conservative	0	0	0	0	0	0	0	0	0	100

The effective yields for each portfolio can be determined on the spreadsheet by creating a compute statement that sums weighted effective yields based on the weights assigned above. These yields are disclosed below:

Portfolio	Portfolio's Effective Yield Under a Strong $ Scenario	Stable $ Scenario	Weak $ Scenario	Expected Value of Effective Yield
Risk Neutral	-0.56%	14.15%	28.07%	14.05%
Balanced	3.18	12.57	24.06	13.20
Conservative	5.99	10.59	16.16	10.88
Ultra-conservative	9.00	9.00	9.00	9.00

Project

a) Use the interest rate and exchange rate data in the back of the text to determine a U.S. firm's effective (exchange rate-adjusted) yield when investing in French francs on a quarterly basis. Identify the periods in which this strategy would have resulted in very low effective yields. Was the dollar strengthening or weakening in those periods? (A computerized spreadsheet could easily be created to reduce your computational time.)

This project allows students to realize how exchange rates can enhance yields of overseas investments, and also how exchange rates can reduce or completely eliminate the yields in some periods.

Integrative Problem for Part IV

Short-Term Asset and Liability Management

Kent Company is a large U.S. firm with no international business. It has two branches within the U.S., an East branch and a West branch. Each branch presently makes investing or financing decisions independently, as if it was a separate entity. The East branch has excess cash of $15 million to invest for the next year. It can invest its funds in Treasury bills denominated in dollars or any of the three foreign currencies in which it does business. The only restriction enforced by the parent is that a maximum of $5,000,000 can be invested or financed in any foreign currency.

The West branch needs to borrow $15 million over one year to support its U.S. operations. It can borrow funds in any currency in which it does business (although any foreign funds borrowed need to be converted to dollars to finance the U.S. operations). The only restriction enforced by the-parent is that a maximum equivalent of $5 million can be borrowed in any single currency.

A large bank serving the Eurocurrency market has offered Kent Company the following terms:

Currency	Annual Interest Rate on Deposits	Annual Interest Rate Charged On Loans
U.S. dollars	6%	9%
Australian dollars	11%	14%
Canadian dollars	7%	10%
German marks	9%	12%
Japanese yen	8%	11%

The parent of Kent company has created one-year forecasts of each currency (shown below) which can be used by the branches in making their investing or financing decisions:

Currency	Spot Exchange Rate	Forecasted Annual Percentage Change in Exchange Rates
Australian dollar	$.70	-4%
Canadian dollar	$.80	-2%
German mark	$.60	+3%
Japanese yen	$.008	0%

1. Determine the investment portfolio composition for Kent's East branch that would maximize the expected effective yield, while satisfying the restriction imposed by the parent.

   When accounting for the interest rate and forecasted exchange rates, the expected effective yields are listed below:

Currency	Expected Effective Yield on Investment
U. S. dollar	6.00%
Australian dollar	6.56%
Canadian dollar	4.86%
German mark	12.27%
Japanese yen	8.00%

ANSWER:

Given these expected effective yields, the investment should be allocated as follows:

$5 million invested in German marks

$5 million invested in Japanese yen

$5 million invested in Australian dollars

2. What is the expected effective yield of the investment portfolio?

   ANSWER: Based on 33.3% allocated to each of three currencies (DM, JY, A$), the portfolio's expected effective yield is:

   (33.3%) (12.27%) + (33.3%) (8.00%) + (33.3%) (6.56%)

   = 4.086% + 2.554% + 2.18%

   = 8.93%

3. Based on the expected effective yield for the portfolio and the initial investment amount of $15 million, determine the annual interest to be earned on the portfolio.

   ANSWER: The expected interest earned is the portfolio's expected effective yield times the initial investment, or:

   8.93% x $15,000,000 = $1,339,500

4. Determine the financing portfolio composition for Kent's West branch that would minimize the expected effective financing rate, while satisfying the restriction imposed by the parent.

When accounting for the interest rate and forecasted exchange rate, the expected effective financing rates are listed below:

Currency	Expected Effective Financing Rate
U.S. dollar	9.00%
Australian dollar	9.44%
Canadian dollar	7.80%
German mark	15.36%
Japanese yen	11.00%

ANSWER:

Given these expected financing rates, the financing should be allocated as follows:

The equivalent of $5 million borrowed in Canadian dollars.

The equivalent of $5 million borrowed in U.S. dollars.

The equivalent of $5 million borrowed in Australian dollars.

5. What is the expected effective financing rate of the total amount of funds borrowed?

ANSWER: Based on 33.3% financed with each of three currencies (C$, U.S.$, A$), the expected financing rate for the entire portfolio of funds borrowed is:

(33.3%) (7.80%) + (33.3%) (9.00%) + (33.3%) (9.44%)

= 2.60% + 3.00% + 3.14%

= 8.74%

6. Based on the expected effective financing rate for the portfolio, and the total amount of $15 million borrowed, determine the expected loan repayment amount beyond the principal borrowed.

ANSWER: The expected loan repayment amount beyond the principal borrowed is the portfolio's expected effective financing rate times the amount borrowed, or:

8.74% x $15,000,000 = $1,311,000

7. When consolidating the expected interest received by the East branch and paid by the West branch of Kent Company, what is the net amount of interest received?

ANSWER:

Net = Interest received by East branch - Interest paid by West branch

= $1,339,500 - $1,311,000

= $28,500

8. If the East branch and West branch worked together, the East branch could have loaned its $15 million to the West branch. Yet, one could argue that the branches could not have taken advantage of interest rate differentials or expected exchange rate effects among currencies. Given the data provided in this example, would you have recommended that the two branches make their short-term investment or financing decisions independently, or should the East branch lend its excess cash to the West branch? Explain.

ANSWER: If one branch lends to another, the interest received by one branch will be exactly equal to the interest paid by the other. yet, the expected interest received is $28,500 above the expected interest to be paid when each branch acts independently.

However, there is much exchange rate risk involved in the investing and financing in foreign currencies, especially when considering that $15 million was to be invested by one branch and another $15 million was to be borrowed by the other branch. Most firms would prefer that one branch lend to the other branch, even if the expected return is slightly lower. This strategy would avoid a substantial amount of exchange rate risk, especially because the firm did not have any international business that could offset foreign investment or financing positions.

Chapter 16

Direct Foreign Investment

Lecture Outline

Corporate Motives for Increasing International Business

Methods to Increase International Business

DFI
Exporting
Licensing
Joint Ventures
Franchising

A Closer Look at Benefits of International Diversification

Numerical Example of Diversification Benefits
Sensitivity of Diversification Benefits to Number of Foreign Projects

The Direct Foreign Investment Decision

Direct Foreign Investment as an Ongoing Decision
Incentives Offered by Host Governments

Chapter Theme

The main purpose of this chapter is to illustrate why MNC's often use DFI, and to suggest the various factors involved in the DFI decision. The specifics involved in quantifying costs and benefits of DFI are discussed in the following chapter. Thus, this chapter should be covered in general terms as to the costs and benefits of DFI. The chapter implicitly suggests that each firm may benefit from DFI by capitalizing on some unique perceived advantages of the foreign market. Yet, all DFI decisions relate to the MNC's overall risk and return objectives.

Topics to Stimulate Class Discussions

1. Why would a large advanced MNC consider DFI in some less developed country?

2. Assume that you produce plastic computer pieces for computer companies. The pieces require very little technology. Where would you like to establish DFI? (The point of this question is to force consideration of various characteristics that are incorporated in a DFI decision).

3. What factors would be considered when deciding whether a subsidiary should reinvest earnings or remit them to the parent?

4. The DFI decision is related to marketing, finance, and management. What is the role of each area in the DFI decision? (This question is not explicitly covered in the text, but allows students to consider the differences in disciplines as related to the broad corporate function of DFI.)

5. Do you think foreign investments are primarily intended to reduce production costs or increase sales? Discuss.

Answers to End of Chapter Questions

1. Describe some potential benefits to the MNC as a result of direct foreign investment (DFI). Elaborate on each type of benefit.

   ANSWER: See Exhibit 16.1 for a complete breakdown.

2. Packer Inc., a U.S. producer of computer diskettes, plans to establish a subsidiary in Germany in order to penetrate the German market. Executives of Packer believe that the mark's value is relatively strong and will weaken against the dollar over time. If their expectations about the mark value are correct, how will this affect the feasibility of the project? Explain.

ANSWER: If the mark's value is relatively strong now, Packer Inc. will incur high costs of establishing a German subsidiary. In addition, if the mark weakens, future remitted earnings by the subsidiary to the parent will be converted to fewer dollars. Packer will be adversely affected by the exchange rate movements (although the project may still be feasible).

3. Bear Company and Viking Inc. are automobile manufacturers that desire to benefit from economies of scale. Bear Company has decided to establish distributorship subsidiaries in various countries, while Viking Inc. has decided to establish manufacturing subsidiaries in various countries. Which firm is more likely to benefit from economies of scale.

   ANSWER: Bear Company is likely to benefit because it is maintaining all of its manufacturing in one area. If Viking Inc. spreads its production facilities, it will incur higher fixed costs of machinery.

4. Raider Chemical Company and Ram Inc. had similar intentions to reduce the volatility of their cash flows. Raider implemented a long-range plan to establish 40 percent of its business in Canada. Ram Inc. implemented a long-range plan to establish 30 percent of its business in Europe and Asia, scattered among 12 different countries. Which company would more effectively reduce cash flow volatility once the plans have are achieved?

   ANSWER: Ram Inc. would likely be more effective because its international business is spread across several major countries, while Raider Chemical Company is concentrated in only one foreign country whose business cycles are related to the U.S.

5. If the United States placed long-term restrictions on imports, would the amount of direct foreign investment by non-U.S. MNCs in the United States increase, decrease, or be unchanged? Explain.

   ANSWER: It would likely increase because the foreign firms would need to replace their exporting business with DFI in order to maintain their business in the U.S.

6. In 1972 Tandy Corporation established a manufacturing facility in South Korea to produce computer components. One of the attractions was the relatively low cost of labor. In 1989 Tandy closed the facility, as the cost advantage dissipated. Why do you think the relative cost advantage has dissipated in South Korea and other Asian countries such as Hong Kong, Singapore, and Taiwan? (Ignore possible exchange rate effects.)

   ANSWER: The labor cost in South Korea rose by 110 percent from 1984 to 1989. This was partially due to the labor shortage, as many MNCs were attempting to capitalize on the low cost labor there during the 1980s. The strong demand for labor caused labor shortages and increased wage rates, thereby reducing any cost advantage.

7. Offer your opinion on why economies of some less developed countries with strict restrictions on international trade and direct foreign investment are somewhat independent from economies of other countries. Why would MNCs desire to enter such countries? If these countries relaxed their restrictions, would their economies continue to be independent of other economies? Explain.

   ANSWER: Countries that are unrelated to other economies are desirable because business in these countries would not be subject to existing business cycles in other countries. Consequently, an MNC's overall cash flow may be more stable. However, a typical reason why these countries' economies are independent of other economies is government restrictions on international trade and DFI. Thus, their economies are insulated from other countries. Yet, this means that while these countries may be desirable to MNCs, they may also be off limits to MNCs. If the governments of these countries loosen restrictions, the MNCs could enter these countries, but the economies of these countries could no longer be as insulated from the rest of the world.

8. Dolphin Inc., a U.S.-based MNC with a German subsidiary, expects that the German mark will appreciate for several years. How might Dolphin Inc. adjust its policy on remitted earnings from the German subsidiary?

   ANSWER: Dolphin Inc. may prefer that its German subsidiary reinvest mark earnings in Germany, and postpone remitting earnings until the time at which the mark's value has strengthened. Ideally, the funds would be remitted when the mark reaches its highest value, so that the funds convert to the maximum number of dollars. This strategy is most preferable when the subsidiary has a use for the marks until they are to be remitted.

9. Bronco Corporation has decided to establish a subsidiary in Taiwan that would produce stereos and sell them in Taiwan. It expects that its cost of producing these stereos will be one-third the cost of producing them in the United States. Assuming that its production cost estimates are accurate, is Bronco's strategy sensible? Explain.

   ANSWER: No. Bronco Corporation recognized an advantage of producing stereos in Taiwan versus the U.S. Yet, this is only an advantage if Bronco sells the stereos produced in Taiwan to the U.S. market. All of Bronco's competition in the Taiwan market will have the same production costs as Bronco's Taiwan subsidiary, so Bronco would not have an advantage in the Taiwan market.

10. What do the studies mentioned in the chapter reveal about the relationship between degree of international business and risk of MNCs? What do these results imply about the feasibility of increasing international business?

    ANSWER: Firms with more international business exhibited less risk. Thus, firms could reduce their risk by increasing their degree of international business.

11. Starter Corporation of New Haven, Connecticut produces sportswear that is licensed by professional sports teams. It recently decided to expand in Europe. What are the potential benefits for this firm to use direct foreign investment?

    ANSWER: The primary reason would be to attract new sources of demand. This type of sportswear is much more popular in the U.S., but the U.S. market is possibly saturated. The European market offers new sources of demand because the European people have not been exposed to this type of sportswear.

12. What potential benefits do you think were most important in the decision of Walt Disney Company to build a theme park in France?

    ANSWER: There is no simple answer to this question, but the question usually leads to an interesting discussion. Some of the more likely motives as related to those discussed in this chapter are:

    1. New sources of demand - another theme park in the U.S. would have less potential, since U.S. tourists are willing to travel to California or Florida to see the theme parks.

    2. Economies of scale should result from the new theme park because much of the costs associated with planning a theme park have already been incurred. Also, the sales of Disney toys will increase, allowing for additional economies of scale in production.

    3. French labor may not necessarily by less costly than U.S. labor, but there may be a cost advantage to the land in France (due to land subsidies provided by the French government).

    4. Exploit monopolistic advantages - there are other theme parks in Europe. Yet, some tourists may feel that no other theme park is an adequate substitute for Disney. Thus Disney can now attract tourists who are unwilling to travel to the U.S.

    5. Diversification - the Disney theme parks in the U.S. have experienced reduced sales when the dollar is strong because foreign tourism in the U.S. declines. A theme park in France may appeal to tourists that decide not to travel to the U.S. when the dollar is strong. In fact, it may even attract more tourists from the U.S. when the dollar is strong.

13. Once an MNC establishes a subsidiary, DFI remains an ongoing decision. What does this statement mean?

    ANSWER: The subsidiary established due to DFI will generate earnings which are to be either reinvested in the host country or remitted to the parent. This reflects a continuous DFI decision of whether to expand in the host country.

14. Why would foreign governments provide MNCs with incentives to undertake DFI there?

    ANSWER: Foreign governments sometimes expect that DFI will provide needed employment or technology for a country. For these reasons, they may provide incentives to encourage DFI.

15. This chapter concentrates on possible benefits to a firm that increases its international business. What are some risks of international business that may not exist when conducting local business?

    ANSWER: Some of the more common risks of DFI are a government takeover, and changing tax laws. There are additional risks (discussed in other chapters) such as currency restrictions, high probability of war, and declining economic conditions.

Solution to WSJ Case : U.S. Direct Foreign Investment in China

1. Explain in general terms the motivation for the recent direct foreign investment by Proctor & Gamble, Unilever, and Colgate-Palmolive Company in China.

   ANSWER: China has 1.2 billion consumers, which represents the potential strong demand for household products. Yet, the supply of these products has been limited because of barriers that were previously enforced. The U.S. firms can sell the household products needed in China.

2. Describe some of the obstacles faced by U.S. firms such as Proctor & Gamble and Colgate-Palmolive Company that have engaged in direct foreign investment in China.

   ANSWER: Obstacles include high inflation in China, difficulties in converting foreign currency, difficulties in efficiently distributing products across small stores, and the lack of disposable income for many China residents.

3. Johnson & Johnson plans a factory in Shanghai to produce baby shampoo. Why do you think Johnson & Johnson produces the shampoo there rather than simply exporting the shampoo from the U.S.?

   ANSWER: By producing the shampoo in China, Johnson & Johnson creates expenses in the Chinese currency to offset some revenue there, which reduces its exposure to exchange rate risk. Second, Johnson & Johnson can reduce its labor costs by producing the shampoo in China. Third, it may be more capable of monitoring the proper distribution of the shampoo by having a subsidiary established in China. Fourth, it can quickly accommodate new orders for shampoo when producing the shampoo locally (in China).

Solution to Case Problem: Blues Corporation

Some possible answers are provided below, although there is no perfect solution to the issues introduced. The main objective of this case is to stimulate discussion and force students to create their own concerns about entering Eastern Europe. Students must learn that some ventures could easily backfire.

a) Blues Corp. should not immediately jump at the opportunity unless it considers the following information. First, while the labor cost is low today, it may increase over time as East and West German economies become more integrated. Second, while the East European facility is inefficient, the potential to remove the inefficiencies may be limited by the government. For example, the government may require that all workers at the facility remain employed. Third, there is much uncertainty about the restrictions that could be enforced as conditions of ownership in East Germany, such as high taxes and environmental restrictions. These factors must be accounted for.

b) While the competition appears overpriced, Blues Corp. must consider how that may change in the long run. Some of the government-owned businesses may be privatized over time, which would likely increase efficiency and reduce prices. Therefore, competition could become more intense in the near future. Blues Corp. could attempt to capitalize on the East European markets by exporting from its West German subsidiary. However, it may not be worthwhile to use a heavy promotion program unless it believes that it can attain a reasonable market share even when some of the competition may reduce prices in the future.

c) Blues Corp. should not forgo its established U.S. business as a means of pursuing business in East Germany. The risks are high. Blues Corp. could test the East German market by exporting, without requiring a major amount of funds. If it decides to make a major investment in an East German facility or promotion program, it should wait until it can raise funds by some means other than divesting U.S. assets.

Solution to Case Problem: Penguin Company

While there is no perfect solution to these questions, the case is intended to stimulate thought and discussion. It is recommended that a diagram be drawn when discussing this case, so that students can grasp the background information provided.

a) The U.S. government could place trade restrictions on the Hong Kong companies. While this seems like a simple solution, there are some serious ramifications to consider. Would the restrictions be placed only on these auto parts? If so, this sets a precedent for any other U.S. companies competing with Hong Kong companies to appeal to the U.S. government for restrictions on products imported by U.S. firms. Furthermore, retaliation by the Hong Kong government is possible, so that whatever Penguin Inc. gains could be lost by a U.S. exporting company that becomes subject to new trade restrictions by Hong Kong.

   If the U.S. government does attempt to enforce trade barriers on the Hong Kong companies, (despite the potential adverse consequences stated above) the Taiwan companies may begin to penetrate the U.S. market. Thus, the problems faced by Penguin Inc. would continue, and could only be resolved if the U.S. government also places trade barriers on Taiwan companies as well. In this case, Penguin Inc. would essentially have a monopoly in its market. This could result in higher costs for the automobile manufacturers that purchase the supplies.

b) The Hong Kong companies must determine the probability that the U.S. government will take any action to restrict their entry into the U.S. market, since such action could cause any marketing efforts to go without any benefits. The Hong Kong companies must also consider their competitive advantage over Penguin Inc. Why does it exist, and will the reasons for its existence continue in the future? For example, if the profit margin of the Hong Kong companies was severely cut in order to generate previous growth, perhaps it should not continue to increase its market share, especially in the U.S. market.

   In addition, what has been the exchange rate trend in recent years? Could the success of the Hong Kong companies be due to a weak currency, which made their product look unusually attractive during the previous years? If so, perhaps the companies should not get carried away with a marketing drive, as their prices from the U.S. perspective could become unattractive as soon as their currency strengthens against the dollar.

   A marketing drive can be considered as a large initial outlay which is only justified if the present value of future cash flows is sufficient to cover the initial outlay. These future cash flows are highly dependent on the factors mentioned above.

c) The big difference between continually exporting versus establishment of a subsidiary is whether the large initial outlay necessary to establish a subsidiary will be offset over time by the savings from reduced transportation costs, or from other factors. Labor costs must be considered. The labor cost of production in the U.S. will likely be higher than in Hong Kong. Also, the quality control costs must be considered. The potential size of the U.S. market that a Hong Kong company expects to control would influence its decision here. Is any one of the several Hong Kong companies large enough to justify establishing a production plant in the U.S.? Without sufficient sales volume, the future cash inflows could not recapture the initial outlay of a new production plant, regardless of the transportation cost savings, or size of profit margin. If no single Hong Kong company is large enough to establish a subsidiary, perhaps they would consider a joint venture. The viability of this idea depends on the ability to equitably allocate tasks and costs among the companies for the creation and management of the subsidiary.

An additional consideration is tax incentives. Some areas of the U.S. may provide tax incentives to the companies if they would set up a subsidiary and hire local labor (much to the dismay of Penguin Co.).

When Hong Kong companies export to the U.S., the expectation of a weaker U.S. dollar suggests the U.S. market will reduce the demand for these goods, unless the Hong Kong companies reduce their price. In addition, any dollars earned in the U.S. by the subsidiary that are remitted to headquarters in Hong Kong will not be worth as much. Yet, earnings generated in the U.S. could possibly be reinvested in the U.S. until the dollar has strengthened.

If a Hong Kong company establishes a subsidiary before the dollar weakens, the U.S. demand for its product will be somewhat insulated from exchange rate movements. However, the cost of establishing the subsidiary when the dollar is relatively strong would be higher.

d) If Penguin Co. cannot convince the U.S. government to impose trade restrictions, it must assess its future competitive position. It should first determine what factors in the last few years caused the Hong Kong companies to steal some of their market share (such as a strong dollar), and if those factors will persist in the future. If it sees a continual advantage of Hong Kong cost-effectiveness, it may consider a joint venture with one or more Hong Kong firms, where it exploits its advantages (such as its facilities and location in the U.S.).

If this effort fails, it may consider selling its plant to a Hong Kong competitor, or divesting its assets. These measures are drastic and should only be considered if Penguin Co. does not foresee an improvement in its efficiency. If the relatively lower efficiency is due to high labor costs, Penguin Co. may consider establishing a subsidiary in another country where wages are low, and exporting from there. It could even sell its U.S. manufacturing plant, and create a subsidiary for all of its production, with an emphasis on penetrating some other markets (such as Europe). However, the same cost advantages of competitors would possibly prevail in these other markets as well.

e) If the U.S. government imposes barriers, Hong Kong may retaliate. As a result, trade between the two countries would be reduced. This could adversely affect both countries. Taiwan could benefit by substituting its products for exports previously provided by Hong Kong companies and Penguin Co. Under this setting, more funds should be invested in Taiwan at the expense of the U.S. and Hong Kong firms that rely on trade to each other.

If government action does not occur, the situation is not likely to have a significant impact on country economies. However, some types of firms may be affected by the situation. For example, any firms that currently do business with Penguin Co. would be affected unfavorably, since Penguin's future is uncertain. Any companies that supply materials to the Hong Kong companies may benefit.

Project

1. Review recent annual reports of an MNC of your choice and summarize why it increased its international operations over time. Various factors that motivate international business were identified in the chapter. Determine which factors were probably most influential in motivating the MNC's expansion into other countries.

   This project shows students that the motives for DFI vary among countries. Students should not focus on memorizing the list of DFI motives, but instead should be able to pinpoint which motives on that list are applicable to a particular situation.

Chapter 17

Multinational Capital Budgeting

Lecture Outline

Subsidiary Versus Parent Perspective
- Tax Differentials
- Restricted Remittances
- Excess Remittances
- Exchange Rate Movements
- Subsidiary Versus Parent Perspective: An Example

Input Used for Multinational Capital Budgeting Decision

Multinational Capital Budgeting: An Example
- Example: Background
- Example: Analysis

Factors to Consider in Multinational Capital Budgeting
- Exchange Rate Fluctuations
- Inflation
- Financing Arrangement
- Blocked Funds
- Remittance Provisions
- Uncertain Salvage Value
- Impact of Project on Prevailing Cash Flows
- Host Government Incentives
- Social Costs
- Threat of Expropriation

Adjusting Project Assessment for Risk
- Risk-Adjusted Discount Rate
- Sensitivity Analysis
- Simulation

Chapter Theme

This chapter identifies additional considerations in multinational capital budgeting versus domestic capital budgeting. These considerations can either be explained briefly or illustrated with the use of an example. The cost of capital discussion in this chapter should be linked to capital budgeting for obvious reasons. An effort should be made to identify factors that affect an MNC's cost of capital which are not relevant for a domestic firm's cost of capital.

Topics to Stimulate Class Discussion

1. Create an idea for a firm to expand its operations overseas. Provide the industry the firm is involved in. Given this information, students should be requested to list all information that needs to be gathered in order to conduct a capital budgeting analysis.

2. How should a firm adjust the capital budgeting analysis for investment in a country where the currency is extremely volatile?

3. How should a firm adjust the capital budgeting for investment in a country where the chance of a government takeover is relatively high?

Answers to End of Chapter Questions

1. Why should capital budgeting for subsidiary projects be assessed from the parent's perspective?

   ANSWER: When a parent allocates funds for a project, it should view the project's feasibility from its own perspective. It is possible that a project could be feasible from a subsidiary's perspective, but be infeasible when considering a parent's perspective (due to foreign withholding taxes or exchange rate changes affecting funds remitted to the parent).

2. What additional factors deserve consideration in multinational capital budgeting that are not normally relevant for a purely domestic project?

   ANSWER: Some of the more obvious factors are (1) exchange rates, (2) whether currency restrictions may exist, (3) probability of a host government takeover, and (4) foreign demand for the product.

3. What is the limitation of using point estimates of exchange rates within the capital budgeting analysis?

ANSWER: Point estimates of exchange rates lead to a point estimate of a project's NPV. It is more desirable to have a feel for a variety of outcomes (NPVs) that could occur.

4. Explain how simulation can be used in multinational capital budgeting.

   ANSWER: Develop a range of possible values that each input variable (such as price, quantity sold, exchange rates) may take on, and apply the simulation model to these ranges. The result is a distribution of NPVs that could occur.

5. Why is simulation applicable to multinational capital budgeting? What can it do that other risk adjustment techniques cannot?

   ANSWER: Simulation is very applicable to multinational capital budgeting since several input variables are unknown and may be best forecasted within a range instead of as a point estimate. Simulation accounts for the uncertainty by generating a range of NPV estimates that could occur.

6. List the various techniques for adjusting risk in multinational capital budgeting. Describe any advantages or disadvantages of each technique.

   ANSWER: The risk adjusted discount rate (RADR) is easy to use, but generates only a single point estimate of the NPV. It may be more desirable to develop a distribution of possible NPVs in order to assess the probability that NPV will be positive. Sensitivity analysis and simulation could be very useful because they generate a distribution of NPVs.

7. Project X has an NPV estimated by your employees to be $1.2 million. Your employees state in their report that they have not accounted for risk, but that with such a large NPV, the project should be accepted, since even a risk-adjusted NPV would likely be positive. You have the final decision as to whether to accept or reject the project. What is your decision?

   ANSWER: The decision should not be made until risk has been considered. If the project has a risk of a government takeover for example), a large estimated NPV may not be a sufficient reason to accept the project.

8. Describe in general terms how future appreciation of the German mark will likely affect the value (from the parent's perspective) of a project established in Germany today by a U.S.-based MNC. Will the sensitivity of the project value be affected by the percentage of earnings remitted to the parent each year?

   ANSWER: Future appreciation of the mark would benefit the parent since the mark earnings would be worth more when remitted and converted to dollars. This is especially true when a large percentage of earnings are sent to the parent.

9. Repeat Question. 8, assuming future depreciation of the German mark.

   ANSWER: Future depreciation of the mark would hurt the parent since the mark earnings would be worth less when remitted and converted to dollars. This is especially true when a large percentage of earnings are sent to the parent.

10. Explain how the financing decision can influence the sensitivity of NPV to exchange rate forecasts.

    ANSWER: By financing the project with the same currency that is received from the project, the firm can reduce the sensitivity of a foreign project's NPV.

11. Wolverine Corporation presently has no existing business in Germany but is considering the establishment of a subsidiary there. The following information has been gathered to assess this project:

    - The initial investment required is DM50 million. Given the existing spot rate of $.50 per mark, the initial investment in dollars is $25 million. In addition to the DM50 million initial investment on plant and equipment, DM20 million is needed for working capital and will be borrowed by the subsidiary from a German bank. The German subsidiary of Wolverine will pay interest only on the loan each year, at an interest rate of 14 percent. The loan principal is to be paid in 10 years.

    - The project will be terminated at the end of year 3, when the subsidiary will be sold.

    - The price, demand, and variable cost of the product in West Germany are as follows:

Year	Price	Demand	Variable Cost
1	DM500	40,000 units	DM30
2	DM511	50,000 units	DM35
3	DM530	60,000 units	DM40

    - The fixed costs, such as overhead expenses, are estimated to be DM6 million per year.

    - The exchange rate of the mark is expected to be $.52 at the end of Year 1, $.54 at the end of Year 2, and $.56 at the end of Year 3.

    - The German government will impose an income tax of 30 percent on income. In addition, it will impose a withholding tax of 10 percent on earnings remitted by the subsidiary. The U.S. government will allow a tax credit on remitted earnings and will not impose any additional taxes.

    - All cash flows received by the subsidiary are to be sent to the parent at the end of each year. The subsidiary will use its working capital to support ongoing operations.

- The plant and equipment are depreciated over 10 years using the straight-line depreciation method. Since the plant and equipment are initially valued at DM50 million, the annual depreciation expense is DM5 million.

- In three years, the subsidiary is to be sold. Wolverine plans to let the acquiring firm assume the existing German loan. The working capital will not be liquidated, but will be used by the acquiring firm. Wolverine expects to receive DM52 million after subtracting capital gains taxes when it sells the subsidiary.

- Wolverine requires a 20 percent rate of return on this project.

a. Determine the net present value of this project. Should Wolverine accept this project?

Capital Budgeting Analysis: Wolverine Corporation

	Year 0	Year 1	Year 2	Year 3
1. Demand		40,000	50,000	60,000
2. Price per unit		DM500	DM511	DM530
3. Total revenue = (1) x (2)		DM20,000,000	DM25,550,000	DM31,800,000
4. Variable cost per unit		DM30	DM35	DM40
5. Total variable cost = (1) x (4)		DM1,200,000	DM1,750,000	DM2,400,000
6. Fixed cost		DM6,000,000	DM6,000,000	DM6,000,000
7. Interest expense of German loan		DM2,800,000	DM2,800,000	DM2,800,000
8. Noncash expense (depreciation)		DM5,000,000	DM5,000,000	DM5,000,000
9. Total expenses = (5)+(6)+(7)+(8)		DM15,000,000	DM15,550,000	DM16,200,000
10. Before-tax earnings of subsidiary = (3)-(9)		DM5,000,000	DM10,000,000	DM15,600,000
11. Host government tax (30%)		DM1,500,000	DM3,000,000	DM4,680,000
12. After-tax earnings of subsidiary		DM3,500,000	DM7,000,000	DM10,920,000
13. Net cash flow to subsidiary = (12)+(8)		DM8,500,000	DM12,000,000	DM15,920,000
14. DM remitted by sub. (100% of CF)		DM8,500,000	DM12,000,000	DM15,920,000
15. Withholding tax imposed on remitted funds (10%)		DM850,000	DM1,200,000	DM1,592,000
16. DM remitted after withholding taxes		DM7,650,000	DM10,800,000	DM14,328,000
17. Salvage value				DM52,000,000
18. Exchange rate of DM		$.52	$.54	$.56
19. Cash flows to parent		$3,978,000	$5,832,000	$37,143,680
20. PV of parent cash flows (20% of discount rate)		$3,315,000	$4,050,000	$21,495,185
21. Initial investment by parent	$25,000,000			
22. Cumulative NPV of cash flows		$-21,685,000	$-17,635,000	$3,860,185

ANSWER: The net present value of this project is $3,860,185. Therefore, Wolverine should accept this project.

b. Assume that Wolverine also considers an alternative financing arrangement, in which the parent invests an additional $10 million to cover the working capital requirements, so that the subsidiary avoids the German loan. If this arrangement is used, the selling price of the subsidiary (after subtracting any capital gains taxes) is expected to be DM18 million higher. Is this alternative financing arrangement more feasible for the parent than the originally proposed arrangement? Explain.

ANSWER: This alternative financing arrangement will have the following effects. First, it will increase the dollar amount of the initial outlay to $35 million. Second, it avoids the annual interest expense of DM2,800,000. Third, it will increase the salvage value from DM52,000,000 to DM70,000,000. The capital budgeting analysis is revised to incorporate these changes.

Capital Budgeting Analysis With An Alternative
Financing Arrangement: Wolverine Corporation

	Year 0	Year 1	Year 2	Year 3
1. Demand		40,000	50,000	60,000
2. Price per unit		DM500	DM511	DM530
3. Total revenue = (1)x(2)		DM20,000,000	DM25,550,000	DM31,800,000
4. Variable cost per unit		DM30	DM35	DM40
5. Total variable cost = (1)x(4)		DM1,200,000	DM1,750,000	DM2,400,000
6. Fixed cost		DM6,000,000	DM6,000,000	DM6,000,000
7. Interest expense of German loan		DM0	DM0	DM0
8. Noncash expense (depreciation)		DM5,000,000	DM5,000,000	DM5,000,000
9. Total expenses = (5)+(6)+(7)+(8)		DM12,200,000	DM12,750,000	DM13,400,000
10. Before-tax earnings of subsidiary = (3)-(9)		DM7,800,000	DM12,800,000	DM18,400,000
11. Host government tax (30%)		DM2,340,000	DM3,840,000	DM5,520,000
12. After-tax earnings of subsidiary		DM5,460,000	DM8,960,000	DM12,880,000
13. Net cash flow to subsidiary = (12)+(8)			DM10,460,000	DM13,960,000
DM17,880,000				
14. DM remitted by sub. (100% of CF)		DM10,460,000	DM13,960,000	DM17,880,000
15. Withholding tax imposed on remitted funds (10%)		DM1,046,000	DM1,360,000	DM1,788,000
16. DM remitted after withholding taxes		DM9,414,000	DM12,564,000	DM16,092,000
17. Salvage value				DM70,000,000
18. Exchange rate of DM		\$.52	\$.54	\$.56
19. Cash flows to parent		\$4,895,280	\$6,784,560	\$48,211,520
20. PV of parent cash flows (20% discount rate)		\$4,079,400	\$4,711,500	\$27,900,185
21. Initial investment by parent	\$35,000,000			
22. Cumulative NPV of cashflows		-\$30,920,600	-\$26,209,100	\$1,691,085

The analysis shows that this alternative financing arrangement is expected to generate a lower net present value than the original financing arrangement.

c. Would the NPV of this project from the parent's perspective be more sensitive to exchange rate movements if the subsidiary used German financing to cover the working capital or if the parent invested more of its own funds to cover the working capital? Explain.

ANSWER: The NPV would be more sensitive to exchange rate movements if the parent uses its own financing to cover the working capital requirements. If it used German financing, a portion of DM cash flows could be used to cover the interest payments on debt. Thus, there would be less marks to be converted to dollars, and less exposure to exchange rate movements.

d. Assume Wolverine used the original proposed financing arrangements and that funds are blocked until the subsidiary is sold. The funds to be remitted are reinvested at a rate of 6 percent (after taxes) until the end of Year 3. How is the project's NPV affected?

ANSWER:

The effects of the blocked funds are shown below:

		Year 1	Year 2	Year 3
13. Net cash flow to subsidiary =(12)+(8)		DM8,500,000	DM12,000,000	DM15,920,000
				DM12,720,000
				DM 9,550,600
14. DM remitted by subsidiary		DM0	DM0	DM38,190,600
15. Withholding tax imposed on remitted funds (10%)				DM 3,819,060
16. DM remitted after withholding taxes				DM34,371,540
17. Salvage value				DM52,000,000
18. Exchange rate of DM				$.56
19. Cash flows to parent				$48,368,062
20. PV of parent cash flows (20% discount rate)		DM0	DM0	$27,990,777
21. Initial investment by parent	$25,000,000			
22. Cumulative NPV of cash flows		$0	$0	$2,990,777

e. What is the break-even salvage value of this project, if Wolverine Corporation uses the original proposed financing arrangement and funds are not blocked?

First, determine the present value of cash flows when excluding salvage value:

End of Year	Present Value of Cash Flows (excluding salvage value)
1	$ 3,315,000
2	4,050,000
3	4,643,333*
	$12,008,333

*This number is determined by converting the third year DM cash flows excluding salvage value (DM14,328,000) into dollars at the forecasted exchange rate of $.56 per mark:

DM14,328,000 x $.56 = $8,023,680

The present value of the $8,023,680 received 3 years from now is $4,643,333.

Then determine the breakeven salvage value:

Breakeven salvage value $= [\text{IO} - (\text{present value of cash flows})](1+k)^n$

$= [\$25{,}000{,}000 - \$12{,}008{,}333](1+.20)^3$

$= \$22{,}449{,}601$

ANSWER: Since the mark is expected to be $.56 in Year 3, this implies that the breakeven salvage value in terms of marks is:

$22,449,601/$.56 = DM40,088,572

f. Assume that Wolverine decides to implement the project, using the original proposed financing arrangement. Also assume that after one year, a German firm offers Wolverine a price of $27 million after taxes for the subsidiary, and that Wolverine's original forecasts for Years 2 and 3 have not changed. Should Wolverine divest the subsidiary? Explain.

Divestiture Analysis One Year After The Project Began

	End of Year 2 (one year from now)	End of Year 3 (two years from now)
Cash flows to parent	$5,832,000	$37,143,680
PV of parent cash flows foregone if project is divested	$4,860,000	$25,794,222

ANSWER: The present value of foregone cash flows is $30,654,22. Since this exceeds the $27,000,000 in proceeds from the divestiture, the project should not be divested.

12. Huskie Industries, a U.S.-based MNC, considers purchasing a small German manufacturing company that sells products only within West Germany. Huskie has no other existing business in West Germany and no cash flows in German marks. Would the proposed acquisition likely be more feasible if the mark is expected to appreciate or depreciate over the long run? Explain.

ANSWER: The proposed acquisition is likely to be more feasible if the mark is expected to appreciate over the long run. Huskie would like to purchase the firm when the mark is weak. Then, after the purchase, a strengthened mark will convert the German firm's earnings remitted to the parent into a larger amount of U.S. dollars.

13. When Walt Disney World considered establishing a theme park in France, were the forecasted revenues and costs associated with the French park sufficient to assess the feasibility of this project? Were there any other "relevant cash flows" that deserved to be considered?

    ANSWER: Other relevant cash flows are Walt Disney World's existing cash flows. The establishment of a theme park in France could reduce the amount of European customers that would have visited Disney's U.S. theme parks. These foregone cash flows should be considered when assessing the feasibility of the theme park in France.

14. Athens Inc. established a subsidiary in the United Kingdom that was independent of its operations in the United States. The subsidiary's performance was well above what was expected. Consequently, when a British firm approached Athens Inc. about the possibility of acquiring it, Athens' chief financial officer implied that the subsidiary was performing so well that it was not for sale. Comment on this strategy.

    ANSWER: Even if the performance is superior, the subsidiary may be worth selling if the price offered for it exceeds the Athens' perceived present value of the subsidiary.

15. Lehigh Company established a subsidiary in Switzerland that was performing below the cash flow projections developed before the subsidiary was established. Lehigh anticipated that future cash flows would also be lower than the original cash flow projections. Consequently, Lehigh decided to inform several potential acquiring firms of its plan to sell the subsidiary. Lehigh then received a few bids. Even the highest bid was very low, but Lehigh accepted the offer. It justified its decision by stating that any existing project whose cash flows are not sufficient to recover the initial investment should be divested. Comment on this statement. (See the appendix).

    ANSWER: Even if the project will not recover its initial outlay, it should only be divested if the price offered for it exceeds Lehigh's estimation of its present value.

16. Flagstaff Corporation is a U.S.-based firm with a subsidiary in Mexico. It plans to reinvest its earnings in Mexican government securities for the next ten years since the interest rate earned on these securities is so high. Then, after ten years, it will remit all accumulated earnings to the United States. What is a drawback of using this approach? (Assume the securities have no default or interest rate risk.)

ANSWER: While the funds are reinvested at high rates, they may be worth less dollars ten years from now. Flagstaff may have been better off if the earnings were remitted in the year they were generated. Even though the funds could not be invested at as high an interest rate in the U.S., the exchange rate effects are reduced when the earnings are remitted each year.

17. Colorado Springs Company (based in the United States) plans to divest either its German or its Canadian subsidiary. Assume that if exchange rates stayed constant, the dollar cash flows each of these subsidiaries provided to the parent over time would be somewhat similar. However, the firm expects the German mark to depreciate against the U.S. dollar, and the Canadian dollar to appreciate against the U.S. dollar. The firm can sell either subsidiary for about the same price today. Which one should it sell? (See the appendix).

    ANSWER: It should sell the German subsidiary because the foregone cash flows to the parent will be less. If the mark depreciates, the dollar cash flows received by the parent will decline.

18. San Gabriel Corporation recently considered divesting its Italian subsidiary, and determined that the divestiture was not feasible. The required rate of return on this subsidiary was 17 percent. In the last week its required return on that subsidiary increased to 21 percent. If the sales price of the subsidiary has not changed, explain why the divestiture may now be feasible.

    ANSWER: As a project's required rate of return increases, the present value of cash flows decreases. Also, the present value of foreign cash flows would decrease, and may now be lower than the proceeds received from the divestitures.

19. Ventura Corporation is a U.S.-based MNC which plans to establish a subsidiary in France. It is very confident that the French franc will appreciate against the dollar over time. The subsidiary will retain only enough revenues to cover expenses and will remit the rest to the parent each year. Would Ventura benefit more from exchange rate effects if its parent provided equity financing for the subsidiary, or if the subsidiary were financed by local banks in France? Explain.

    ANSWER: Ventura would benefit more from exchange rate effects if its parent uses an equity investment in the subsidiary. This would result in larger remittance that would be favorably affected by the appreciation of the French franc (as the francs are converted to dollars).

    If financing was provided by local banks in France, interest payments to these banks would reduce the amount remitted to the U.S. each year. Therefore, the effect of the franc would be less favorable because it would be applied to a smaller amount of funds.

20. Santa Monica Company is a U.S.-based MNC that was considering establishing a consumer products division in West Germany, which would be financed by German banks. It completed its capital budgeting analysis in August 1989. Then, in November 1989, there was evidence of possible reunification between East and West Germany. In response, it increased its expected cash flows by 20 percent and did not adjust the discount rate applied to the project. Why was the discount rate affected by reunification?

    ANSWER: The possibility of reunification led to a surge in economic activity, which caused an increase in German interest rates. Therefore, Santa Monica's cost of funds for the German project should rise as well, and its discount rate should be adjusted to incorporate a higher interest rate.

21. Assume a less developed country called LDC removes its barriers to encourage direct foreign investment (DFI) in order to reduce its unemployment rate, presently at 15 percent. Also assume that several MNCs are likely to consider DFI in LDC. The inflation rate in recent years has averaged 4 percent. The hourly wage in LDC for manufacturing is the equivalent of about $5 per hour. As Piedmont Company developed cash flow forecasts to perform a capital budgeting analysis for a project in LDC, it assumed a wage rate of $5 in Year 1, and applied a 4 percent increase to each of the next ten years. The components produced are to be exported to its headquarters in the United States, where they will be used in the production of computers. Do you think Piedmont will overestimate or underestimate the net present value of this project? Why? (Assume that LDC's currency is tied to the dollar and will remain that way.)

    ANSWER: The net present value will likely be overestimated because the labor costs in LDC will probably increase at a higher rate than 4 percent per year. As DFI increases, the demand for labor will be much greater than in previous years, and future wage rates will reflect the strong demand. This example is analogous to situations in South Korea, Hong Kong, and Singapore, in which the desire by MNCs to capitalize on low-cost labor caused wage rates to increase between from 50 percent and 110 percent over the 1984-1989 period.

22. Using the capital budgeting framework discussed in this chapter, explain the sources of uncertainty surrounding a proposed project in Hungary by a U.S. firm. In what ways is the estimated NPV of this project more uncertain than that of a similar project in a more developed European country?

    ANSWER: The estimated NPV is more uncertain because cash flows are more uncertain. The high degree of uncertainty surrounding the cash flows is attributed to uncertain economic conditions (especially given the shift to a market-oriented economy), and to an uncertain degree of competition (the competitive structure is changing substantially because of the removal of barriers).

Solution to WSJ Case: PepsiCo's Investment in Poland

1. Given that the investment by PepsiCo Inc. in Poland was entirely in dollars, describe the exposure to exchange rate risk resulting from the project. Explain how the size of the parent's initial investment and the exchange rate risk would have been affected if PepsiCo Inc. had financed much of the investment with loans from banks in Poland.

   ANSWER: As the earnings in Poland are remitted, they will be converted to dollars. If Poland's currency depreciates against the dollar over time, there will be less dollar earnings received.

   If PepsiCo Inc. borrowed funds from banks in Poland, the parent's initial investment would have been smaller. Also, the payments by the Polish subsidiary on loans in Poland would cause less remitted earnings over time, and therefore less exchange rate risk.

2. Describe the factors that were likely considered by PepsiCo Inc. when estimating the future cash flows of the project in Poland.

   ANSWER: The demand in Poland for the soft-drinks and snacks produced by PepsiCo Inc. is dependent on the economy in Poland, consumer habits, country regulations, and the competition. PepsiCo apparently expects an increased demand for soft drinks and snacks as the economy improves. Yet, Coca Cola is positioned to absorb some of the increased demand.

3. What factors were likely considered by PepsiCo Inc. in deriving its required rate of return on the project in Poland?

   ANSWER: PepsiCo planned to use $500 million for investment in Poland. Its funds may have been derived from retained earnings and loans from creditors. PepsiCo would have estimated a cost of each source of funds, and determined the weighted average cost of these funds. It would have attached a risk premium on to the cost to reflect the risk of investment in Poland.

Solution to Case Problem: North Star Company

a) The analysis based on total parent financing is shown below using the somewhat stable exchange rate scenario:

	0	1	2	3	4	5	6
DM Cash Flows (excluding DM interest payments)		DM8,000	DM10,000	DM14,000	DM16,000	DM16,000	DM16,000
DM Interest Payments		0	0	0	0	0	0
DM Cash Flows (after accounting for interest payments)		DM8,000	DM10,000	DM14,000	DM16,000	DM16,000	DM16,000
DM Cash Flows to be remitted (50% of CF)		DM4,000	DM 5,000	DM 7,000	DM 8,000	DM 8,000	DM 8,000
Withholding Tax (10%)		DM400	DM500	DM700	DM800	DM800	DM800
DM Cash Flows to be converted to $		DM3,600	DM4,500	DM6,300	DM7,200	DM7,200	DM7,200
Salvage Value							DM30,000
Exchange Rate of DM		$.50	$.51	$.48	$.50	$.52	$.48
$ Cash Flows		$1,800	$2,295	$3,024	$3,600	$3,744	$17,856
Present Value Interest Factor (18%)		.847	.718	.609	.516	.437	.370
Present Value		$1,525.424	$1,648.233	$1,840.499	$1,856.840	$1,636.537	$6,614.425
Initial Outlay	$15,000						
NPV							$121.959

Applying the same procedure from the previous table, the NPV for each exchange rate scenario is:

Exchange Rate Scenario	Probability	NPV
I. Somewhat stable mark	60%	$ 121,959
II. Weak mark	30%	$-1,692,980
III. Strong mark	10%	$4,895,436

The analysis based on partial financing by the subsidiary is shown below using the somewhat stable exchange rate scenario.

(Cash amounts in thousands)

	0	1	2	3	4	5	6
DM Cash Flows (excluding DM interest payments)		DM8,000	DM10,000	DM14,000	DM16,000	DM16,000	DM16,000
DM Interest Payments		DM1,600	DM 1,600	DM 1,600	DM 1,600	DM 1,600	DM 1,600
DM Cash Flows (after accounting for interest payments)		DM6,400	DM 8,400	DM12,400	DM14,400	DM14,400	DM14,400
DM Cash Flows to be remitted (50%)		DM3,200	DM4,200	DM6,200	DM7,200	DM7,200	DM7,200
Withholding Tax (10%)		DM320	DM420	DM620	DM720	DM720	DM720
DM Cash Flows to be converted to $		DM2,880	DM 3,780	DM5,580	DM ,480	DM6,480	DM6,480
Salvage Value							DM20,000
Exchange Rate of DM		$.50	$.51	$.48	$.50	$.52	$.48
$ Cash Flows		$1,440	$1,927.8	$2,678.4	$3,240	$3,369.6	$12,710.4
Present Value Interest Factor (18%)		.847	.718	.609	.516	.437	.370
Present Value		$1,219.68	$1,384.16	$1,631.145	$1,671.84	$1,472.515	$4,702.848
Initial Outlay	$10,000						
NPV							2082.189

Applying the same procedure from the previous table, the NPV for each exchange rate scenario is:

Exchange Rate Scenario	Probability	NPV
I. Somewhat stable mark	60%	$2,082,189
II. Weak mark	30%	$ 649,840
III. Strong mark	10%	%5,767,235

For each possible scenario, partial subsidiary financing leads to more favorable results. Thus, this method of financing should be chosen.

b) The parent's required rate of return may increase if the borrowed funds by the subsidiary creates a higher degree of financial leverage for the MNC as a whole, which could increase the risk perception of the MNC. If so, the discount rate used should reflect the higher required rate of return.

c) When using a 20 percent withholding tax instead of a 10 percent withholding tax, the results change as follows (based on partial financing by the subsidiary:

Exchange Rate Scenario	Probability	NPV
I. Somewhat stable mark	60%	$1,139,090
II. Weak mark	30%	$-196,292
III. Strong mark	10%	4,599,202

The results suggest that with a 20 percent withholding tax, there is a 70 percent chance that the subsidiary will still generate a positive NPV. The potential negative NPV in the event of a weak mark is not as pronounced as the positive NPVs if either of the other events occur. Most managers would likely still recommend accepting the project under these circumstances.

d) The estimate of net cash flows could be revised, which would result in a lower NPV for each exchange rate scenario. The accept/reject decision would be based on the overall distribution of possible NPVs.

e) As of the end of Year 2, the present value of foregone cash flows for the following 4 years (including the foregone salvage value at the end of Year 6) is $13,203,674. Therefore, North Star should receive at least this amount in order to divest the subsidiary as of the end of Year 2.

Project

1. Assume that your firm's British subsidiary has been able to remit earnings of 400,000 pounds at the end of each year since 1980. Based on the exchange rate at about that time each year, determine the dollar cash flows.

   Repeat this analysis for your firm's Canadian subsidiary, which was able to remit C$800,000 at the end of each year since 1980. Is the standard deviation of the dollar cash flows higher for the British subsidiary or the Canadian subsidiary? Why? What does this project tell you about the exchange rate risk of a Canadian project versus a British project (from a U.S. perspective)?

   This project is intended to show the potential impact of exchange rate fluctuations on the level of remitted earnings.

Chapter 18

Multinational Cost of Capital and Capital Structure

Lecture Outline

Cost of Capital for MNCs versus Domestic Firms
  Cost of Capital Comparison Using the CAPM

Costs of Capital Across Countries
  Country Differences in the Cost of Debt
  Country Differences in the Cost of Equity
  Combining the Costs of Debt and Equity

Using the Cost of Capital for Assessing Foreign Projects

The Capital Structure Decision
  Corporate Characteristics That Affect Capital Structure
  Country Characteristics That Affect Capital Structure

Creating a Target Capital Structure

Capital Structure Across Countries

Chapter Theme

This chapter explains why the capital structure and the cost of capital of MNCs may vary with those of domestic firms. It also explains why the cost of capital varies across countries. The disparity in the cost of capital across countries is important because it can influence the MNC's decisions on where to establish subsidiaries and where to obtain funds.

Topics to Stimulate Class Discussion

1. Why don't all MNCs attempt to obtain funds in countries where the cost of capital is very low?

2. The cost of capital is very high in Latin American countries. Yet, many MNCs continue to establish subsidiaries there. What underlying factor that causes a high cost of capital can also enhance the revenues of subsidiaries over time?

3. Explain why a firm's capital structure may be dependent on the countries in which it operates.

Answers to End of Chapter Questions

1. Create an argument in support of an MNC's favoring a debt-intensive capital structure.

   ANSWER: MNCs that are well-diversified across countries would have somewhat stable cash flows and may therefore be able to handle a high level of debt. They may use substantial foreign debt financing to reduce their subsidiary exposure to exchange rate risk and country risk.

2. Create an argument in support of an MNC's favoring an equity- intensive capital structure.

   ANSWER: MNCs that are highly exposed to exchange rate movements or have subsidiaries located in politically unstable countries may experience very volatile cash flows. These MNCs could not handle high periodic debt payments, and may be better off with an equity intensive capital structure.

3. Do U.S.-based MNCs in general have a higher or lower degree of financial leverage than U.S. domestic firms (based on recent research)?

ANSWER: Recent research has found that U.S.-based MNCs have a lower degree of financial leverage than domestic firms, on average.

4. Describe general differences between the capital structures of firms based in the United States and those of firms based in Japan. Offer an explanation for this difference.

   ANSWER: Japanese firms tend to have a higher degree of financial leverage. This may be because the government of Japan is more likely to rescue a troubled firm. Also, creditors may be more patient there, allowing a firm more time to recover.

5. Why might a firm use a "local" capital structure at a particular subsidiary that differs substantially from its "global" capital structure?

   ANSWER: A particular country's characteristics can cause the MNC's subsidiary to use mostly debt or mostly equity, even if the MNC's "global" target capital structure is more balanced. For example, if the country's stock market is not well developed, the MNC may prefer not to issue stock there, as an inactive secondary market may make it difficult to place stock in that country. In this case, the subsidiary may be financed mostly with debt (such as loans from local banks).

6. Explain how characteristics of MNCs can affect the cost of capital.

   ANSWER: The following characteristics of MNCs can influence the cost of capital:

   - Size. MNCs have more opportunities to grow, and larger, better known firms may receive preferential treatment by creditors.

   - Access to international capital markets. MNCs have access to more sources of funds than domestic firms. To the extent that financial markets are segmented, MNCs may be able to obtain financing from various sources at a lower cost.

   - International diversification. If MNCs can achieve more stable cash flows through their international diversification, their probability of bankruptcy is reduced. Creditors and shareholders may therefore accept a lower rate of return when providing funds to the MNCs, which reflects a lower cost of capital for MNCs.

   - Exchange rate risk. MNCs that are highly exposed to exchange rate movements may be more likely to experience financial problems (if they do not hedge the risk). Thus, they may incur a higher cost of capital.

- Country risk. MNCs with subsidiaries in politically unstable countries may experience volatile cash flows over time and be more susceptible to financial problems. Thus, they may incur a higher cost of capital.

7. Explain why managers of a wholly-owned subsidiary may be more likely to satisfy the shareholders of the MNC.

   ANSWER: Managers of a wholly-owned subsidiary can more easily focus on the objective of satisfying the MNCs shareholders. If the subsidiary is partly-owned, this implies that these are minority shareholders who have an interest in the subsidiary. In this case, the managers may attempt to satisfy both the majority and minority shareholders. However, they cannot satisfy both groups simultaneously. Some decisions made to satisfy minority shareholders will adversely effect majority shareholders.

8. LaSalle Corporation is a U.S.-based MNC with subsidiaries in various less developed countries where stock markets are not well established. How can LaSalle still attempt to achieve its "global" target capital structure of 50 percent debt and 50 percent equity, even if it plans to use only debt financing for the subsidiaries in these countries?

   ANSWER: LaSalle Corporation can use mostly equity financing for its U.S. operations. When consolidated with the debt financing of its subsidiaries, its "global" target capital structure is balanced. The heavy emphasis on equity financing in the U.S. offsets the heavy emphasis on debt financing in the foreign countries.

9. Drexel Company is a U.S.-based company that is establishing a project in a politically unstable country. It is considering two possible sources of financing. Either the parent could provide most of the financing, or the subsidiary could be supported by local loans from banks in that country. Which financing alternative is most appropriate to protect the subsidiary?

   ANSWER: Drexel should let local banks support the subsidiary since it would be in the interest of the banks to see that the subsidiary performs well. If the host government imposed restrictions that reduced the subsidiary's profits, the banks could be adversely affected as well.

   Financing from the MNC parent would not provide such protection since the local banks would have less interest in protecting the subsidiary from host government restrictions.

10. Charleston Corporation has considered establishing a subsidiary in either Germany or the United Kingdom. The subsidiary would be mostly financed with loans from the local banks in the host

country chosen. It determined that the revenue generated from a British subsidiary would be slightly more favorable than the revenue generated by the German subsidiary, even after considering tax and exchange rate effects. The initial outlay is the same, and both countries appear to be politically stable. Charleston recently chose to establish the subsidiary in the United Kingdom because of the revenue advantage. Do you agree with its decision? Explain.

ANSWER: Charleston neglected the cost of financing the subsidiary. It may be more costly to finance a subsidiary in the United Kingdom than a subsidiary in Germany when using the local debt of the host country as the primary source of funds. When considering the cost of financing, a subsidiary in the United Kingdom could be less favorable than a subsidiary in Germany, based on the information provided in this question.

11. Fairfield Corporation, a U.S. firm, just established a subsidiary in a less developed country that consistently experiences an annual inflation rate of 80 percent or more. The country does not have an established stock market, but loans by local banks are available with a 90 percent interest rate. Fairfield has decided to use a strategy in which the subsidiary is financed entirely with funds from the parent. It believes that in this way it can avoid the excessive interest rate in the host country. What is a key disadvantage of using this strategy that may cause Fairfield to be no better off then if it paid the 90 percent interest rate?

    ANSWER: The local currency of the host company will likely depreciate consistently and substantially against the dollar because of the pressure caused by high inflation. Consequently, the cash flows remitted over time will be converted at an unfavorable exchange rate. If the subsidiary was financed with local funds, the interest would be paid on loans prior to remitting funds to the U.S. so that a smaller amount of funds would be affected by the unfavorable exchange rate.

12. Veer Company is a U.S.-based MNC that has most of its operations in Japan. Noticing that the Japanese companies with which it competes use more financial leverage, it has decided to adjust its financial leverage to be in line with theirs. In this way, it should reap more tax advantages with the heavy emphasis on debt. It believes that the market's perception of its risk will remain unchanged, since its financial leverage is still no higher than that of Japanese competitors. Comment on this.

    ANSWER: Japanese corporations can use a higher degree of financial leverage because of their relationships with creditors and the government. The Japanese government may be willing to bail out a Japanese company whose shares are held by Japanese investors and institutions. Yet, it is less likely to bail out a subsidiary of a U.S. corporation. The Japanese subsidiary does not receive the same protection that other Japanese firms receive. Therefore, if this subsidiary attempts to use as much financial leverage, its risk will be higher than that of the Japanese competitors.

13. Pullman Inc., a U.S. firm, has had much profitability, but prefers not to pay out higher dividends because its shareholders desire that the funds be reinvested. It plans for large growth in several less developed countries. Pullman Inc. would like to finance the growth with local debt in the host countries of concern to reduce exposure to country risk. Explain the dilemma faced by Pullman, and possible solutions.

    ANSWER: Pullman Inc. has retained earnings that it must reinvest. Yet, if it uses the retained earnings to finance the growth, it will be more exposed to country risk. Pullman may consider using retained earnings, but allowing for other local institutions in the host countries to invest in their projects as well. In this way, retained earnings are used while tying some local institutions into the project for negotiating power in case the host government imposes severe restrictions on the subsidiaries.

14. Forest Company produces goods in the U.S., Germany, and Australia, and sells the goods in the areas where they are produced. Foreign earnings are periodically remitted to the U.S. parent. As German interest rates have declined to a very low level, Forest Company has decided to finance its German operations with borrowed funds in place of the parent's equity investment. Forest will transfer the U.S. parent's equity investment in the German subsidiary over to its Australian subsidiary. These funds will be used to pay off a floating-rate loan, as Australian interest rates have been high and are rising. Explain the expected effects of these actions on the consolidated capital structure and cost of capital of Forest Company.

    ANSWER: While the capital structure is now more equity intensive in Australia and more debt-intensive in Germany, its consolidated capital structure is not necessarily affected. The MNC's cost of capital may have been reduced, because of the transfer of debt to a country where interest rates were low.

15. Using the information in Question 14, explain how the exposure of Forest Company to exchange rate risk may have changed.

    ANSWER: The exposure of Forest resulting from German operations may have decreased, because the German mark inflows are now more offset by the mark outflows on the German debt. Thus, a smaller amount of earnings is remitted to the U.S. parent. The exposure of Forest resulting from Australian operations may have increased because the Australian dollars to be remitted to the U.S. will increase once the Australian dollar loan is paid off.

16. Explain why the cost of capital for a U.S.-based MNC with a large subsidiary in Brazil is larger than for a U.S.-based MNC in the same industry with a large subsidiary in Japan. Assume the subsidiary operations for each MNC are financed with local debt in the host country.

    ANSWER: The risk-free interest rate is much higher in Brazil than in Japan. In addition, the risk premium on the business in Brazil may be higher than the risk premium on the business in Japan.

Solution to WSJ Case: The Cost of Capital for Subsidiaries in Mexico

1. Explain how the cost of capital for U.S. firms such as GTE Corporation and Underwriters Laboratories, Inc. is affected by expansion into Mexico.

   ANSWER: Interest rates are higher in Mexico, causing the cost of funds to be higher in Mexico than in the U.S. Thus, U.S. firms that borrow funds in Mexico will experience a higher cost of capital on those projects, other things being equal.

2. Explain the logic behind why the Mexican government's reluctance to quickly reduce interest rates? Is there any disadvantage associated with a policy of allowing interest rates to remain high?

   ANSWER: Higher interest rates in Mexico attracts more foreign investment in interest-bearing securities, which can be used to finance development in Mexico. However, such high interest rates may reduce the amount of development in Mexico because financing costs are higher, and some possible projects may not be feasible as a result.

3. How might U.S.-based MNCs expand in Mexico without incurring the high Mexican interest expenses when financing the expansion? Are there any disadvantages associated with this strategy?

   ANSWER: The parents of the MNCs could provide funding for the subsidiaries by investing their own capital. This involves converting dollars to pesos for use in Mexico. In this case, the parent has more at stake. As the Mexican subsidiary remits funds back to the U.S. parent, it will remit larger amounts if it does not finance with pesos because the financing came from the U.S. (no cash outflows are needed to cover interest payments in pesos). Thus, MNC is exposed to a higher level of exchange rate risk.

4. Are there any additional alternatives for the Mexican subsidiary to finance its business itself after it has been well established? How might this strategy affect the subsidiary's capital structure?

   ANSWER: Once the subsidiary has generated earnings, it can retain the earnings and reinvest them to finance future operations. This strategy emphasizes equity financing, and would result in an equity-intensive capital structure for the subsidiary.

Solution to Case Problem: Sabre Computer Corporation

a) The cost of financing is composed of a risk-free rate and a risk premium. The Mexican joint venture would likely have a higher risk-free rate since its inflation rate is usually much higher than Germany's. The risk premium should probably be higher on the German venture because there is more uncertainty about the revenue to be generated from that venture. However, the advantage on the risk premium for the Mexican venture will be overwhelmed by the disadvantage on the risk-free rate. Overall, the cost of financing the Mexican project will be higher.

b) While the Mexican venture will have higher financing costs, the Mexican subsidiary will not necessarily experience lower returns. The high inflation that causes a high risk-free rate also can inflate periodic cash flows. Thus, there may be an offsetting effect. Recall that the price of computers in Mexico is tied to the inflation rate.

c) If the debt is backed by the parent, the creditors may be less inclined to charge a high risk premium.

d) The German subsidiary may have to pay a higher interest rate, because it would not have the implicit backing of the German government. The German-owned companies could possibly receive some government support if they experienced financial problems. Therefore, they may be able to obtain funds at a lower cost.

e) The risk-free interest rate is likely to rise in response to an increase in inflation. Therefore, the cost of funds should rise as well. The cost of production may also rise by a similar degree. The revenue from selling the computers is not tied to German inflation because the computers are sold in other countries. Those countries are not expected to experience inflated economies. Overall, the costs should increase, without any impact on revenue.

Project

Review the annual report of an MNC of your choice. Offer your opinion as to whether this MNC's cost of capital is higher or lower than what it would have been if all of its operations were in the U.S.

This project forces students to apply the theory of how international factors affect the cost of capital to a particular MNC.

Chapter 19

Country Risk Analysis

Lecture Outline

Why Country Risk Analysis is Important

Increased Awareness of Country Risk

Political Risk Factors

"Purchase Homemade Products" Philosophy
Attitude of Public
Attitude of Host Government
Blockage of Fund Transfers
Currency Inconvertibility
War
Bureaucracy

Financial Risk Factors

Types of Country Risk Assessment

Macro-Assessment of Country Risk
Micro-Assessment of Country Risk

Techniques to Assess Country Risk

Checklist Approach
Delphi Approach
Quantitative Analysis
Inspection Visits
Combination of Techniques

Comparing Country Risk Ratings Among Countries

Quantifying Country Risk: An Example

Use of Country Risk Assessment

Incorporating Country Risk in Capital Budgeting
Applications of Country Risk Analysis

Chapter Theme

This chapter attempts to acquaint the student with various forms of risk that must be considered by a multinational corporation. Methods used to assess country risk are defined. It should be emphasized that country risk is often difficult to assess. Furthermore, it may change over time. A firm should incorporate the country risk assessment in its decision of whether to begin (or continue) business in a particular country. If it decides to conduct business there, it should consider the various defenses against a host government takeover (which are listed in the chapter).

Topics to Stimulate Class Discussion

1. How would you rate the country risk of the U.S.? Would your rating change if you lived in a foreign country? Why?

2. Some people say that you cannot separate the political and financial risk of a country. What does this mean?

3. If you use a country risk rating system based on a scoring range of 0 to 100 (100 representing a very safe country), and Country Z earns a score of 77, are you going to invest in that country? Explain your answer.

Answers to End of Chapter Questions

1. List some forms of country risk other than a takeover of a subsidiary by the host government.

   ANSWER: Other forms include the possibility of (1) blocked funds, (2) changing tax laws, (3) public revolt against the firm, (4) war, and (5) a changing attitude of the host government toward the MNC.

2. Identify common political factors for an MNC to consider when assessing country risk. Briefly elaborate on how each factor can affect the risk to the MNC.

   ANSWER: The forms of political risk mentioned in Question 1 can cause reduced demand for the subsidiary's product, or higher taxes, or restrictions of fund transfers.

3. Identify common financial factors for an MNC to consider when assessing country risk. Briefly elaborate on how each factor can affect the risk to the MNC.

   ANSWER: Financial factors include inflation, interest rates, GNP growth, and labor costs. These factors can affect the cost of production, or revenues to the subsidiary.

4. Discuss the use of the foreign investment risk matrix (FIRM) to compare country risk among countries. Why do firms have different acceptable zones when using this matrix?

   ANSWER: The FIRM allows an MNC to compare political and financial risks of various countries. Firms have different acceptable zones because different projects may have different risk tolerance. In addition, firms have different degrees of risk tolerance.

5. Describe the steps involved in assessing country risk once all relevant information has been gathered.

   ANSWER: First, a rating must be assigned to each factor. Then a weight must be assigned. Finally, the weighted ratings can be consolidated to derive an overall political risk and financial risk rating, and (if desired) an overall country risk rating.

6. Describe the possible errors involved in assessing country risk. In other words, explain why country risk analysis is not always accurate.

   ANSWER: Errors occur due to (1) assigning inaccurate ratings to factors, and (2) weighting the importance of the factors improperly.

7. Explain an MNC's strategy of diversifying projects internationally in order to maintain a low level of overall country risk.

   ANSWER: If the MNC can set up foreign projects in countries whose country risk levels are not highly correlated over time, then it reduces the exposure to the possibility of high country risk in all of these areas simultaneously.

8. Once a project is accepted, country risk analysis for the foreign country involved is no longer necessary, assuming that no other proposed projects are being evaluated for that country. Do you agree with this statement? Why or why not?

   ANSWER: Disagree! The country risk must be monitored continuously, since if risk becomes too high, the MNC should divest its subsidiaries in that country.

9. If the potential return is high enough, any degree of country risk can be tolerated. Do you agree with this statement? Why or why not?

   ANSWER: Disagree! If country risk is so high that there is great danger to employees, no expected return is high enough to warrant the project.

10. An MNC has decided to call a well-known country risk consultant to conduct a country risk analysis in a small country in which the MNC plans to develop a large subsidiary. The MNC prefers to hire the consultant since it plans to use its employees for other important corporate functions. The consultant uses a computer program which has assigned weights of importance linked to the various factors. The consultant will evaluate the factors for this small country and insert a rating for each factor into the computer. While the assigned weights to the factors are not adjusted by the computer, the factor ratings are adjusted for each particular country which the consultant assesses. Do you think the MNC should use this consultant? Why or why not?

    ANSWER: No! The consultant's program has not allowed for the weights on importance for each rating to be flexible, depending on the country or firm project of concern. Therefore, the program will definitely assign improper weights to some factors.

11. Explain the micro-assessment of country risk.

    ANSWER: A micro-assessment of country risk assesses risk factors as related to the firm's particular projects.

12. How could a country risk assessment be used to adjust a project's required rate of return? How could such an assessment be used to instead adjust a project's estimated cash flows?

    ANSWER: For countries with a lower country risk rating (implying high risk), the project's required rate of return could be increased (by increasing the discount rate on NPV analysis).

    To adjust cash flows, consider each key form of country risk and re-estimate cash flows if that form of risk occurs. For example, if the host government may block funds temporarily, estimate the NPV of the project if that occurs. Re-estimate the NPV for any other forms of country risk as well. This process results in a distribution of possible NPVs that can be assessed to determine whether a project should be accepted.

13. Explain some methods of reducing exposure to existing country risk, while maintaining the same amount of business within a particular country.

    ANSWER:

    Some of the more common methods to reduce country risk are:

    1. use a short-term horizon
    2. hire local labor
    3. borrow local funds
    4. obtain insurance
    5. create joint ventures

    These and other methods are discussed in the chapter.

14. Why do some subsidiaries maintain a low profile as to where their parent are located?

    ANSWER: Some subsidiaries are concerned that the public in the country where they are located will harm their employees or damage the facilities as an act of protest against the home country of subsidiaries.

15. Do you think that a proper country risk analysis can replace a capital budgeting analysis of a project considered for a foreign country? Explain.

    ANSWER: No. Country risk analysis is not intended to estimate all project cash flows and determine the present value of these cash flows. It is intended to identify forms of country risk, and their potential impact. This is important information for capital budgeting but is not a substitute for capital budgeting.

16. NYU Corporation considered establishing a subsidiary in Zenland; it performed a country risk analysis to help make the decision. It first retrieved a country risk analysis performed about one year earlier, when it had planned to begin a major exporting business to Zenland farms. Then it updated the analysis by incorporating all current information on the key variables that were used in that analysis, such as Zenland's willingness to accept exports, its existing quotas, and existing tariff laws. Is this country risk analysis adequate? Explain.

    ANSWER: No. A country risk analysis used for an exporting project incorporates different information than a country risk analysis used to assess the feasibility of establishing a subsidiary.

17. In the early 1990s, MNCs such as Alcoa DuPont, Heinz, and IBM donated products and technology to foreign countries where they have subsidiaries. How could these actions reduce some forms of country risk?

    ANSWER: When MNCs donate products and/or technology to foreign countries where they have subsidiaries, they may receive more favorable treatment from the consumers in that country, their employees that work for their subsidiaries, and the host governments.

18. A U.S. firm plans a project in the United Kingdom, in which it would lease space for one year in a shopping mall to sell expensive clothes manufactured in the U.S. The project would end in one year, when all earnings would be remitted to the U.S. firm. Assume no additional corporate taxes are incurred beyond those imposed by the British government. Since the firm would rent space, it would not have any long-term assets in the United Kingdom, and expects the salvage (terminal) value of the project to be about zero.

    Assume that the project's required rate of return is 18 percent. Also assume that the initial outlay required by the parent to fill the store with clothes is $200,000. The pre-tax earnings are expected to the £300,000 at the end of one year. The British pound is expected to be worth $1.60 at the end of one year, when the after-tax earnings are converted to dollars and remitted to the U.S. The following forms of country risk must be considered:

    - The British economy may weaken (probability = 30%), which would cause the expected pre-tax earnings to be £200,000.

    - The British corporate tax rate on income earned by U.S. firms may increase from 40% to 50% (probability = 20%).

    These two forms of country risk are indpendent. Calculate the expected value of the project's net present value (NPV) and determine the probability that the project will have a negative NPV.

    ANSWER: Sensitivity analysis can be used to measure the net present value under each possible scenario, as shown in the attached exhibit. There are four possible scenarios. The most favorable scenario is a strong British economy and a relatively low (40%) British tax rate. This scenario results in after-tax dollar earnings of $288,000 in one year. The NPV is determined by obtaining the present value of these earnings (discounted at the required rate of return of 18%) and subtracting the initial outlay of $200,000. The NPV resulting from the most favorable scenario is $44,068. The joint probability of a strong British economy and the 40% tax rate is the product of the probabilities of these two situations (assuming that the situations are independent). Given a 70 percent probability for the strong British economy and an 80 percent probability for the 40% British tax rate, the joint probability is (70%) x (80%) = 56%.

The NPV and joint probability for each of the other three scenarios are also estimated in the exhibit, following the same process as discussed above. The expected value of the project's NPV can be determined as the sum of the products of each scenario's NPV and joint probability, as shown below:

E(NPV) = ($44,068) (56%) + ($3,390) (14%) + (-$37,288) (24%) + (-$64,407) (6%)

= ($24,678) + ($475) + (-$8,949) + (-$3,864)

= $12,340

The expected net present value of the project is positive. Yet, the NPV is expected to be negative for two of the four possible scenarios that could occur. Since the joint probabilities of these two scenarios add up to 30 percent, this implies that there is a 30 percent chance that the project will result in a negative NPV.

The example was simplified in that the project has a planned life of only one year, and there was no terminal value for the project. However, a more complicated example could be analyzed by using spreadsheet software to conduct the sensitivity analysis. The analyst would need to develop some "compute" statements that lead to an estimate of NPV. Each scenario causes a change in one or more of the numbers to be input when estimating the NPV.

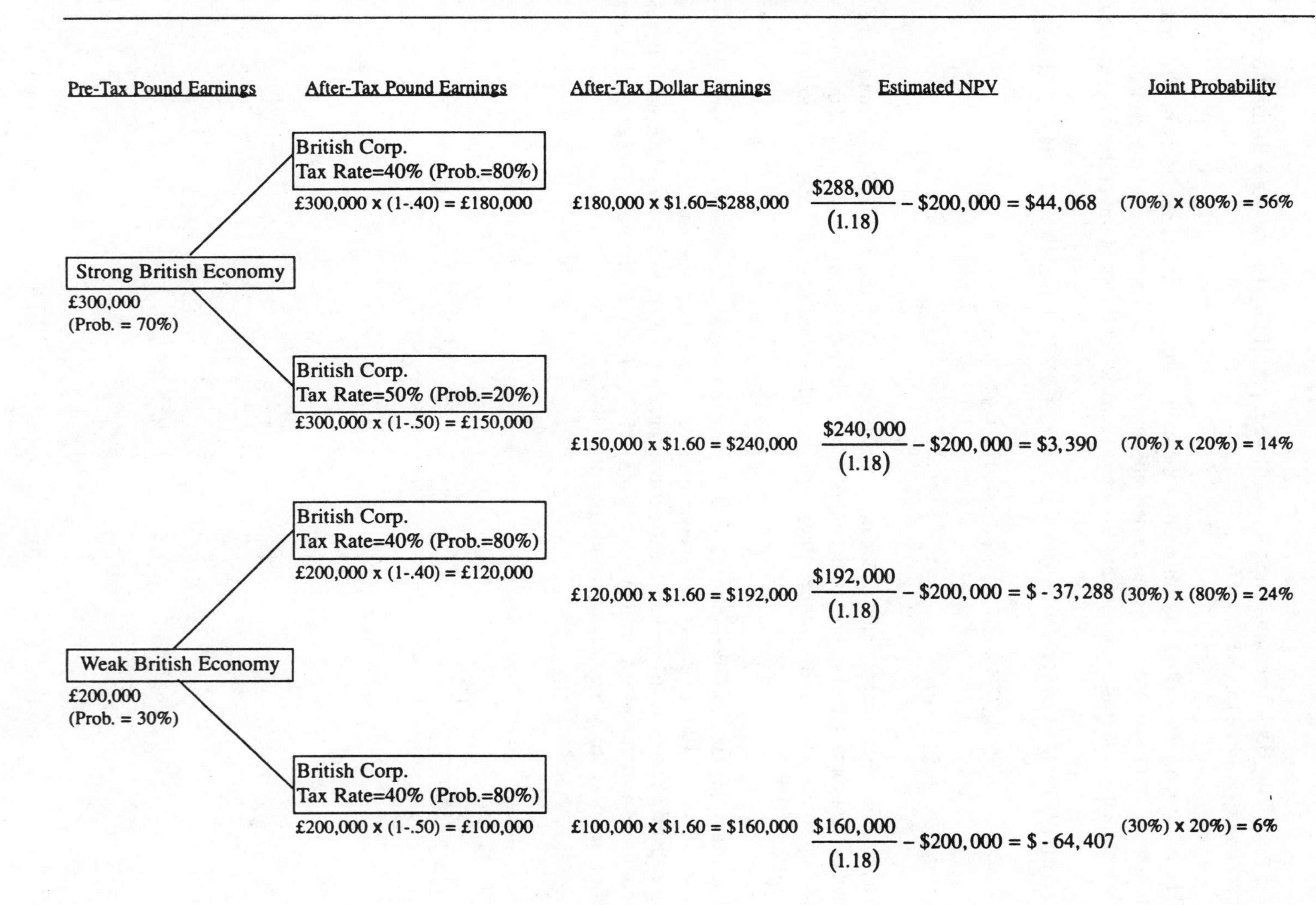
EXHIBIT FOR THE ANSWER TO QUESTION 18
Pre-Tax Pound Earnings
After-Tax Pound Earnings
After-Tax Dollar Earnings
Estimated NPV
Joint Probability
British Corp.
Tax Rate=40% (Prob.=80%)
£300,000 x (1-.40) = £180,000
£180,000 x $1.60=$288,000
$288,000 / (1.18) - $200,000 = $44,068
(70%) x (80%) = 56%
Strong British Economy
£300,000
(Prob. = 70%)
British Corp.
Tax Rate=50% (Prob.=20%)
£300,000 x (1-.50) = £150,000
£150,000 x $1.60 = $240,000
$240,000 / (1.18) - $200,000 = $3,390
(70%) x (20%) = 14%
British Corp.
Tax Rate=40% (Prob.=80%)
£200,000 x (1-.40) = £120,000
£120,000 x $1.60 = $192,000
$192,000 / (1.18) - $200,000 = $ - 37,288
(30%) x (80%) = 24%
Weak British Economy
£200,000
(Prob. = 30%)
British Corp.
Tax Rate=40% (Prob.=80%)
£200,000 x (1-.50) = £100,000
£100,000 x $1.60 = $160,000
$160,000 / (1.18) - $200,000 = $ - 64,407
(30%) x 20%) = 6%

19. Explain how capital budgeting analysis would need to be adjusted for Question 18 if there were three possible outcomes for the British pound along with the possible outcomes for the British economy and corporate tax rate.

    ANSWER: A simplification of the example provided is that only one expectation for the British pound's value was assumed. In reality, the MNC may create a probability distribution for the pound's value one year from now. If the MNC used three possible outcomes for the pound, this would expand the number of possible scenarios. For each of the four scenarios in Question 18, there would now be three possible outcomes for the pound's value, resulting in a total of 12 possible scenarios.

Solution to WSJ Case: Country Risk in China

1. Explain why China's tightening of restrictions on currency convertibility can make some projects of U.S.-based MNCs unfeasible.

   ANSWER: The projects could have been feasible when assuming that the profits in yuan (the Chinese currency) were remitted to the parent. The new Chinese policy restricts remittances, which forces the earnings in China to be reinvested in China.

2. Explain how a U.S.-based MNC could have attempted to account for this type of country risk (tighter restrictions on currency convertibility), even if it was not sure that China would tighten restrictions.

   ANSWER: The MNC could have used sensitivity analysis to determine how the forecasted cash flows of the Chinese project would be adjusted when accounting for tighter restrictions on currency convertibility. For example, it could have determined the NPV of the Chinese project assuming that earnings would have to remain in China for various time horizons. MNCs cannot predict every government policy, but since China's currency convertibility system was not clearly established, it would be natural for MNCs to at least account for such a possibility. If the possible scenario of tighter restrictions had a severe impact on a project's NPV, the MNC could have decided not to implement the project.

3. It is sometimes argued that projects considered for China could be assessed using a higher discount rate to capture the possibility of new government policies, in order to account for this risk when estimating a project's NPV. Would this method properly distinguish between projects in China that will be worthwhile and those that will not?

ANSWER: This method will not be very effective because it does not directly measure the impact of the country risk of concern. If China imposes restrictions on currency convertibility and the MNC has no other reasonable use of the funds that are restricted in China, it may be devastated by the project. Yet, adding a few percentage points to a discount rate when assessing the NPV of the project may suggest that the project is worthwhile. There may be some MNCs that are affected less by the restrictions because they may be able to more capably reinvest the earnings in China. Thus, the best way to account for the country risk in the NPV estimation is to re-estimate the NPV based on scenarios that reflect the country risk. In this way, the firm has directly accounted for the impact of country risk.

Solution to Case Problem: King, Incorporated

a) There are several government-related issues to consider. Some of these issues are listed below:

(1) Will Bulgaria's government allow the firm to establish the firm? Or will it require that King Inc. participate in a joint venture with the government? This issue is relevant because it could affect the risk and return of the project.

(2) What is the corporate tax rate to be charged on profits earned by King Inc. in Bulgaria?

(3) What is the withholding tax rate to be imposed on profits remitted to the parent of King Inc.?

(4) What are Bulgaria's plans regarding privatization? If Bulgaria encourages privatization, this may allow for other competitors to compete against King Inc.

(5) Will Bulgaria require King Inc. to incur any additional expenses for environmental reasons? In past years, Eastern Bloc countries have not focused on environmental problems, but this issue is now receiving more attention.

(6) What is the government's monetary and fiscal policy? Any effect that these policies have on the economy could influence the demand for the food products to be marketed by King Inc.

(7) What are the political relations between Bulgaria and other Eastern Bloc countries? Will King Inc. be able to transport the products produced in Bulgaria to other countries without incurring any taxes or bureaucratic inconveniences?

(8) Would King Inc. be able to sell the subsidiary at market value if it desired to divest the project in the future? Or would the selling price be dictated by the government?

b) The demand could be affected by:

(1) The economies of the various Eastern Bloc countries (not just Bulgaria) that are targeted for this project; all the factors that affect economic conditions such as government policies, interest rates, etc. need to be assessed for each of these countries.

(2) Consumer preferences for the food products; King Inc. must assess consumer preferences in these countries.

c) The cost of production could be affected as follows:

(1) Changes in wage rates in Bulgaria would affect the labor cost incurred by King Inc.

(2) Changes in inflation could affect the cost of obtaining the necessary ingredients for production.

(3) The cost of leasing the plant may be dictated by the government or be influenced by inflation.

Project

Review the annual report of an MNC of your choice. Summarize the forms of country risk that the MNC is exposed to according to the report.

This project will allow students to realize that country risk is a realistic concern of MNCs, as MNCs typically discuss the types of country risk they are exposed to in the annual report.

Chapter 20

Long-Term Financing

Lecture Outline

Long-Term Financing Decision
  Financing with a Stable Currency
  Financing with a Strong Currency
  Financing with a Weak Currency

Actual Bond Financing Costs

Comparing Bond Denomination Alternatives
  Use of Exchange Rate Probabilities
  Use of Simulation

Financing with Floating-Rate Eurobonds

Exchange Rate Risk of Foreign Bonds
  Hedging Exchange Rate Risk

Long-Term Financing in Multiple Currencies
  Currency Cocktail Bonds

Using Swaps to Hedge Financing Costs
  Interest Rate Swaps
  Currency Swaps

Chapter Theme

This chapter introduces the long-term sources of funds available to MNCs. Should the MNC choose bonds as a medium to attract long-term funds, a currency for denomination must be chosen. This is a critical decision for the MNC. While there is no clear-cut solution, this chapter illustrates how such a problem can be analyzed. A suggested method of presenting this analysis is to run through an example under assumed exchange rates. Then stress that future exchange rates are not known with certainty. Therefore, the firm should consider the possible costs of financing under a variety of exchange rate scenarios.

Topics to Stimulate Class Discussion

1. Why would U.S. firms consider issuing bonds denominated in a foreign currency?

2. What are the desirable characteristics related to a currency's interest rate (high or low) and value (strong or weak) that would make the currency attractive from a borrower's perspective? How about from an investor's perspective?

Answers to End of Chapter Questions

1. What factors should be considered by a U.S. firm which plans to issue a floating rate Eurobond?

   ANSWER: A U.S. firm should consider the interest rate for each possible currency as well as forecasts of the exchange rate relative to the firm's home currency. The firm should also determine whether it has future cash inflows in any foreign currencies that could denominate the bond. Finally, the firm should forecast the future path of the coupon rate.

2. What is the advantage of using simulation to assess the bond financing position?

   ANSWER: Unlike point forecasts, simulation provides a distribution of possible outcomes. Thus, the firm can determine the probability that a particular Eurobond will be a less expensive source of funds than a locally issued bond.

3. Explain the difference in the cost of financing with foreign currencies during the 1981-1984 (strong dollar) period, and the 1990-1993 (weak dollar) period for a U.S. firm.

ANSWER: The cost of financing was high in the 1976-1980 period and in the 1985-1988 period, since the dollar weakened against foreign currencies. However, the cost of financing was low in the 1981-84 period because the dollar strengthened in this period.

4. Explain how a U.S.-based MNC issuing bonds denominated in German marks may be able to offset a portion of this exchange rate risk.

   ANSWER: It may offset some exchange rate risk if it has cash inflows in marks. These marks could be used to make coupon payments.

5. Is the risk of issuing a floating rate Eurobond higher or lower than the risk of issuing a fixed rate Eurobond? Explain.

   ANSWER: The risk from issuing a floatingrate Eurobond is that the interest rate may rise over time. The risk from issuing a fixed rate Eurobond is that the firm is obligated to pay that coupon rate even if interest rates decline. Some firms may feel that a fixed-rate Eurobond is less risky since at least they know with certainty the coupon rate they must pay in the future. This question is somewhat open-ended.

6. Columbia Corporation is a U.S. company with no foreign- currency cash flows. It plans to either issue (1) a bond denominated in German marks with a fixed interest rate or (2) a bond denominated in U.S. dollars with a floating interest rate. It estimates its periodic dollar cash flows for each bond. Which bond do you think would have greater uncertainty surrounding these future dollar cash flows? Explain.

   ANSWER: Exchange rates are generally more volatile than interest rates over time. Therefore the dollar payments made on mark-denominated bonds would likely be more uncertain than the dollar payments made on floating-rate bonds denominated in dollars. Also, the principal payment is subject to exchange rate risk, but not to interest rate risk.

7. Why would a U.S. firm consider issuing bonds denominated in multiple currencies?

   ANSWER: The firm may issue bonds in multiple currencies to reduce exchange rate risk. This is especially possible when the currencies used to denominate bonds are not highly correlated.

8. Why is the ECU bond popular?

   ANSWER: The ECU bond reflects the currency denomination of several European currencies. European firms like it since the exchange rate of the ECU relative to their home currency is relatively stable.

9. Assume you are assessing the potential cost of financing with Eurobonds denominated in a foreign currency. What is the most critical point in time at which the exchange rate will have the greatest impact?

   ANSWER: The most critical time is maturity, since the principal will be paid back at that time.

10. How would an investing firm differ from a borrowing firm in the features (i.e., interest rate and currency's future exchange rates) it would prefer a floating rate Eurobond to exhibit?

    ANSWER: An investing firm prefers a bond denominated in a currency that is expected to appreciate, and with an interest rate that is high and expected to increase. A borrowing firm prefers a bond denominated in a currency that is expected to depreciate, and with an interest rate that is low, and expected to decrease.

11. Assume that Seminole Inc. considers issuing a mark-denominated bond at its present coupon rate of 7 percent, even though it has no incoming mark cash flows to cover the bond payments. It is attracted to the low financing rate, since dollar bonds issued in the United States would have a coupon rate of 12 percent. Assume that either type of bond would have a four-year maturity and could be issued at par value. Seminole needs to borrow $10 million. Therefore, it will either issue dollar bonds with a par value of $10 million or mark bonds with a par value of DM20 million. The spot rate of the mark is $.50. Seminole has forecasted the mark's value at the end of each of the next four years, when coupon payments are to be paid:

End of Year	Exchange Rate of DM
1	$.52
2	.56
3	.58
4	.53

Determine the expected annual cost of financing with marks. Should Seminole Corporation issue bonds denominated in dollars or marks? Explain.

ANSWER:

	End of Year:			
	1	2	3	4
DM payment	DM1,400,000	DM1,400,000	DM1,400,000	DM21,400,000
Exchange rate	$.52	$.56	$.58	$.53
$ Payment	$728,000	$784,000	$812,000	$11,342,000

The annual cost of financing with DM is determined as the discount rate that equates the dollar payments resulting from payments on the mark-denominated bond to the amount of dollars borrowed. Using a calculator, this discount rate is 8.97%. Thus, the expected annual cost of financing with a mark-denominated bond is 8.97%, which is less than the 12% cost of financing with U.S. dollars. However, there is some uncertainty associated with mark-financing. Seminole, Inc. must weigh the expected savings from financing in marks with the uncertainty associated with such financing.

12. Assume that Hurricane Inc. is a U.S. company that exports products to Great Britain, invoiced in dollars. It also exports products to Germany, invoiced in dollars. It presently has no cash outflows in foreign currencies, and it plans to issue bonds in the near future. It could likely issue bonds at par value in (1) dollars with a coupon rate of 12 percent, (2) marks with a coupon rate of 9 percent, or (3) in pounds with a coupon rate of 15 percent. It expects that the mark and pound will strengthen over time. How could Hurricane revise its invoicing policy and make its bond denomination decision to achieve low financing costs without excessive exposure to exchange rate fluctuations?

    ANSWER: Hurricane could invoice goods exported to Germany in marks instead of dollars. Thus, it would now have mark inflows that could be used to make coupon payments on mark-denominated bonds that it could issue. This strategy allows to achieve a cost of financing of 9 percent, which is lower than the cost of other financing alternatives. To the extent that the mark inflows can cover bond payments, this strategy is not exposed to exchange rate risk.

Solution to WSJ Case: EuroDisney's Financing Dilemma

1. When bonds are issued across countries, and a separate prospectus is needed per country, the provisions may be inconsistent. Explain how the provisions of EuroDisney's convertible bonds were more complicated because of the discrepancies in the prospectuses.

ANSWER: The prospectus written in English stated that the provisions of the bonds can only be changed if all bondholders agree. The French version stated that a change in the provisions of the bonds requires a majority vote among bondholders.

2. Who is responsible to incur the losses associated with EuroDisney's financial problems? The creditors? Walt Disney (the parent)? Explain the controversy and offer your opinion.

   ANSWER: The creditors believe that Walt Disney (the parent) is responsible. Yet, Walt Disney has only limited ties to EuroDisney, and could argue that it does not need to back EuroDisney, which places the financial burden on the creditors.

3. The case of EuroDisney illustrates how disagreements can occur among creditors about provisions of the credit (bonds, loans) and also between the parent of a firm and the creditors. Why are these disagreements more likely for MNCs than for purely domestic firms? Is there a solution to avoid such disagreements?

   ANSWER: The disagreements are more likely for MNCs because of the differences among prospectuses distributed across countries. They are also because of the possible limited financial support provided by the parent to a foreign subsidiary, which can cause the foreign subsidiary to be legally separated from the parent. This complicates the issue of whether the parent backs the subsidiary.

   One solution is to develop one homogenous international language of law so that discrepancies regarding provisions of credit and whether the parent is responsible for a foreign subsidiary can be avoided.

Solution to Case Problem: Devil VCR Corporation

a) It could issue mark-denominated bonds, and convert the proceeds into British pounds to cover the new investment in the facility. Since 1 pound = DM4, it would need to issue DM80 million to achieve 20 million pounds. Over time, the marks received from export sales can be used to repay the coupon payments of DM8.8 million (11% of DM80 million) per year. Some of the additional marks received can be converted to pounds at the forward rate to cover the annual production expenses (2 million pounds per year), while the remaining marks can be remitted to the U.S. at the forward rate. These annual transactions would have been agreed upon at the inception of the exporting program to lock in the applicable forward rate for each year.

b) Based on the approach described in Part (a), the mark cash flows would be distributed as follows:

Year	Thousands of Marks Received	Thousands of Marks Needed to Cover Bond Payment	Thousands of Marks Converted to 2 Million Pounds at Appropriate Forward Rate to Pay Annual Expenses	Thousands of Marks Converted to Dollars at Appropriate Forward Rate as Remitted Earnings	Thousands of Dollars Received by Parent
1	DM25,000	DM8,800	DM7,880	DM8,320	$4,118.4
2	DM25,000	DM8,800	DM7,640	DM8,560	$4,237.2
3	DM25,000	DM8,800	DM7,600	DM8,600	$4,214.0
4	DM25,000	DM8,800	DM7,480	DM8,720	$4,272.8
5	DM25,000	DM8,800	DM7,320	DM8,880	$4,306.8

c. While Devil Corp. can attempt to hedge all currency transactions, it is not sure of the actual amounts for some transactions. For example, the annual sales of DM$25 million may be wrong. In addition, the annual expenses of 2 million pounds may be wrong. Consider the end of Year 1, when it would have been obligated to exchange DM8.32 million for dollars. If its sales were below expectations, it would need to purchase some marks in the spot market at the end of Year 1 just to have enough marks to complete its forward transaction.

Project

1. Review the annual report of an MNC of your choice. Did the MNC issue any bonds denominated in foreign currencies? Does the MNC generate cash flows in that currency that could be used to cover the coupon payments? (Use your opinion if this is not clear from the annual report.) Summarize any statements made regarding the MNC's decision to finance with U.S. dollars versus foreign currencies.

   This project is intended to make students realize that many U.S.-based MNCs obtain some of their funds by issuing bonds denominated in foreign currencies. These MNCs frequently have cash inflows in some or all of the currencies that are used to denominate the bonds, and therefore may somewhat offset the exchange rate risk resulting from issuing the bonds.

Chapter 21

Global Strategic Planning

Lecture Outline

International Tax Characteristics
- Corporate Income Tax
- Withholding Taxes
- Provision for Carrybacks and Carryforwards
- Tax Treaties
- Tax Credits

Use of Transfer Pricing to Reduce Taxes

Influence of Tax Laws on MNC Policies
- Short-Term Financing
- Working Capital Management
- Capital Structure Policy
- Capital Budgeting

Multinational Corporate Policy
- Agency Costs of International Business
- Subsidiary Versus Centralized Management
- Role of Subsidiary Due to Centralization
- Conflict of Interests Among Corporate Departments
- Accounting and Control

Chapter Theme

This chapter provides just enough information on international taxation to make students dangerous. The emphasis should be placed not on memorizing tax laws, but on the importance of tax differentials in the final corporate policy decisions.

In addition, the conflict of interests between individual subsidiaries and centralized management should be emphasized, since this is a common problem for many firms.

Topics to Stimulate Class Discussion

1. If you are considering the establishment of a plant in various countries, what tax characteristics must be examined?

2. Based on information in this chapter as well as in other chapters, which area of business (accounting, finance, management, and marketing) is most critical to the MNC's success. (NOTE: There is no solution to this question, but it forces students to think of the roles each department has in an MNC).

Answers to End of Chapter Questions

1. Discuss how the importance of tax planning at MNCs would change if tax rules were identical among all countries and did not change over time. (Your answer should imply why tax planning is critical to the MNC in reality.)

   ANSWER: Tax planning would not be necessary since it would have no impact.

2. What corporate decisions can be affected when incorporating taxes into the decision? Briefly elaborate on how each decision is affected by taxes.

   ANSWER: First, short-term financing can be affected since the MNC may attempt to increase interest payment liabilities in high-tax countries in favor of lower taxes elsewhere. Second, cash management may be affected since excess cash in high-tax countries may be used to provide low interest loans to subsidiaries in other countries. Capital structure and capital budgeting decisions are also affected since the feasibility of sources of funds and locations for direct foreign investment is affected by tax differences among alternatives.

3. In what general ways do countries differ with regard to their tax systems?

   ANSWER: Countries can differ in their corporate taxes, withholding taxes, and provision for carrybacks and carryforwards.

4. How can tax treaties between countries be beneficial to MNCs?

   ANSWER: Tax treaties will often allow countries to give tax breaks to firms of other countries within the treaty.

5. Explain how transfer pricing can be used to reduce the MNC's overall tax liability.

   ANSWER: The MNC could set up pricing (within provisions set forth by the governments) to impose high prices or interest costs on goods or funds transferred to those subsidiaries that are in high-tax countries.

6. Briefly describe the role of tax planning by the MNC. What are its two key functions?

   ANSWER: Tax planning involves (1) knowing the tax laws of each country and (2) using the tax laws to analyze the feasibility of alternative policies.

7. Describe the possible conflict of interests between a subsidiary and centralized management.

   ANSWER: If centralized management makes decisions to benefit the overall MNC, they may hamper one subsidiary at the expense of another (transfer pricing as an example). The subsidiary adversely affected by the policy may disapprove the MNC's strategy, thereby creating a conflict.

8. How could an MNC avoid a conflict of interests between a subsidiary and centralized management?

   ANSWER: The MNC using centralized management could reward subsidiaries not by profit level but by other means. Profits can be distorted at the subsidiary level, so any distortion must be measured and accounted for.

9. Explain why a conflict of interests can often arise between corporate departments at an MNC.

   ANSWER: A conflict of interest between corporate departments occurs because each department has its own objectives. The production department may prefer a minimal inventory but this doesn't accommodate a loose credit policy (where sales may be erratic).

10. How could an MNC avoid conflicts of interests between the various corporate departments at an MNC.

 ANSWER: To avoid conflicts, the MNC should not impose individual objectives on each department. All departments should work together, since decisions of one department can affect another's importance.

Solution to WSJ Case: International Reorganization of AT&T

1. Why could AT&T benefit from its international reorganization?

 ANSWER: The reorganization gives more power to the executives overseas, so that these executives can make decisions that are based on country-specific conditions. Decisions can be made more quickly because they will not require approval from the parent.

2. Why do you think AT&T consolidated its overseas facilities?

 ANSWER: Consolidation may remove redundant operations and increase efficiency.

3. Why would AT&T grant a special autonomy to the China unit, independent of the Asian region?

 ANSWER: China is a special case because of the growth potential and its unique political characteristics. Thus, the management style for the China unit may not follow the general style used in other Asian countries.

Solution to Case Problem: Redwing Technology Company

a) The earnings performance translated in dollars is misleading because they are distorted by varying exchange rates. The actual earnings in each local currency in each subsidiary should be assessed, since the subsidiary has no control over the exchange rate used for translation. The translation causes earnings to be overstated when the local currency is strong (against the dollar) and understated when the local currency is weak. The following table shows the earnings of each subsidiary when measured in the local currency. Based on this table, the Canadian subsidiary experienced a consistent growth in earnings over time, averaging about a 14 percent increase per year. Conversely, the French subsidiary experienced consistent declines in earnings over time, with an average annual earnings growth rate of -4.38%. The Japanese subsidiary experienced a decline in earnings in all but one year, and its average annual earnings growth rate was -1.03%. When measured in this way, the executive in charge of the Canadian subsidiary appears to have achieved the best performance. The results are much different when earnings are measured in U.S. dollars for all subsidiaries. The Canadian performance would not be as high while the French and Japanese performance would be higher. Yet, the chief executives of the respective subsidiaries cannot control the translated exchange rate. It can be argued that they should not be rewarded or penalized because of the translation effect caused by a volatile exchange rate (although there could be exceptions when they are personally responsible for hedging any remitted earnings or any inflows of funds coming from other countries).

EARNINGS (IN MILLIONS) DENOMINATED IN THE LOCAL CURRENCY

Years Ago	Canada	Annual Percentage Increase	France	Annual Percentage Increase	Japan	Annual Percentage Increase
5	C$16.80	-	FF210.00	-	Y7,500.00	-
4	19.92	18.57%	200.00	-4.76%	7,441.86	-.77%
3	22.68	13.85	187.50	-6.25	7,608.69	2.24
2	25.92	14.28	180.00	-3.74	7,454.54	-2.03
1	28.44	9.72	175.00	-2.78	7,187.50	-3.58

b) Based on its high annual growth rate of earnings, the Canadian subsidiary would likely deserve a cash infusion from the parent to push for additional growth. The parent would probably feel that its funds are more likely to generate decent returns there than in other countries.

c) Even if the earnings are remitted, Canada would still be the best bet. There was an assumption that last year's exchange rate would be a reasonable guess for exchange rates in future years for each currency. This means that the parent will invest funds at the same exchange rate as the rate in which subsidiary earnings will be converted back to dollars in the future, for each subsidiary. Thus, no subsidiary is expected to have an exchange rate advantage over the others.

d) The earnings of the Canadian and French subsidiaries only appear to be highly correlated when translated in U.S. dollars. Their earnings in local currencies were not highly correlated. Thus, some diversification benefits would be lost if the Canadian subsidiary was sold (not to mention that it is the best-performing subsidiary), or if the French subsidiary was sold.

Project

1. Review the annual report of an MNC of your choice. Based on the annual report, does it appear that the decision making is centralized or decentralized? Elaborate.

   This project gives a student experience in assessing managerial policies of an MNC. MNCs may not precisely state whether their decision making is decentralized or centralized, but the discussion about its operations may offer an indication. Some of an MNC's policies may be centralized while others are decentralized.

Integrative Problem for Part V

Long-Term Asset and Liability Management

Gandor Company is a U.S. firm that is considering a joint venture with a Chinese firm to produce and sell video cassettes. Gandor will invest $12 million in this project, which will help to finance the Chinese firm's production. For each of the first three years, 50 percent of the total profits will be distributed to the Chinese firm, while the remaining 50 percent will be converted to dollars to be sent to the U.S. The Chinese government intends to impose a 20 percent income tax on the profits distributed to Gandor. The Chinese government has guaranteed that the after-tax profits (denominated in renminbi, the Chinese currency) can be converted to U.S. dollars at an exchange rate of RM 1 = $.20 per unit and sent to Gandor Company each year. At the present time, there is no withholding tax imposed on profits to be sent to the U.S. as a result of joint ventures in China. Assume that even after considering the taxes paid in China, there is an additional 10 percent tax imposed by the U.S. government on profits received by Gandor Company. After the first three years, all profits earned are allocated to the Chinese firm.

The expected total profits resulting from the joint venture per year are as follows:

Year	Total Profits from Joint Venture (in renminbi, RM)
1	RM60 million
2	RM80 million
3	RM100 million

Gandor's average cost of debt is 13,8 percent before taxes. Its average cost of equity is 18 percent. Assume the corporate income tax rate imposed on Gandor is normally 30 percent. Gandor uses a capital structure composed of 60 percent debt and 40 percent equity. Gandor automatically adds 4 percentage points to its cost of capital when deriving its required rate of return on international joint ventures. While this project has particular forms of country risk that are unique, Gandor plans to account for these forms of risk within its estimation of cash flows.

There are two forms of country risk that Gandor is concerned about. First, there is the risk that the Chinese government will increase the corporate income tax rate from 20 percent to 40 percent (20 percent probability). If this occurs, additional tax credits will be allowed, resulting in no U.S. taxes on the profits from this joint venture. Second, there is the risk that the Chinese government will impose a withholding tax of 10 percent on the profits that are sent to the U.S. (20 percent probability). In this case, additional tax credits will not be allowed, and Gandor will still be subject to a 10 percent U.S. tax on profits received from China. Assume the two types of country risk are mutually exclusive. This is, the Chinese government will only adjust one of its tax guidelines (the income tax or the withholding tax), if any.

1. Determine Gandor's cost of capital. Also determine Gandor's required rate of return for the joint venture in China.

   ANSWER: Gandor's weighted average cost of capital is:

$$k_c = \left(\frac{D}{D+E}\right)k_d(1-t) + \left(\frac{E}{D+E}\right)k_e$$

$$= (60\%)(13.8\%)(70\%) + (40\%)(18\%)$$

$$= 5.8\% + 7.2\%$$

$$= 13\%$$

Since Gandor applied a premium of 4 percentage points to its cost of capital for joint ventures in foreign countries, its required rate of return on this joint venture is 17 percent. Gandor also attempts to explicitly capture some types of country risk in the estimated cash flows, as explained shortly.

2. Determine the probability distribution of Gandor's net present values for the joint venture.

   ANSWER: The capital budgeting analyses are shown for the three scenarios:

Scenario 1	Based on original assumptions.
Scenario 2	Based on an increase in the corporate income tax by the Chinese government.
Scenario 3	Based on the imposition of a withholding tax by the Chinese government.

SCENARIO 1: BASED ON ORIGINAL ASSUMPTIONS
(Probability = 60%)

	Year 0	Year 1	Year 2	Year 3
Total Profits (in RM)		RM60,000,000	RM80,000,000	RM100,000,000
Profits allocated to Gandor Co. (50% of total)		RM 30,000,000	RM 40,000,000	RM 150,000,000
Corporate income taxes imposed by Chinese Government (20%)		RM 6,000,000	RM 8,000,000	RM 10,000,000
Profits to Gandor after paying corporate income taxes in China		RM 24,000,000	RM 32,000,.000	RM 40,000,000
Gandor's dollar profits received from China (based on exchange rate of RM 1 = $.20)		$4,800,000	$6,400,000	$8,000,000
U.S. taxes paid (10%)		$480,000	$640,000	$8,000,000
Cash flows from joint venture		$4,320,000	$5,760,000	$7,200,000
PV of cash flows (using a 17% discount rate)		$3,692,308	$4,207,758	$4,495,468
Initial Investment	$12,000,000			
Cumulative NPV of cash flows		-$8,307,692	-$4,099,934	$395,534

SCENARIO 2: BASED ON INCREASE IN CORPORATE INCOME TAX BY CHINESE GOVERNMENT
(Probability = 20%)

	Year 0	Year 1	Year 2	Year 3
Total Profits (in RM)		RM60,000,000	RM80,000,000	RM100,000,000
Profits allocated to Gandor Co. (50% of total)		RM 30,000,000	RM 40,000,000	RM 50,000,000
Corporate income taxes imposed by Chinese Government (40%)		RM 12,000,000	RM 16,000,000	RM 20,000,000
Profits to Gandor after paying corporate income taxes in China		RM 18,000,000	RM 24,000,.000	RM 30,000,000
Gandor's dollar profits received from China (based on exchange rate of RM 1 = $.20)		$3,600,000	$4,800,000	$6,000,000
U.S. taxes paid (0%)		—	—	—
Cash flows from joint venture		$3,600,000	$4,800,000	$6,000,000
PV of cash flows (using a 17% discount rate)		$3,076,923	$3,506,465	$3,746,223
Initial Investment	$12,000,000			
Cumulative NPV of cash flows		-$8,923,077	-$5,416,612	-$1,670,389

SCENARIO 3: IMPOSITION OF A WITHHOLDING TAX BY CHINESE GOVERNMENT
(Probability = 20%)

	Year 0	Year 1	Year 2	Year 3
Total Profits (in RM)		RM60,000,000	RM80,000,000	RM100,000,000
Profits allocated to Gandor Co. (50% of total)		RM30,000,000	RM40,000,000	RM50,000,000
Corporate income taxes imposed by Chinese Government (20%)		RM6,000,000	RM8,000,000	RM10,000,000
Profits to Gandor after paying corporate income taxes in China		RM24,000,000	RM32,000,.000	RM40,000,000
Withholding tax (10%)		RM2,400,000	RM3,200,000	RM4,000,000
Profits to be sent to the U.S.		RM21,600,000	RM28,800,000	RM36,000,000
Gandor's dollar profits received from China (based on exchange rate of RM 1 = $.20)		$4,320,000	$5,760,000	$7,200,000
U.S. taxes paid (10%)		$432,000	$576,000	$7,200,000
Cash flows from joint venture		$3,888,000	$5,184,000	$6,480,000
PV of cash flows (using a 17% discount rate)		$3,323,077	$3,786,982	$4,045,921
Initial Investment	$12,000,000			
Cumulative NPV of cash flows		-$8,676,923	-$4,889,941	-$844,020

SUMMARY OF SCENARIOS

Scenario	NPV for this scenario	Probability that this scenario will occur
Original scenario	$ 395,534	60%
Increase in corporate income tax by Chinese Government	-$1,670,389	20%
Imposition of withholding tax by Chinese Government	-$844,020	20%

Expected value of NPV = 60% ($395,534) + 20% (-$1,670,389) + 20% (-$844,020)

= $237,320 + (-$334,078) + (-$168,804)

= -$265,562

3. Would you recommend that Gandor participate in the joint venture? Explain.

   ANSWER: The expected value of the NPV is negative. In addition, there is a 40 percent chance that the joint venture will have a negative NPV for Gandor. Thus, the project does not appear to be feasible for Gandor.

4. What do you think would be the key underlying factor that would have the most influence on the profits earned in China as a result of the joint venture?

   ANSWER: The key influential factor in this joint venture is probably the future economic conditions in China, which affects the demand for video cassettes, and therefore affects profits to be received. Since economic conditions in most countries (especially those that are not fully developed) are uncertain, there is much uncertainty about the profit estimates used in this example.

5. Is there any reason for Gandor to revise the composition of its capital (debt and equity) obtained from the U.S. when financing joint ventures like this?

   ANSWER: Gandor may consider using more equity if it believes that the cash flows from joint ventures like this are very uncertain, in order to assure that it maintains sufficient cash flows to cover its debt.

6. When Gandor was assessing this proposed joint venture, some of the managers of Gandor Company recommended that it borrow the Chinese currency rather than dollars to obtain some of the necessary capital for its initial investment. They suggested that such a strategy can reduce Gandor's exchange rate risk. Do you agree? Explain.

   ANSWER: In this case, the exchange rate is guaranteed by the government, so the concept of borrowing in the foreign currency to reduce exchange rate risk does not apply here (unless there is some chance that the Chinese government will not fulfill its promise).

Chapter 22

International Banking

Lecture Outline

Motivation for International Banking
- Effects of East European Reform
- Effects of NAFTA
- Migration of Non-U.S. Banks in the U.S.

The Eurocurrency Market
- Development of the Eurocurrency Market
- Reasons for Attractive Eurobank Rates
- Risks to Depositors
- Syndicated Eurocurrency Loans
- Regulations in the Eurocurrency Market

Risks Incurred by a Eurobank
- Default Risk of Loans Provided by Eurobanks
- Exchange Rate Risk of Eurobanks
- Interest Rate Risk of Eurobanks
- All Risks Combined

Banking Regulations Among Countries
- Standardizing Regulations Across Countries

Chapter Theme

This chapter provides an overview of how international banking grew and the key parts of the international banking network. A lecture related to this chapter should emphasize the risks that a Eurobank is exposed to and illustrate examples of this risk. Students should understand that banks perceive the home potential opportunities and risks from international business just like non-bank MNCs. Some banks are motivated to spread overseas in order to capture new business. Yet, there are risks to this strategy. A risk-return tradeoff must be examined by each bank.

Topics to Stimulate Class Discussion

1. Why would a large U.S. bank consider setting up branches in foreign countries?

2. Would a large corporation be less likely to repay a loan if the loan came from a single Eurobank or a syndicate? Explain.

Answers to End of Chapter Questions

1. Discuss the motives that led to the growth of international banking.

   ANSWER: Regulation differences encouraged large depositors to place funds in Eurobanks where a maximum ceiling did not exist. Reserve requirements were nonexistent for Eurocurrency deposits, so Eurobanks could pay higher rates in deposits, and charge less on loans. MNCs were requested to obtain financing outside of the U.S. All of these factors encouraged the growth of international banking.

2. What are IBFs and how can they serve MNCs?

   ANSWER: International banking facilities (IBFs) are part of existing banks. They are allowed to accept deposits from or make loans to nonresidents of the U.S. They are free from reserve requirements and interest ceilings but must follow various guidelines.

3. In what ways do banking regulations differ among countries?

   ANSWER: First, countries differ in the types of regulatory agencies that oversee the system. Second, they differ in the maximum allowable loan by a bank to a single borrower. Third, they differ in the maximum allowable amount by a bank to specific countries. Fourth, they differ in terms of what activities a bank can or cannot engage in (underwriting securities, stock ownership, etc.).

4. Describe how a bank can become exposed to exchange rate risk.

   ANSWER: When a bank provides loans in currencies that do not perfectly correspond to deposits, it is exposed to exchange rate risk. It is adversely affected when currencies representing its long positions depreciate or currencies representing its short positions appreciate.

5. Describe how a bank can reduce exposure to exchange rate risk.

   ANSWER: A bank can attempt to match its asset side (loans) to its liability side (deposits). Alternatively, it could use currency swaps to reduce its exposure.

6. Describe how a bank can become exposed to interest rate risk.

   ANSWER: When a bank's loan maturities differ from its deposit maturities, it is exposed to interest rate risk. If its deposit maturities are shorter (longer) than its loan maturities, it is adversely affected by rising (declining) interest rate movements.

7. Describe how a bank can reduce exposure to interest rate risk.

   ANSWER: A bank can attempt to match the loan maturities with its deposit maturities. Alternatively, it can provide floating rate loans so that the interest rate on long-term loans will fluctuate in accordance with short-term deposits. It could also set up interest rate swaps with other banks.

8. Why did the Eurocurrency market become so popular?

   ANSWER: Its popularity is due to the nonexistence of restrictions, which led to attractive deposit rates for savers and loan rates for borrowers.

9. What is syndicated lending? Why do banks sometimes prefer this form of lending?

   ANSWER: Syndicated lending reflects a group of banks (called a syndicate) providing a large loan to a customer. This is sometimes desirable since a single lender may be highly hampered if the borrower defaulted on the loan. With a syndicate, the potential loss to any bank is limited.

10. Describe the possible differences in risk between a purely domestic bank and an international bank.

    ANSWER: The common forms of risk to a Eurobank are default risk on loans, interest rate risk, and exchange rate risk. While domestic banks are exposed to default risk and interest rate risk, they are not normally as exposed to exchange rate risk as a Eurobank.

11. Why might a venture seem feasible for a Japanese bank, but not for a U.S. bank, even if the cash flows are similar? (Ignore exchange rate effects.)

    ANSWER: The cost of capital is normally lower for Japanese banks than U.S. banks, which can cause them to identify more feasible ventures. This partially explains the growth of Japanese banks in various countries. Their low rates charged on loans and other bank services has helped fuel the growth, but these low rates are made possible by the low cost of capital.

12. Why might a bank be able to achieve greater economies of scale in Europe now than it could in the 1980s?

    ANSWER: The uniform regulations across countries enforced by the Single European Act allow a bank to more easily offer a product or service across Europe without costly adjustments.

13. Why did differences in capital requirements give some banks a competitive advantage over others?

    ANSWER: Banks in countries where capital requirements were lower could more easily achieve a respectable return on equity, since they did not hold much equity. Conversely, banks in countries that required more capital could only achieve a similar return on equity if they generated a higher return on assets than the banks operating where capital requirements were lower. Uniform capital requirements are being phased in, which will allow for a more level playing field.

14. Even with uniform capital requirements, some banks may have competitive advantage over others because of differences in laws across countries. Explain.

    ANSWER: Differences in tax laws across countries could cause banks based in some countries to have a competitive advantage. They are taxed at a lower rate and can therefore survive with a lower profit margin, which allows them to charge lower rates for loans and services.

15 Loras Bank planned to establish subsidiaries in various East European countries during the 1990s, even though it did not expect these subsidiaries to be profitable. Its logic was that this action was necessary to retain existing business. Interpret this statement.

ANSWER: Loras Bank could have major MNCs as clients that plan to establish businesses in Eastern Europe. These MNCs may desire to have most or all of their banking needs accommodated by banks that have branches in every country in which they operate.

Solution to WSJ Case: Evolution in International Banking

1. Explain why the large international banks may consider focusing less on traditional lending and more on the trading of derivatives products. That is, what underlying factors could cause this strategy to be more profitable?

   ANSWER: The large amount of potential lenders creates a high degree of competition in the loan market, so the profit is minimal. Capital requirements have increased for banks that focus on loans. Demand for loans has been somewhat weak, and bad debt from unpaid loans is usually high in recessionary periods. In contrast, the demand for derivatives products has been high, and the number of banks providing these services has been limited (although the number is growing).

2. Explain how financial statement items might change for the large international banks that focus less on traditional lending and more on the trading of derivatives products.

   ANSWER: Regarding the balance sheet, the asset size may decline, as banks would have fewer loans. Loan loss reserves would decline. The amount of required capital would be less.

   Regarding the income statement, non-interest income (fee income) would increase because of fees from facilitating the client's use of derivative products. The loan losses would decline. Non-interest expenses would likely increase, because of the high-paid experts in derivative products that would be hired by international banks.

3. What is a potential benefit to the international banks that plan to do more subcontracting (outsourcing)?

   ANSWER: The banks will only incur the costs of operations that they are using. Thus they can reduce non-interest expenses. They can avoid some fixed expenses of maintaining specific divisions that would be costly even if these divisions were not productive.

4. Given the potential changes in emphasis by international banks, offer your opinion on what the global banking environment will be like over the next decade.

   ANSWER: This question is open-ended, but any answer should include some recognition that there is a movement from international lending to international investment banking. It appears that the loan markets are saturated, which causes the international banks to look for other services that are needed by clients.

5. How might some international banks attempt to benefit from the development of emerging markets around the world?

   ANSWER: Open-ended question. International banks may accommodate loan demand by firms, households, or governments in emerging markets. In addition, they may provide business consulting services, and help governments facilitate the privatization of state-owned companies. They may also help facilitate the offerings of securities such as stocks and bonds.

Solution to Case Problem: Bank of Chicago

a) The Bank of Chicago may be forgoing many opportunities by maintaining the exact same currency composition on both sides of the balance sheet. For example, it has a strong demand for French franc denominated loans. Therefore it is forced to use the interbank market for loans, which reduces its returns.

b) The bank has an excess of marks and Swiss francs. If these currencies were converted into French francs to accommodate loan demand, there would not be excessive exchange rate risk. The exchange rate between these currencies is quite stable.

c) The bank is not insulated from interest rate risk. If the interest rates of most of its currencies rose, it would be adversely affected because its liabilities are more rate-sensitive than its assets. However, if the interest rate of the pound decreased, it would be adversely affected because its pound-denominated liabilities are less rate-sensitive than its pound-denominated assets. The British interest rates will not necessarily move in perfect tandem with other interest rates, so that a perfect offsetting effect is unlikely. If British interest rates decline while other interest rates rise, the bank will be adversely affected by all interest rate movements.

Project

1. Once a year, special issues of *Business Week*, *Forbes*, and *Fortune* review the performance of numerous firms in the previous year. These issues normally come out in April. Find the section in each that is devoted to banking, and assess the performance of the ten largest banks that conduct a significant amount of international business. How did these banks perform relative to smaller banks? Attempt to explain why the international banks did better or worse than smaller banks.

   This project helps students realize why the performance of international banks is much different than the performance of domestic banks.

Chapter 23

The International Debt Crisis and Bank Assessment of Country Risk

Lecture Outline

The International Debt Crisis

The Debt Crisis From a Banker's Perspective

Government Intervention in the Crisis

Impact of the Debt Crisis on Non-Bank MNCs

Loan Management Since the Debt Crisis
- Sale of LDC Loans
- Increasing Loan Loss Reserves
- Use of Debt-Equity Swaps
- Implementation of the Brady Plan

Bank Assessment of Country Risk
- Political Risk Factors
- Financial Risk Factors

Country Risk Assessment Procedure
- Limitations and Solutions to Country Risk Analysis

Chapter Theme

This chapter has various intentions. First, it gives the student a background of the international debt crisis, which demonstrates the importance of an adequate country risk assessment system. It also raises several questions to ignite the student's interest (although there are no obvious answers to the questions). The students can make up their own mind as to whether the banks should be rescued, or whether future loans should be provided to LDCs, etc.

Topics to Stimulate Class Discussion

1. Do you think political or financial factors are more critical to the assessment of a country's creditworthiness? Discuss.

2. Do you think political or financial factors are more critical to the assessment of a foreign corporation's creditworthiness? Discuss.

Answers to End of Chapter Questions

1. Discuss the developments that led to the international debt crisis.

   ANSWER: Due to the global recession in the early 1980s, industrialized countries reduced their imports. Demand for goods produced in LDCs declined and unemployment in these countries rose. These countries were not able to pay back the large loans extended to them. In addition, oil prices were falling, so export revenues by oil-producing LDCs were lower than expected.

2. Discuss the IMF's role in attempting to resolve the international debt crisis.

   ANSWER: The IMF provided funds to LDCs in exchange for an obligation by the LDCs to work themselves out of the problem. The IMF provided guidelines to some LDCs for improving their economy.

3. What does the existence of the international debt crisis suggest about the previous country risk assessments conducted by banks?

ANSWER: Banks apparently were unable to detect problems, since they continued to lend freely to LDCs prior to announcements by the LDCs of their problems. In some cases, potential problems were detected but banks often ignored such signals and provided loans anyway.

4. Identify factors that would likely be used by banks to assess a government's creditworthiness.

   ANSWER: Some obvious factors that affect a government's creditworthiness are: (1) Its feeling of obligation to repay loans, (2) government turnover (a measure of stability), (3) potential for war, (4) tax revenue potential, (5) strength of economy.

5. Identify factors that would likely be used by banks to assess a foreign corporation's creditworthiness.

   ANSWER: Some of the more obvious factors affecting a foreign corporation's ability to repay loans include: (1) potential for political revolt against the corporation, (2) strength of the economy, and (3) extent or potential of currency blockage restrictions.

6. Why are country risk assessments by banks not always accurate?

   ANSWER: Past data are not always indicative of the future changes in government ideology, in the economy, or in the public's attitude that can disrupt the current conditions.

7. With regard to the international debt crisis, would banks be better off acting as a group or individually in negotiating the rescheduling of loans? Discuss.

   ANSWER: Banks have more negotiating power as a group. The LDCs will not be hampered by the threat of a few banks that they will never receive loans again if they don't pay up what they owe now. However, if all banks made this threat, there would be more room for a compromise.

8. When a crisis (such as international debt crisis) develops, should international banks receive any help from their governments to resolve the problem? To what extent should their governments become involved?

ANSWER: If a government rescues its home banks, this could encourage banks to take high risks in the future (expecting to be rescued if they experience problems). However, if the government doesn't rescue banks, the entire banking system could be at stake. There is no simple solution. The ideal solution (if possible) would be for the government to resolve the current problems without encouraging banks to take excessive risk in the future.

9. Why do banks sometimes rate countries differently? That is, what components of the country risk rating procedure can lead to different overall ratings among banks for a particular country?

   ANSWER: Banks may vary in the factors they believe are important to assess a country's creditworthiness. Alternatively, they may consider the same factors but weigh them differently. Finally, even if they weigh all factors similarly, they may rate the factors differently.

10. Two common mistakes due to inaccurate country risk assessment by a bank are:

    Providing a loan which it should not have
    Not providing a loan which it should have

    Which of these mistakes is more critical? Elaborate.

    ANSWER: A bank that does not provide a loan can lose a customer. A bank that provides bad loans is more likely to go bankrupt. However, this does not mean that banks should only give loans to top quality borrowers (since there are not enough of them).

11. There are a variety of statistical techniques (such as discriminant analysis) that are used to identify characteristics that can correctly discriminate between countries that have had debt repayment problems and countries that have not. Explain why such techniques may not correctly predict which countries will experience debt repayment problems in the future.

    ANSWER: Some factors that have historically been relevant for discriminating between "safe" and "risky" countries may not continue to have the same impact. For example, a country with a high percentage of floating-rate debt may be adversely affected by this characteristic during a period of rising interest rates but favorably affected during a period of declining interest rates.

12. Explain debt-equity swaps and how they increase activity in the secondary loan market.

ANSWER: Debt-equity swaps allow the lender (or whoever has a claim on the debt) to exchange the claim for an equity investment in the borrower's assets. MNCs may consider purchasing claims on LDC debt in the secondary market in order to then swap the claims for an equity investment in the LDC's assets. In this way, debt-equity swaps can increase activity in the secondary loan market.

13. Why do you think the market did not react negatively to money center banks that boosted their loan loss reserves in 1987 and again in 1989? After all, didn't the boost in loan loss reserves signal problems involving LDC debt?

ANSWER: If the market already anticipated the LDC debt problems, the share prices would have already reflected these problems prior to the increase in loan loss reserves.

14. It has been suggested that the next international debt crisis could result from economic problems in Eastern European countries. Do you think that the Eastern European countries are as exposed to economic problems as the Latin American countries?

ANSWER: This question does not have a concise answer. It is simply intended to make students think about conditions that cause systematic loan repayment problems across countries. Some students may suggest that the East European countries are not, as a group, as susceptible to debt repayment problems as the Latin American countries because (1) they do not rely on oil export revenues as some Latin American countries do, (2) they have significantly less inflation than Latin American countries, (3) their economies are not driven by exports, and (4) their currencies may be less volatile than those of Latin American countries.

15. Briefly describe how the Brady Plan was intended to resolve international debt repayment problems.

ANSWER: The Brady Plan is intended to create a compromise between banks and the less developed countries. The specifics of any agreement between a bank and a country will vary across countries. In the case of Mexico, banks holding Mexican debt could (1) take a cut in the principal or interest on outstanding loans, or (2) grant additional loans to Mexico.

Solution to WSJ Case: New Wave of Loans to Less Developed Countries

1. Why do you think Chase Manhattan, J.P. Morgan, Citicorp, and other commercial banks offer bridge loans to less developed countries?

   ANSWER: These bridge loans offer a relatively high return for banks. In addition, these banks have had excess funds (because loan demand was weak), which caused them to search for ways to use the funds. Furthermore, banks may establish new business relationships.

2. Do you believe these bridge loans offered by Bankers Trust New York Corporation, Citicorp, and other banks to less developed countries (LDCs) are less risky than the loans previously provided to LDCs in the 1970s and 1980s? Explain.

   ANSWER: Bridge loans are short-term loans, and therefore are not considered to be as risky as the long-term loans provided to LDCs in the 1970s and 1980s. Banks can more easily assess the financial condition of the LDCs for a short-term period than for several years.

3. Would banks use the same type of country risk analysis for bridge loans to less developed countries that they used for longer-term loans to LDCs?

   ANSWER: The analysis would focus more on political and financial conditions over a short-term horizon.

Solution to Case Problem: Bank of Baltimore

a) The sale of loans in the secondary market appears to be more appropriate than a debt-equity swap in this case. The debt-equity swap will achieve an expected 1,000,000 million Austral, which at the end of the year would be converted to about $138.88 million (using an exchange rate of 7,200 Austral = $1, which reflects 50% depreciation). This is about the same as what it expected to receive from selling the loans in the secondary market ($500 million book value x $.28 on the dollar = $140 million). Yet, the proceeds to be received from selling the loan in the secondary market are less uncertain, and the funds would arrive soon rather than one year from now.

b) This business has a present value in U.S. dollars of $150 million (computed as 720,000 million Austral/4800 Austral per dollar). However, should a bank be running a sheet metal business? Based on the information, it does not appear that the bank could sell it immediately. That means that the Austral cannot be converted to dollars immediately and will probably depreciate until they are converted. Overall, this venture has substantial risk, which some students will detect, while other students ignore when they estimate the value of the business. Conservative managers would probably not choose this alternative.

Project

1. Review the annual report of a large U.S. bank that historically provided loans to less developed countries. Summarize any statements made regarding these loans. Is the bank offering new loans to these countries? Has it reduced its foreign loan exposure by selling loans? Has it increased its loan loss reserves in anticipation that loans may default?

   This project allows students to see actual examples of how banks are attempting to reduce their exposure to LDC loans.

IMPORTANT: PLEASE READ BEFORE OPENING THIS PACKAGE
THIS PACKAGE IS NOT RETURNABLE IF SEAL IS BROKEN.

West Publishing Corporation
620 Opperman Drive
P.O. Box 64779
St. Paul, Minnesota 55164-0779

Instructor's Manual to Accompany
International Financial Management

LIMITED USE LICENSE